D0430467

Southeast
Asia
PHRASEBOOK & DICTIONARY

Acknowledgments

Associate Publisher Mina Patria
Managing Editor Angela Tinson
Editors Branislava Vladisavljevic
Series Designer Mark Adams
Managing Layout Designer Chris Girdler
Layout Designer Joseph Spanti
Cover Image Researcher Naomi Parker

Thanks

Carol Jackson, Chris Love, Wayne Murphy, Jeanette Wall

Published by Lonely Planet Publications Pty Ltd
ABN 36 005 607 983

3rd Edition – Sep 2013
ISBN 978 1 74321 019 2
Text © Lonely Planet 2013
Cover Image U-Bein's Bridge, Amarapura, Myanmar (Burma), Kylie Mc Laughlin/Getty Images ©

Printed in China   10 9 8 7 6 5 4 3

MIX
Paper from
responsible sources
FSC™ C021741

acknowledgments

This book was based on the current editions of Lonely Planet's phrasebooks for the relevant languages and developed with the help of the following people. Thanks to:

San San Hnin Tun for translating the Burmese content in this book. San San is a senior lecturer in Burmese at Cornell University in New York.

Jason Roberts for translating the Khmer phrases. Jason is an American writer & interpreter who spent nearly six years living and working for various humanitarian agencies in Cambodia.

Natrudy Saykao for translating the Lao chapter. Natrudy is originally from Laos and works as a freelance translator and interpreter in Melbourne.

Bruce Evans for translating the Thai content and for proofing Lao. Bruce lived in Thailand for over 20 years and has translated a number of books from Thai to English. He works as a managing editor at Lonely Planet.

Ben Handicott for producing the Vietnamese section. Ben lived in Vietnam for three years and now works as a publisher at Lonely Planet.

Editor Branislava Vladisavljevic would also like to thank Mark Germanchis for technical assistance and Wendy Wright for the inside illustrations.

make the most of this phrasebook ...

Anyone can speak another language! It's all about confidence. Don't worry if you can't remember your school language lessons or if you've never learnt a language before. Even if you learn the very basics (on the inside covers of this book), your travel experience will be the better for it. You have nothing to lose and everything to gain when the locals hear you making an effort.

finding things in this book

This book is divided into five chapters – for ease of navigation, each chapter has its own colour and all chapters have the same structure. The sound system of each language and the most important grammar rules are explained at the start of the chapter in Pronunciation and the Phrase-builder. For each language we've provided you with practical phrases for basic travel situations, as well as conversational phrases so you can get to know people. Local dishes are listed in the Menu decoders and the most important health and police phrases are included too, just in case. Remember the colours of each chapter and you'll find everything easily; or use the comprehensive Index. Otherwise, check the traveller's Dictionaries included at the end of each chapter for the word you need.

being understood

Throughout this book you'll see coloured phrases on each page. They're phonetic guides to help you pronounce the language – you don't even need to look at the language if you're not familiar with the script. For ease of pronunciation, we've split up the words in syllables with dots for Burmese, Khmer and Vietnamese – for Lao and Thai we've used hyphens instead, and dots to further divide the vowel sound combinations. For Vietnamese we've sometimes given examples of both the northern and southern dialect – the two options are marked as ⓝ and ⓢ.

abbreviations used in this book

a	adjective	m	masculine
adv	adverb	n	noun
excl	exclusive of listener	pl	plural
f	feminine	pol	polite
incl	inclusive of listener	sg	singular
inf	informal	v	verb

contents

language map

Bhutan

India

Bangladesh

China

250 km
150 mi

Mandalay

Sittwe

MYANMAR
(BURMA)

Sapa

Hanoi

Bay
of
Bengal

Luang
Prabang

Bago

Chiang Mai

LAOS

Gulf
of
Tonkin

Yangon
(Rangoon)

Vientiane

Savannakhet

Hué

ANDAMAN
SEA

THAILAND

Pakse

Hoi An

Andaman
Islands
(India)

Dawei

Bangkok

VIETNAM

Mergui
Archipelago

Pattaya

Siem
Reap

Angkor Wat

Nha Trang

Ka Chang
Gulf of
Thailand

CAMBODIA
Phnom
Penh

Dalat

Sihanoukville

Kampot

Ho Chi
Minh City
(Saigon)

Ko Pha-Ngan
Ko Samui

Phu Quoc

Phuket
Ko Phuket

SOUTH
CHINA
SEA

Hat Yai

Indonesia

Strait of
Malacca

Malaysia

	burmese		thai
	khmer		vietnamese
	lao		

For more details, see the relevant **introduction**.

Burmese

consonants

က ká·jì	ခ ká·gwày	ဂ gá·nge	ဃ gá·jì	c ngá
စ sá·lòhng	ဆ sá·layng	ဇ zá·gwè	ဈ zá·mying·zwè	ည nyá
ဋ tá·tuh·ling·jay'	ဌ tá·wung·bè	ဍ dá·ying·gow'	ဎ dá·yay·hmoh'	ဏ ná·jì
တ tá·wùng·boo	ထ tá·sing·dòo	ဒ dá·dwày	ဓ dá·óo·chai'	န ná·nge
ပ pá·zow'	ဖ pá·óo·toh'	ဗ bá·luh·chai'	ဘ bá·gòhng	မ má
ယ yá·puh·le'	ရ yá·gow'	လ lá	ဝ wá·lòhng	သ thá
ဟ há	ဠ lá·jì	အ á		

vowels (the hyphen is used as the consonant base)

creaky high

-́ á	ိ í	̄ óo	̣- áy	̀́ é	̣̈ óh	◌ ◌ áw
◌ ◌ íng	◌ ◌ áyng	◌ ◌ áng	◌ ◌ óhng	◌ ◌ úng	◌ áing	◌ ◌ ówng

low

-ː ◌ː à	◌ː ì	̄ː òo	◌-ː ày	̀ è	◌ː òh	◌ ◌ àw
◌ː ◌ː ìng	◌ː ◌ː àyng	◌ː ◌ː àng	◌ː ◌ː òhng	◌ː ◌ː ùng	◌ː àing	◌ː ◌ː òwng

plain high

◌ ◌ a	◌ i	◌ oo	̄◌ ay	◌- e	-◌ oh	◌ ◌ aw
◌ ◌ ing	◌ ◌ ayng	◌ ◌ ang	◌ ◌ ohng	◌ ◌ ung	◌◌ aing	◌ ◌ owng

stopped (ie followed by the sound heard between 'uh-oh')

◌ i'	◌ ◌ ay	◌ e'	◌ ◌ a'
◌ ◌ oh	◌ ◌ u'	◌ aï'	◌-◌ ow'

introduction

Burmese is part of the Tibeto-Burman language family. As the national language of Myanmar (Burma), it has over 40 million speakers, of whom more than 30 million use it as their first language. The variety of Burmese of Mandalay and Yangon, which is spoken throughout the central area of Myanmar, is considered the standard language and is taught in schools everywhere. Many other languages, such as Rakhine, Tavoyan, Intha, Yaw, Danu and Taungyo, are spoken in Myanmar, but nearly everyone in the country knows Burmese, and widespread literacy has been achieved through schools and adult literacy programmes. With Burmese you'll be understood everywhere in Myanmar.

There are two varieties of Burmese – one used in writing and associated formal situations, the other in speaking and informal situations. The main differences are in vocabulary, especially the most common words and particles (eg 'this' is di in spoken Burmese, but i in the written language). The phrases in this chapter are in the informal spoken variety, which is appropriate for all situations you're likely to encounter as a traveller. Many Burmese nouns are borrowed from English, though the meaning and sound may be somewhat different. There are also some loan words from Hindi. Much of the more formal vocabulary comes from Pali, the language of Theravada Buddhism, but is pronounced in a Burmese way, and so sounds different from Thai, Sri Lankan or other Pali pronunciation.

Burmese was one of the earliest Tibeto-Burman languages to develop a writing system. The earliest surviving inscription, known as the Rajakumar, dates from AD 1112 and is written in four languages: Pali, Mon, Pyu and Burmese. The writing system used in this chapter is the revised spelling introduced in 1980, as formulated by the Myanmar (Burma) Language Commission. We have included the Burmese alphabet on the page opposite. There are various combinations of consonants, and the vowel sound of each syllable is written by adding one or more symbols above, below, before, or after the consonant. Additional markings are used to represent the tones. The three tones and other aspects of pronunciation can best be learned by listening and imitation. You should be understood just fine if you follow our coloured pronunciation guides.

The outline of Burmese grammar included in this chapter only gives the basic rules and shows you how to put together your own phrases. Once you become familiar with these rules, you'll find it easy to explore further and learn sentence patterns for specific situations.

introduction – ဗမာစကား

pronunciation

vowel sounds

Accents above vowels (like à and é) relate to the tones (see below).

symbol	english equivalent	burmese example	symbol	english equivalent	burmese example
a	father	sa-oh'-ṣaing	oh	go	uh-koh
ai	aisle	ṣày-zaing	oo	zoo	mòo-de
aw	law	layng-maw-yay	ow	brown	nguh-pí-gowng
ay	hay	òhng-yay	u	put	uh-wu'-uh-sà
e	bet	móhng-che'-ú	uh	fun	bí'-suh-kí-móhng
i	sin	now'-hní'			

tones

There are three distinct tones in Burmese. The accent marks above the vowel remind you which one to use. Note that the low tone has no accent.

tone	symbol (accent)	burmese example
high, creaky tone, as in 'heart'	acute accent (eg á)	òhn-nó
plain high tone, as in 'car'	grave accent (eg à)	ngà-bòwn
low tone	plain vowel (eg a)	we'-thuh-ni

consonant sounds

In Burmese, there's a difference between the aspirated consonants (pronounced with a puff of air after the sound) and the unaspirated ones – you'll get the idea if you hold your hand in front of your mouth to feel your breath, and say 'pit' (where the 'p' is aspirated) and 'spit' (where it's unaspirated).

symbol	english equivalent	burmese example
b	**b**ook	towng·**b**e'
ch	**ch**urch (with a puff of air afterwards)	chòwng·ṣòh·de
d	**d**og	**d**uh·zowng·mòhng
g	**g**ate	cha·zuhng·hìng·**gà**
h	**h**ello	**h**oh'·ké
hl	**l**ife (with a puff of air before)	ṣuhng·**hl**aw·hìng·joh
hm	**m**e (with a puff of air before)	le'·**hm**a'·duh·zowng
hn	**n**ot (with a puff of air before)	na·u'·**hn**i'
hng	si**ng** (with a puff of air before)	uh·**hng**à·kà
hny	ca**ny**on (with a puff of air before)	ka·u'·**hny**ìng·nguh·chay'
j	ridge	móhng·**j**aw
k	**k**ite (with a puff of air afterwards)	uh·**k**ùhng
l	**l**ife	ping·**l**e·za
m	**m**e	uh·ày·**m**í·bi
n	**n**ot	chuh·**n**aw
ng	si**ng**	**ng**à
ny	ca**ny**on	**ny**i·má
p	**p**ig	uh·**p**yu
'	the sound heard between 'uh-oh'	sa·oh'·ṣaing
s	**s**ee	**s**uh·nay·náy
ṣ	**s**ick (with a puff of air afterwards)	tuh·**ṣ**ei'·low'
sh	**sh**ip	**sh**a·luh·ka·yay
t	**t**alk (with a puff of air afterwards)	**t**aìng
th	**th**in	**th**uh·mì
ṭh	**th**eir	kyòwng·**ṭh**à
w	**w**atch	**w**e'·thà
y	**y**es	**y**ay
z	**z**oo	ṭhuh·dìng·**z**a·ṣuh·ya

phrasebuilder

be

For the verb 'be', use ba (ပါ) after nouns and de (တယ်) after adjectives:

I'm a student.	ကျနော်/ကျမ	chuh·naw/chuh·má
	ကျောင်းသား/ကျောင်းသူ ပါ။	chòwng·ṭhà/chòwng·ṭhu ba m/f
		(lit: I-m/f student-m/f ba)
I'm hot.	ကျနော်/ကျမ ပူ တယ်။	chuh·naw/chuh·má poo de m/f
		(lit: I-m/f hot de)

counters/classifiers

Burmese nouns are the same in singular and plural. However, when counting things, you need to use an extra word which 'classifies' the noun. It always goes after the noun and the number. The box on page 38 has some examples of classifiers and the categories of nouns they refer to.

| three tickets | လက်မှတ် သုံး စောင် | le'·hma' thòhng zowng |
| | | (lit: ticket three written-thing) |

have

The word for 'have' is shí (ရှိ). To say someone owns something, add hma (မှာ) before the thing that's owned and de (တယ်) at the end of the sentence.

I have a visa.
ကျနော်/ကျမ မှာ ဗီဇာ ရှိ တယ်။   chuh·náw/chuh·má hma bi·za shí de m/f
(lit: I-m/f hma visa have de)

negatives

To negate a sentence, place muh (မ) before the verb and pòe (ဘူး) at the end of the sentence.

I don't like this room.
ဒီ အခန်း မ ကြိုက် ဘူး။   di uh·kàng muh chai' pòe
(lit: this room muh like pòe)

pronouns

The pronouns 'I', 'we', and 'you' have different forms depending on the person's gender. On the other hand, the same word is used for both 'he' and 'she'. For a list of Burmese pronouns, see the table on page 31.

questions

To form a yes/no question, place ţhuh·là (သလား) at the end of a statement. To answer 'yes' say hoh' ké (ဟုတ်က) and to answer 'no' say muh hoh' pòo (မဟုတ်ဘူး).

Do you have a free room?	အခန်းအား ရှိ သလား။	uh·kàng·á shí ţhuh·là (lit: room free have ţhuh·là)
Yes.	ဟုတ်ကဲ့။	hoh' ké (lit: true ké)
No.	မဟုတ်ဘူး။	muh hoh' pòo (lit: muh true pòo)

requests

To make a polite request, add ba (ပါ) after the verb.

Please come in.	ဝင် လာ ပါ။	wing la ba (lit: enter come ba)

verbs

Burmese verbs don't change according to tense – instead, a tense particle (an ending which specifies when the action takes place) is added to the end of the word – de (တယ်) for the present, me (မယ်) for future tense, and bi (ပြီ) for the past.

I'm staying at the hotel.
ဟိုတယ် မှာ တည်း ပါ တယ်။
hoh·te hma tè ba de
(lit: hotel hma stay ba de)

They'll come by train.
သူတို့ ရထား နဲ့ လာ မယ်။
thu·dóh yuh·tà né la me
(lit: they train with come me)

It's paid.
ပိုက်ဆံ ရှင်း ပြီး ပြီ။
pai'·şang shìng pì bi
(lit: money pay finish bi)

basics

language difficulties

Do you speak English?
အင်္ဂလိပ်လို ပြောတတ်သလား။   ìng·guh·lay'·loh pyàw·da'·thuh·là

Do you understand?
နားလည်သလား။   nà·le·thuh·là

I understand.
နားလည်တယ်။   nà·le·de

I don't understand.
နားမလည်ဘူး။   nà·muh·le·bòo

What does (puh·yà) mean?
(ဘုရား) ဆိုတာ ဘာလဲ။   (puh·yà) ṣoh·da ba·lè

How do you pronounce this?
ဒါ ဘယ်လို အသံ ထွက်သလဲ။   da be·loh uh·thuhng twe'·thuh·lè

How do you write (Mandalay)?
(မန္တလေး)ကို ဘယ်လို ရေးသလဲ။   (muhng·duh·làỵ)·goh be·loh yàỵ·thuh·lè

Could you please ...?   --- ပါ။   ... pa
   repeat that   ထပ်ပြော   tuh'·pyàw
   speak more slowly   ဖြည်းဖြည်းပြော   pyàỵ·pyàỵ·pyàw
   write it down   ရေးမှတ်ထား   yàỵ·hmuh'·tà

essentials		
Yes.	ဟုတ်ကဲ့။	hoh'·ké
No.	ဟင့်အင်း။	híng·ìn
Please.	တဆိတ်လောက်။	tuh·ṣay'·low'
Thank you (very much).	ကျေးဇူး (အများကြီး)	chàỵ·zù (uh·myà·ji)
	တင်ပါတယ်။	ting·ba·deh
You're welcome.	ရပါတယ်။	yà·ba·de
Excuse me.	ဆောရီးနော်။	saw·ri·naw
Sorry.	ဆောရီးနော်။	saw·ri·naw

numbers

0	သုည	thohn·nyá		17	ဆယ့်ခုနစ်	şé·kung
1	တစ်	ti'		18	ဆယ့်ရှစ်	şé·shi'
2	နှစ်	hni'		19	ဆယ့်ကိုး	şé·kòh
3	သုံး	thòhng		20	နှစ်ဆယ်	hnuh·şe
4	လေး	làypanel		21	နှစ်ဆယ်တစ်	hnuh·şé·ti'
5	ငါး	ngà		22	နှစ်ဆယ့်နှစ်	hnuh·şé·hni'
6	ခြောက်	chow'		30	သုံးဆယ်	thòhng·ze
7	ခုနှစ်	kung·ni'		40	လေးဆယ်	lày·ze
8	ရှစ်	shi'		50	ငါးဆယ်	ngà·ze
9	ကိုး	kòh		60	ခြောက်ဆယ်	chow'·şe
10	တစ်ဆယ်	tuh·şe		70	ခုနှစ်ဆယ်	kung·nuh·şe
11	ဆယ့်တစ်	şé·ti'		80	ရှစ်ဆယ်	shi'·şe
12	ဆယ့်နှစ်	şé·hni'		90	ကိုးဆယ်	kòh·ze
13	ဆယ့်သုံး	şé·thòhng		91	ကိုးဆယ့်တစ်	kòh·zé·ti'
14	ဆယ့်လေး	şé·lày		100	တစ်ရာ	tuh·ya
15	ဆယ့်ငါး	şé·ngà		1000	တစ်ထောင်	tuh·towng
16	ဆယ့်ခြောက်	şé·chow'		1,000,000	တစ်သန်း	tuh·thùhng

numerals

0	1	2	3	4	5	6	7	8	9
၀	၁	၂	၃	၄	၅	၆	၇	၈	၉

time & dates

What time is it?
အခု ဘယ်အချိန်လဲ။ — uh·gú be·uh·chayng·lè

It's (one) o'clock.
တစ်နာရီ (ရှိပြီ)။ — (tuh·na·yi) shí·bi

It's (two) o'clock.
နှစ်နာရီ (ရှိပြီ)။ — (hnuh·na·yi) shí·bi

Quarter past (one).
(တစ်နာရီ) ဆယ့်ငါး မိနစ်။ — (tuh·na·yi) şé·ngà muh·ni'

Half past (one).
(တစ်နာရီ) ခွဲ။ — (tuh·na·yi) gwè

Quarter to (eight).

⟨ရှစ်နာရီ⟩ ထိုးဖို့ ဆယ့်ငါး မိနစ်။   (shí·na·yi) tòh·bó şé·ngà muh·ni'

At what time ...?

ဘယ်အချိန် ---   be·uh·chayng ...

At ...

--- မှာ   ... hma

am (morning)	မနက် --- နာရီ	muh·ne' ... na·yi
pm (afternoon)	နေ့ လည် --- နာရီ	náy·le ... na·yi
pm (evening)	နေ့ လည် --- နာရီ	nyá·nay ...na·yi

Monday	တနင်္လာနေ့	tuh·nìng·la·náy
Tuesday	အင်္ဂါနေ့	ing·ga·náy
Wednesday	ဗုဒ္ဓဟူးနေ့	boh'·duh·hòo·náy
Thursday	ကြာသပတေးနေ့	chà·thuh·buh·dày·náy
Friday	သောကြာနေ့	thow'·cha·náy
Saturday	စနေနေ့	suh·nay·náy
Sunday	တနင်္ဂနွေနေ့	tuh·nìng·guh·nway·náy

January	ဇန္နဝါရီလ	zuhn·nuh·wa·yi·lá
February	ဖေဖော်ဝါရီလ	pay·paw·wa·yi·lá
March	မတ်လ	ma'·lá
April	ဧပြီလ	ay·pyi·lá
May	မေလ	may·lá
June	ဇွန်လ	jung·lá
July	ဂျူလိုင်လ	joo·laing·lá
August	ဩဂုတ်လ	àw·goh'·lá
September	စက်တင်ဘာလ	se'·ting·ba·lá
October	အောက်တိုဘာလ	ow'·toh·ba·lá
November	နိုဝင်ဘာလ	noh·wing·ba·lá
December	ဒီဇင်ဘာလ	di·zing·ba·lá

What date is it today?

ဒီနေ့ ဘယ်နှစ်ရက်နေ့လဲ။   di·náy be·hnuh·ye'·náy·lè

(It's) 15 December.

ဒီဇင်ဘာလ ဆယ့်ငါးရက်နေ့။   di·zing·ba·lá şé·ngà·ye'·náy

since (May)	⟨မေလ⟩ ကတည်းက	(may·lá) guh·dè·gá
until (June)	⟨ဇွန်လ⟩ အထိ	(jung·lá) uh·tí
last night	မနေ့ညက	muh·náy·nyá·gá

last …	အရင် --- က	uh·ying … ká
next …	နောက် ---	now' …
week	အပတ်	uh·puh'
month	လ	lá
year	နှစ်	hni'
yesterday …	မနေ့က ---	muh·náy·gá …
tomorrow …	မနက်ဖန် ---	muh·ne'·puhng …
morning	မနက်	muh·ne'
afternoon	နေ့လည်	náy·le
evening	ညနေ	nyá·nay

weather

What's the weather like?
ရာသီဥတု ဘယ်လိုလဲ။ ya·ţhi·ú·dú be·loh·lè

It's …

cold	အေးတယ်။	ày·de
(very) hot	〈သိပ်〉 ပူတယ်။	(thay') poo·de
rainy	မိုးရွာနေတယ်။	mòh·ywa·nay·de
warm	နည်းနည်း ပူတယ်။	nè·nè poo·de
windy	လေတိုက်တယ်။	lay·tai'·te
autumn	ဆောင်းဦးရာသီ	şowng·òo·ya·ţhi
cool season (winter)	ဆောင်းရာသီ	şowng·ya·ţhi
dry season (summer)	နွေရာသီ	nway·ya·ţhi
rainy season	မိုးရာသီ	mòh·ya·ţhi
spring	နွေဦးရာသီ	nway·òo·ya·ţhi

border crossing

I'm …	ကျနော်/ကျမ က ---	chuh·naw/chuh·má gá … **m/f**
in transit	ခရီး ဆက်သွားမှာ	kuh·yì şe'·thwà·hma
on business	အလုပ်ကိစ္စနဲ့လာတာ	uh·loh'·kay'·sá·né la·da
on holiday	အလည်လာတာ	uh·le la·da

I'm here for ... ကျနော်/ကျမ ဒီမှာ --- နေမယ်။ chuh·naw/chuh·má di·hma ... nay·me m/f

(10) days	(ဆယ်)ရက်	(şe)·ye'
(two) months	(နှစ်)လ	(hnuh)·lá
(three) weeks	(သုံး)ပတ်	(thòhng)·buh'

I'm going to (Maymyo).
(မေမြို့)ကို သွားမယ်။ (may·myó)·goh thwà·me

I'm staying at the (Kandawgyi Hotel).
(ကန်တော်ကြီးဟိုတယ်)မှာ တည်းနေတယ်။ (kuhn·daw·jì hoh·te)·hma tè·nay·de

I have nothing to declare.
ကြေညာဖို့ ပစ္စည်း မပါဘူး။ chay·nya·bóh pyi'·sì muh·pa·bòo

I have something to declare.
ကြေညာဖို့ ပစ္စည်း ပါတယ်။ chay·nya·bóh pyi'·sì pa·de

That's mine.
ဒါ ကျနော့်/ကျမ ပစ္စည်းပါ။ da chuh·náw/chuh·má pyi'·sì·ba m/f

That's not mine.
ဒါ ကျနော့်/ကျမ ပစ္စည်း မဟုတ်ပါဘူး။ da chuh·náw/chuh·má pyi'·sì muh·hoh'·pa·bòo m/f

I didn't know I had to declare it.
ဒါ ကြေညာရမယ် ဆိုတာ မသိဘူး။ da chay·nya·yá·me şoh·da muh·thí·bòo

transport

tickets & luggage

Where can I buy a ticket?
လက်မှတ် ဘယ်မှာ ဝယ်ရမလဲ။ le'·hma' be·hma we'·yá·muh·lè

Do I need to book?
ထိုင်ခုံ ကြိုယူစရာ လိုသလား။ taing·gohng choh·yoo·zuh·ya loh·ţuh·là

One ... ticket to (Taunggyi), please. (တောင်ကြီး) ---လက်မှတ် တစ်စောင် ပေးပါ။ (towng·jì) ... le'·hma' duh·zowng pày·ba

one-way	အသွား	uh·thwà
return	အသွား အပြန်	uh·thwà uh·pyang

I'd like to ...	ကျနေ့/ကျမ လက်မှတ်	chuh·náw/chuh·má le'·hma'
my ticket, please.	--- ချင်ပါတယ်။	... ching·ba·de m/f
cancel	ဖျက်	pye'
change	ပြောင်း	pyòwng
collect	အခု ယူ	uh·gú yoo
confirm	ကွန်ဖမ်းလုပ်	kung·pang·loh'

I'd like a ...	ဆေးလိပ် --- နေရာ	şày·lay' ... nay·ya
seat, please.	ပေးပါ။	pày·ba
nonsmoking	မသောက်ရတဲ့	muh·thow'·yá·dé
smoking	သောက်လို့ရတဲ့	thow'·lóh·yá·dé

How much is it?
ဘယ်လောက်လဲ။ — be·low'·lè

Is there air conditioning?
အဲကွန်း ပါသလား။ — è·kùng pa·ṭhuh·là

Is there a toilet?
အိမ်သာ ပါသလား။ — ayng·ṭha pa·ṭhuh·là

How long does the trip take?
ဒီခရီးက ဘယ်လောက် ကြာမလဲ။ — di·kuh·yì·gá be·low' cha·muh·lè

Is it a direct route?
ဒါ တိုက်ရိုက်လမ်းလား။ — da dai'·yai'·làng·là

I'd like a luggage locker.
သေတ္တာသော့ လိုချင်ပါတယ်။ — thí'·ta·tháw loh·jing·ba·de

My luggage	ကျနေ့/ကျမ	chuh·náw/chuh·má
has been ...	သေတ္တာ ---	thí'·ta ... m/f
damaged	ပျက်စီးနေတယ်	pye'·si·nay·de
lost	ပျောက်နေတယ်	pyow'·nay·de
stolen	ခိုးခံရတယ်	kòh·kang·yá·de

getting around

Where does flight (TG 132) arrive?
လေယာဉ် နံပါတ် (တီဂျီ ၁၃၂) — lay·ying nang·ba' (ti·ji tuh·ya·thòhng·zé·hni')
ဘယ်မှာ ဆိုက်မလဲ။ — be·hma şai'·muh·lè

Where does flight (TG 132) depart?
လေယာဉ် နံပါတ် (တီဂျီ ၁၃၂) — lay·ying nang·ba' (ti·ji tuh·ya·thòhng·zé·hni')
ဘယ်က ထွက်မလဲ။ — be·gá twe'·muh·lè

Where's (the) …?	--- ဘယ်မှာလဲ။	… be·hma·lè
arrivals hall	ဆိုက်တဲ့နေရာ	şai'·té·nay·ya
departures hall	ထွက်တဲ့နေရာ	twe'·té·nay·ya
duty-free shop	ဂျူတီဖရီးဆိုင်တွေ	joo·ti·puh·yí·şaing·dway
gate (12)	ဂိတ်နံပါတ် ⟨ဆယ့်နှစ်⟩	gay'·nang·ba' (şé·hni')

Is this the … to (Moulmein)?	ဒါ ⟨မော်လမြိုင်⟩ သွားတဲ့ --- လား။	da (maw·luh·myaing) thwà·dé … là
boat	သင်္ဘော	thìng·bàw
bus	ဘတ်စကား	ba'·suh·kà
plane	လေယာဉ်	lay·ying
train	ရထား	yuh·tà

At what time's the … bus?	--- ဘတ်စကား ဘယ်အချိန် ထွက်မလဲ။	… ba'·suh·kà be·uh·chayng twe'·muh·lè
first	ပထမ	puh·tuh·má
last	နောက်ဆုံး	now'·şòhng
next	နောက်	now'

At what time does it leave?
ဘယ်အချိန် ထွက်သလဲ။ — be·uh·chayng twe'·thuh·lè

How long will it be delayed?
ဘယ်လောက် နောက်ကျမလဲ။ — be·low' now'·chá·muh·lè

What station is this?
ဒါ ဘာဘူတာလဲ။ — da ba·boo·da·lè

What's the next station?
နောက်ဘူတာက ဘာဘူတာလဲ။ — now'·boo·da·gá ba·boo·da·lè

Does it stop at (Bago)?
⟨ပဲခူး⟩မှာ ရပ်သလား။ — (buh·gòh)·hma ya'·thuh·là

Please tell me when we get to (Myitkyina).
⟨မြစ်ကြီးနား⟩ ရောက်ရင် ပြောပါ။ — (myi'·chì·nà) yow'·ying pyàw·ba

How long do we stop here?
ဒီမှာ ဘယ်လောက်ကြာကြာ ရပ်မလဲ။ — di·hma be·low'·cha·cha ya'·muh·lè

Is this seat available?
ဒီနေရာ အားသလား။ — di·nay·ya à·ţhuh·là

That's my seat.
ဒါ ကျနော့်/ကျမ နေရာပါ။ — da chuh·náw/chuh·má nay·ya·ba **m/f**

I'd like a taxi ...	တက္ကစီလိုချင်ပါတယ်။	te'·kuh·si loh·jing·ba·de
at (9am)	(မနက် ၉နာရီ)မှာ	(muh·ne' kòh·na·yi)·hma
now	အခု	uh·gú
tomorrow	မနက်ဖြန်	muh·ne'·pang

Is this ... available?	ဒီ --- အားသလား။	di ... à·ṭhuh·là
motorcycle-taxi	အငှား	uh·hngà
	မော်တော်ဆိုင်ကယ်	maw·taw·ṣaing·ke
rickshaw	ဆိုက်ကား	ṣai'·kà
taxi	တက္ကစီ	te'·kuh·si

How much is it to ...?
--- ကို ဘယ်လောက်လဲ။   ... koh be·low'·lè

Please put the meter on.
မီတာ စမှတ်ပါ။   mi·ta sá·hma'·ba

Please take me to (this address).
(ဒီလိပ်စာ)ကို ပို့ပေးပါ။   (di·lay'·sa)·goh póh·pày·ba

Please ...	--- ပါ။	... ba
slow down	ဖြည်းဖြည်းသွား	pyày·byày·thwà
stop here	ဒီမှာ ရပ်	di·hma ya'
wait here	ဒီမှာ စောင့်	di·hma sówng

car, motorbike & bicycle hire

I'd like to hire a ...	--- ငှားချင်ပါတယ်။	... hngà·jing·ba·de
bicycle	စက်ဘီး	se'·bàyng
car	ကား	kà
motorbike	မော်တော်ဆိုင်ကယ်	maw·taw·ṣaing·ke

with ...	--- နဲ့	... né
air conditioning	အဲကွန်း	è·kùng
a driver	ဒရိုင်ဘာ	duh·yaing·ba

How much for	--- ငှားရင်	... hngà·ying
... hire?	ဘယ်လောက်လဲ။	be·low'·lè
hourly	တစ်နာရီ	tuh·na·yi
daily	တစ်ရက်	tuh·ye'
weekly	တပတ်	duh·ba'

air	လေ	lay
oil	ဆီ	şi
petrol	ဓါတ်ဆီ	da'·şi
tyre	ဘီး	bàyng

I need a mechanic.
မက္ကင်းနစ် လိုချင်ပါတယ်။ — muh·kìng·ni' loh·jing·ba·de

I've run out of petrol.
ဓါတ်ဆီ ကုန်သွားပြီ။ — da'·şi kohng·thwà·bi

I have a flat tyre.
ဘီးပေါက်နေတယ်။ — bàyng·pow'·nay·de

directions

Where's a/the ...?	--- ဘယ်မှာလဲ။	... be·hma·lè
bank	ဘဏ်တိုက်	bang·dai'
city centre	မြို့ထဲ	myóh·dè
hotel	ဟိုတယ်	hoh·te
market	ဈေး	zày
police station	ရဲစခန်း	yè·suh·kàng
post office	စာတိုက်	sa·dai'
public toilet	အများသုံး အိမ်သာ	uh·myà·thòhng ayng·ţha
tourist office	တိုးရစ်ရုံး	tòh·yi'·yòhng

Is this the road to (Moulmein)?
ဒါ 〈မော်လမြိုင်〉 သွားတဲ့လမ်းလား။ — da (maw·luh·myaing) thwà·dé·làng·là

Can you show me (on the map)?
〈မြေပုံပေါ်မှာ〉 ညွှန်ပြပေးပါ။ — (myay·bohng·baw·hma) hnyung·pyá·pày·ba

What's the address?
လိပ်စာက ဘာလဲ။ — lay'·sa·gá ba·lè

How far is it?
ဘယ်လောက် ဝေးသလဲ။ — be·low' wày·ţhuh·lè

How do I get there?
ဘယ်လို သွားရမလဲ။ — be·loh thwà·yá·muh·lè

Turn ...	--- ချိုး·ပါ॥	... chòh·ba
at the corner	လမ်း·ထောင့်မှာ	làng·dá·ung·hma
at the traffic lights	မီး·ပွိုင့်မှာ	mì·pwáing·hma
left/right	ဘယ်ဘက်/ညာဘက်	be·be'/nya·be'

It's ...		
behind ...	--- အနောက်မှာ॥	... uh·now'·hma
far away	အရမ်း·ဝေး·တယ်॥	uh·yàng·wày·de
here	ဒီမှာ॥	di·hma
in front of ...	--- ရှေ့မှာ॥	... sháy·hma
left	ဘယ်ဘက်မှာ॥	be·be'·hma
near ...	--- နား·မှာ॥	... nà·hma
next to ...	--- ဘေး·မှာ॥	... bày·hma
opposite ...	--- မျက်နှာချင်း·ဆိုင်·မှာ॥	... mye'·hnuh·jing·ṣaing·hma
right	ညာဘက်မှာ॥	nya·be'·hma
straight ahead	ရှေ့·တည်·တည်·မှာ॥	sháy·té·dé·hma
there	ဟိုမှာ॥	hoh·hma

by bus	ဘတ်စ်ကား·နဲ့	ba'·suh·kà·né
by taxi	တက္ကစီ·နဲ့	te'·kuh·sì·né
by train	ရထား·နဲ့	yuh·tà·né
on foot	ခြေကျင်	chay·jing

north	မြောက်ဘက်မှာ	myow'·pe'·hma
south	တောင်ဘက်မှာ	towng·be'·hma
east	အရှေ့ဘက်မှာ	uh·sháy·be'·hma
west	အနောက်ဘက်မှာ	uh·now'·pe'·hma

signs

အဝင်/အထွက်	uh·wing/uh·twe'	**Entrance/Exit**
ဖွင့်/ပိတ်ထားသည်	pwing/pay'·tà·ṭhi	**Open/Closed**
အခန်းအား ရှိသည်	uh·kàng·à shí·ṭhi	**Vacancies**
အခန်းအား မရှိပါ	uh·kàng·à muh·shí·ba	**No Vacancies**
စုံစမ်း·ရန်	sohng·zàng·yang	**Information**
ရဲစခန်း	yè·suh·kàng	**Police Station**
တားမြစ်နယ်မြေ	tà·myi'·ne'·myay	**Prohibited**
အိမ်သာ	ayng·ṭha	**Toilets**
ကျား/မ	chà/má	**Men/Women**
ပူ/အေး	poo/àr	**Hot/Cold**

accommodation

finding accommodation

Where's a ...?	--- ဘယ်မှာလဲ။	... be·hma·lè
bungalow	ဘန်ဂလို	buhng·guh·loh
guesthouse	တည်းခိုခန်း	tè·koh·gàn
hotel	ဟိုတယ်	hoh·te

Can you recommend somewhere ...?	--- တဲ့နေရာ ညွှန်ပေးနိုင်မလား။	... te·nay·ya hnyun·pày·nayng·muh·là
cheap	ဈေးပေါ	zày·pàw
good	ကောင်း	kòwng
nearby	နီး	nì

Do you have a ... room?	--- ရှိသလား။	... shí·ţhuh·là
single	တစ်ယောက်ခန်း	tuh·yow'·kàng
double	နှစ်ယောက်ခန်း	hnuh·yow'·kàng
twin	ခုတင်နှစ်လုံး	guh·ding·hnuh·lòhng·
	ပါတဲ့အခန်း	pa·dé·uh·kàng

I'd like to book a room, please.
အခန်းတစ်ခန်း ကြိုယူချင်ပါတယ်။ — uh·kàng·tuh·kàng choh·yoo·jin·ba·de

I have a reservation.
ကျွန်တော်/ကျွန်မ — chuh·naw/chuh·má
ဘွတ်ကင် လုပ်ထားတယ်။ — bu'·king loh'·tà·de m/f

My name is ...
ကျွန်တော်/ကျွန်မ နာမည်က --- ပါ။ — chuh·náw/chuh·má nang·me·gá ...ba m/f

How much is it per night/person?
တစ်ည/တစ်ယောက် ဘယ်လောက်လဲ။ — tuh·nyá/tuh·yow' be·low'·lè

Can I see it?
ကြည့်လို့ ရမလား။   chí·lóh yá·muh·là

I'd like to stay for (two) nights.
(နှစ်)ည နေချင်ပါတယ်။   (hnuh)·nyá nay·jing·ba·de

From (July 2) to (July 6).
(ဂျူလိုင်လ ၂ရက်နေ့,)က   (joo·layng·lá hnuh·ye'·né)·gá
(ဂျူလိုင်လ ၆ရက်နေ့,)အထိ။   (joo·layng·lá chow'·ye'·né)·uh·tí

Am I allowed to camp here?
ဒီမှာ စခန်းချလို့ ရမလား။   di·hma suh·kàng·chá·lóh yá·muh·là

Is there a camp site nearby?
ဒီနားမှာ စခန်းချစရာနေရာ   di·nà·hma suh·kàng·chá·zuh·ya·nay·ya
ရှိသလား။   shí·ṭhuh·là

Can I pay ...?   --- ပေးနိုင်သလား။   ... pày·naing·ṭhuh·là
    by credit card   ခရက်ဒစ်ကဒ်နဲ့,   kuh·ye'·di'·ka'·né
    with a travellers   ခရီးသွား   kuh·yì·ṭhwà
    cheque   ချက်လက်မှတ   che'·le'·hma'

requests & queries

When's breakfast served?
မနက်စာ ဘယ်အချိန်မှာ   muh·ne'·sa be·uh·chayng·hma
ကျွေးသလဲ။   chwày·ṭhuh·lè

Where's breakfast served?
မနက်စာ ဘယ်မှာ ကျွေးသလဲ။   muh·ne'·sa be·hma chwày·ṭhuh·lè

Please wake me at (seven).
(၇နာရီ)မှာ နှိုးပါ။   (kung·nuh·na·yi)·hma hnòh·ba

Could I have my key, please?
ကျနော်/ကျမ သော့ ပေးပါ။   chuh·náw/chuh·má tháw pày·ba m/f

Do you have a ...?   --- ရှိသလား။   ... shí·ṭhuh·là
    mosquito net   ခြင်ထောင်   ching·downg
    safe   မီးခံသေတ္တာ   mì·gang·thí'·ta

The room is too ...   အခန်းက ---   uh·kàng·gá ...
    expensive   ဈေးကြီးလွန်းတယ်   zày·chì·lùng·de
    noisy   ဆူညံလွန်းတယ်   ṣoo·nyang·lùng·de
    small   သေးလွန်းတယ်   thày·lùng·de

The ... doesn't work.	- - - ပျက်နေတယ်။	... pye'·nay·de
air conditioner	အဲကွန်း	è·kùng
fan	ပန်ကာ	pang·ka
toilet	အိမ်သာ	ayng·tha

This ... isn't clean.	ဒီ - - - ညစ်ပတ်နေတယ်။	di ... nyi'·pa'·nay·de
pillow	ခေါင်းအုံး	gòwng·òhng
sheet	အိပ်ရာခင်း	ay'·yuh·gìng
towel	မျက်နှာသုတ်ပုဝါ	mye'·hnuh·thoh'·puh·wa

checking out

What time is checkout?
ဘယ်အချိန် အခန်းက ထွက်ရမလဲ။ be·uh·chayng·uh·kàng·gá·twe'·yá·muh·lè

Can I leave my luggage here?
သေတ္တာ ဒီမှာ ထားခဲ့လို့ရမလား။ thi'·ta·di·hma·tà·gé·lóh·yá·muh·là

Could I have my ..., please?	ကျနော်/ကျမ - - - ...	chuh·náw/chuh·má ... pày·ba m/f
	ပေးပါ။	
deposit	စရံငွေ	zuh·yang·ngway
passport	ပတ်စပို့	pa'·suh·pó
valuables	အဖိုးတန် ပစ္စည်းတွေ	uh·pòh·tang·pyi'·sì·dway

communications & banking

the internet

Where's the local Internet café?
အင်တာနက် ကဖေး ဘယ်မှာလဲ။ ing·ta·ne'·ká·pày·be·hma·lè

How much is it per hour?
တစ်နာရီ ဘယ်လောက်လဲ။ tuh·na·yi·be·low'·lè

I'd like to ...	- - - ချင်ပါတယ်။	... ching·ba·de
check my email	အီးမေးလ်ကြည့်	ì·màyl·chí
get Internet access	အင်တာနက်ချိတ်	ing·ta·ne'·chay'
use a printer	ပရင်တာသုံး	puh·ying·ta·thòhng
use a scanner	စကင်နာသုံး	suh·king·na·thòhng

mobile/cell phone

I'd like a mobile/cell phone for hire.
ဆဲလ်ဖုံး ငှားချင်ပါတယ်။ — şèl·pòhng hngà·jing·ba·de

I'd like a SIM card for your network.
ဒီနယ်က ဆင်းမ်ကတ် လိုချင်ပါတယ်။ — di·ne·gá sim·ka' loh·jing·ba·de

What are the rates?
နှုန်းက ဘယ်လောက်လဲ။ — hnòhng·gá be·low'·lè

telephone

What's your phone number?
တယ်လီဖုန်းနံပါတ် ဘယ်လောက်လဲ။ — te·li·pòhng·nang·ba' be·low'·lè

The number is …
နံပါတ်က --- ပါ။ — nang·ba'·ká … ba

Where's the nearest public phone?
အနီးဆုံး အများသုံး တယ်လီဖုန်း ဘယ်မှာလဲ။ — uh·nì·zòhng uh·myà·thòhng te·li·pòhng be·hma·lè

I'd like to buy a phonecard.
ဖုန်းကတ် ဝယ်ချင်ပါတယ်။ — pòhng·ka' we·jing·ba·de

I want to …	--- ချင်ပါတယ်။	… jing·ba·de
call (Singapore)	(စင်ကာပူ)ကို ခေါ်	(sing·guh·poo)·goh kaw
make a local call	မြို့တွင်း တယ်လီဖုန်းခေါ်	myóh·dwìng te·li·pòhng·kaw
reverse the charges	ဟိုဘက်ကလူကို ဖုန်းခ ပေးစေ	hoh·be'·ká·loo·goh pòhng·gá pày·zay

How much does … cost?	--- ဘယ်လောက် ကျမလဲ။	… be·low' chá·muh·lè
a (three)-minute call	(၃)မိနစ် ခေါ်ရင်	(thòhng)·muh·ni' kaw·ying
each extra minute	နောက်တစ်မိနစ်ကို	now'·tuh·muh·ni'·koh

(30c) per (30) seconds.	(၃၀) စက္ကန့်ကို ဆင့်(၃၀)။	(thòhng·ze) se'·káng·goh şíng·(thòhng·ze)

post office

I want to send a …	--- ပို့ချင်ပါတယ်။	…póh·jing·ba·de
fax	ဖက်စ်	faks
letter	စာ	sa
parcel	ပါဆယ်	pa·şe
postcard	ပို့စကတ်	póh·suh·ka'
I want to buy a/an …	--- ဝယ်ချင်ပါတယ်။	… we·jing·ba·de
envelope	စာအိတ်	sa·ay'
stamp	တံဆိပ်ခေါင်း	duh·zay'·gòwng
Please send it (to Australia) by …	(ဩစတြေးလျကို) --- နဲ့ ပို့ပေးပါ။	(aw·suh·tray·lyá·koh) … né póh·pày·ba
airmail	လေကြောင်းစာ	lay·jòwng·za
express mail	အမြန်	uh·myang
registered mail	မှတ်ပုံတင်စာ	hma'·pohng·ting·za
surface mail	ရိုးရိုး	yòh·yòh

Is there any mail for me?

ကျနော့်/ကျမ အတွက် စာရှိသလား။	chuh·náw/chuh·má uh·twe' sa·shí·ţhuh·là m/f

bank

I'd like to …	--- ချင်ပါတယ်။	… ching·ba·de
Where can I …?	ဘယ်မှာ --- လို့ရမလဲ။	be·hma … lóh·yá·muh·lè
arrange a transfer	ငွေလွှဲ	ngway·hlwè
cash a cheque	ချက်လက်မှတ်ကို ငွေလ	che'·le'·hma'·koh ngway·lè
change money	ငွေလဲ	ngway·lè
change a travellers cheque	ခရီးချက်လက်မှတ်လဲ	kuh·yì·che'·le'·hma'·lè
What's the …?	--- ဘယ်လောက်လဲ။	… be·low'·lè
charge for that	အဲဒါအတွက် အခကြေးငွေက	è·da·uh·twe' uh·ká·chày·ngway·gá
exchange rate	ငွေလဲလှယ်နှုန်းက	ngway·lè·hle·hnòhng·gá
It's …		
(12) kyat	(၁၂) ကျပ်	(şé·hnuh) cha'
free	အလကားပေးတယ်	uh·luh·gà pày·de

personal & possessive pronouns		
I	ကျနော်/ကျမ	chuh·naw/chuh·má m/f
my	ကျနော့်/ကျမ	chuh·náw/chuh·má m/f
you sg	ခင်ဗျား/ရှင်	king·myà/shing m/f
your sg	ခင်ဗျား/ရှင့်	king·myà/shíng m/f
he/she/it	သူ	thoo
his/her	သူ့	thóo
we	ကျနော်တို့/ကျမတို့	chuh·naw·dóh/chuh·má·dóh m/f
our	ကျနော်တို့/ကျမတို့	chuh·naw·dóh/chuh·má·dóh m/f
you pl	ခင်ဗျားတို့/ရှင်တို့	king·myà·dóh/shing·dóh m/f
your pl	ခင်ဗျားတို့/ရှင်တို့	king·myà·dóh/shing·dóh m/f
they/their	သူတို့	thu·dóh

sightseeing

getting in

What time does it open/close?
ဘယ်အချိန် ဖွင့်/ပိတ်သလဲ။ — be·uh·chayng pwíng/pay'·ţhuh·lè

What's the admission charge?
ဝင်ကြေး ဘယ်လောက်လဲ။ — wing·jày be·low'·lè

Is there a discount for students/children?
ကျောင်းသား/ကလေး အတွက် လျှော့ဈေး ရှိသလား။ — chòwng·ţhà/kuh·lày uh·twe' sháw·zày shí·ţhuh·là

I'd like a ...	--- လိုချင်ပါတယ်။	... loh·jing·ba·de
guide	လမ်းညွှန်တစ်ယောက်	làng·hnyung·tuh·yow'
local map	ဒီနေရာကမြေပုံ	di·nay·ya·gá myay·bohng

I'd like to see ...	--- ကြည့်ချင်ပါတယ်။	... chí·jing·ba·de
Can I take a photo?	ဓါတ်ပုံရိုက်လို့ ရသလား။	da'·pohng·yai'·lóh yá·là

tours

When's the next ...?	နောက် --- က ဘယ်အချိန်လဲ။	now' ... ká be·uh·chayng·lè
boat trip	သင်္ဘော	thìng·bàw
day trip	နေ့ချင်းပြန် ခရီး	né·jìng·byang kuh·yì

Is (the) ... included?	--- အပါအဝင်လား။	... uh·pa·uh·wing·là
accommodation	တည်းခိုခ	tè·koh·gá
admission charge	ဝင်ကြေး	wing·jày
food	အစားအသောက်	uh·sà·uh·thow'
transport	ခရီးစရိတ်	kuh·yì·zuh·yay'

How long is the tour?
ဒီခရီးစဉ်က ဘယ်လောက် ကြာမလဲ။   di·kuh·yì·zing·gá be·low' cha·muh·lè

What time should we be back?
ဘယ်အချိန် ပြန်လာရမလဲ။   be·uh·chayng pyang·la·yá·muh·lè

monument	အထိမ်းအမှတ် ကျောက်တိုင်	uh·tàyng·uh·hma' chow'·taing
museum	ပြတိုက်	pyá·dai'
old city	မြို့ဟောင်း	myóh·hòwng
palace	နန်းတော်	nàng·daw
ruins	အပျက်အစီး	uh·pye'·uh·sì
statues	ရုပ်ထု	yoh'·tú
temple	စေတီ	zay·di

shopping

enquiries

Where's a ...?	--- ဘယ်မှာလဲ။	... be·hma·lè
bank	ဘဏ်တိုက်	bang·dai'
bookshop	စာအုပ်ဆိုင်	sa·oh'·saing
camera shop	ကင်မရာဆိုင်	king·muh·ya·zaing
department store	ကုန်တိုက်	kohng·dai'
(floating) market	(ရေပေါ်)ဈေး	(yay·baw·)zày
supermarket	ဆူပါမားကက်	şoo·pa·mà·ke'

Where can I buy (a padlock)?
(သော့ခလောက်) ဘယ်မှာ
ဝယ်လို့ရမလဲ။

(tháw·guh·low') be·hma
we·lóh·yá·muh·lè

Can I look at it?
ကြည့်လို့ ရမလား။

chí·lóh yá·muh·là

Do you have any others?
တခြား ရှိသေးလား။

tuh·chà shí·thày·là

Does it have a guarantee?
ဝါရံတီ ရှိသလား။

wuh·yang·ti shí·thuh·là

Can I have it sent overseas?
နိုင်ငံခြားကို ပို့လို့ရမလား။

naing·ngan·jà·goh póh·lóh·yá·muh·là

Can I have my ... repaired?
ဒီ --- ပြင်ပေးနိုင်မလား။

di ... pying·pày·naing·muh·là

It's faulty.
ပျက်နေတယ်။

pye'·nay·de

I'd like a bag, please.
အိတ်တစ်အိတ် လိုချင်ပါတယ်။

ay'·tuh·ay' loh·jing·ba·de

I'd like a refund.
ပိုက်ဆံ ပြန်အမ်းပါ။

pai·şang pyang·àng·ba

I'd like to return this.
ပြန်ပေးချင်ပါတယ်။

pyang·pày·jing·ba·de

paying

How much is it?
ဒါ ဘယ်လောက်လဲ။

da be·low'·lè

Can you write down the price?
ဈေး ချရေးပေးပါ။

zày chá·yày·pày·ba

That's too expensive.
ဈေးကြီးလွန်းတယ်။

zày·chì·lùng·de

What's your lowest price?
အနည်းဆုံးဈေးက ဘယ်လောက်လဲ။

uh·nè·zòhng·zày·gá be·low'·lè

I'll give you (480) kyat.
(၄၈၀) ကျပ် ပေးမယ်။

(làx·yá·shì'·şe) cha' pày·me

There's a mistake in the bill.
ဒီပြေစာမှာ အမှား ပါနေတယ်။

di·pyay·za·hma uh·hmà pa·nay·de

Do you accept ...?	--- လက်ခံသလား။	... le'·kang·ṭhuh·là
credit cards	ခရက်ဒစ်ကဒ်	kuh·ye'·di'·ka'
debit cards	ဒဲဘစ်ကဒ်	dè·bi'·ka'
travellers cheques	ခရီးချက်လက်မှတ်	kuh·yì·che'·le'·hma'

I'd like ..., please.	--- လိုချင်ပါတယ်။	... loh·jing·ba·de
a receipt	ဘောက်ချာ	bow'·cha
my change	ကျနော့်/ကျမ	chuh·náw/chuh·má
	အကြွေ	uh·chway m/f

clothes & shoes

Can I try it on?
ဝတ်ကြည့်လို့ ရမလား။
wu'·chí·lóh yá·muh·là

My size is (42).
ကျနော့်/ကျမ ဆိုက်က (၄၂)။
chuh·náw/chuh·má ṣai'·ká (lày·zé·hnì') m/f

It doesn't fit.
မတော်ဘူး။
muh·taw·bòo

small	အသေး	uh·thày
medium	အလတ်	uh·la'
large	အကြီး	uh·chì

books & music

I'd like a ...	--- လိုချင်ပါတယ်။	... loh·jing·ba·de
newspaper (in English)	(အင်္ဂလိပ်) သတင်းစာ	(ing·guh·lay') ṭhuh·dìng·za
pen	ဘောပင်	bàw·ping

Is there an English-language bookshop?
အင်္ဂလိပ် စာအုပ်ဆိုင် ရှိသလား။
ing·guh·lay' sa·oh'·ṣaing shí·ṭhuh·là

I'm looking for something by (Zaw Gyi).
(ဇော်ဂျီ) ရေးတဲ့စာအုပ် ရှာနေပါတယ်။
(zaw·ji) yày·dé·sa·oh' sha·nay·ba·de

Can I listen to this?
ဒါ ခဏ နားထောင်လို့ ရမလား။
da kuh·ná nà·towng·lóh yá·muh·là

photography

Can you ...?	--- နိုင်သလား။	... naing·ṭhuh·là
burn a CD from	မယ်မိုရီကတ်ကနေ	me·moh·yi·ka'·ká·nay
my memory card	စီဒီ ပြောင်းပေး	si·di·pyòwng·pày
develop this film	ဒီဖလင်ကူးပေးဖလင	di·puh·ling·kòo·pày puh·ling
load my film	ကျနော်/ကျမ	chuh·náw/chuh·má
	ဖလင် ထည့်ပေး	puh·ling té·pày m/f

I need a/an ... film	ဒီ ကင်မရာအတွက် ---	di king·muh·ya·uh·twe' ...
for this camera.	ဖလင် လိုနေတယ်။	puh·ling loh·nay·de
APS	အေပီအက်စ်	ay·pi·es
B&W	ဘလက်အင်ဝိုက်	buh·le'·ing·wai'
colour	ကာလာ	ka·la
slide	ဆလိုက်	ṣuh·lai'
(200) speed	(၂၀၀) စပိဒ်	(hnuh·ya) suh·píd

When will it be ready?	ဘယ်တော့ ရမလဲ။	be·dáw yá·muh·lè

toiletries

condoms	ကွန်ဒုံ	kung·dung
conditioner	ဆံပင်ပျော့ဆေး	zuh·bing·pyáw·ṣày
deodorant	ချွေးနံ့ပျောက်ဆေး	chwày·náng·pyow'·ṣày
insect repellent	ပိုးကောင် မလာတဲ့ဆေး	pòh·gowng muh·la·dé·ṣày
razor blades	မုတ်ဆိတ်ရိတ်ဓား	moh'·ṣay'·yay'·dà
sanitary napkins	အမျိုးသမီး	uh·myòe·thuh·mì
	လစဉ်သုံး ပစ္စည်း	lá·zing·thòhng pyi'·sì
shampoo	ခေါင်းလျှော်ရည်	gòwng·shaw·yay
shaving cream	မုတ်ဆိတ်ရိတ် ဆပ်ပြာ	moh'·ṣay'·yay' ṣa'·pya
soap	ဆပ်ပြာ	ṣa'·pya
sunscreen	နေပူခံ လိမ်းဆေး	nay·poo·gang làyng·zày
toilet paper	အိမ်သာသုံး စက္ကူ	ayng·ṭha·thòhng se'·koo
toothbrush	သွားတိုက် သွားပွတ်တံ	thwà·tai' ṭhuh·bu'·tang
toothpaste	သွားတိုက်ဆေး	thwà·dai'·ṣày

meeting people

greetings, goodbyes & introductions

| Hello/Hi. | မင်္ဂလာပါ။ | ming·guh·la·ba |
| Goodbye. | သွားမယ်နော်။ | thwà·me·naw |

| Mr | ဦး | òo |
| Mrs/Miss | ဒေါ်/မ | daw/má |

How are you?
နေကောင်းလား။ — nay·kòwng·là

Fine. And you?
ကောင်းပါတယ်။ — kòwng·ba·de
ခင်ဗျား/ရှင်ရော။ — king·myà/shing·yàw m/f

What's your name?
နာမည် ဘယ်လို ခေါ်သလဲ။ — nang·me be·loh kaw·thuh·lè

My name is ...
ကျွန်တော်/ကျွန်မ နာမည်က --- ပါ။ — chuh·náw/chuh·má nang·me·gá ... ba m/f

I'm pleased to meet you.
တွေ့ရတာ ဝမ်းသာပါတယ်။ — twáy·yá·da wùng·tha·ba·de

This is my ...	ဒါ ကျွန်တော်/ကျွန်မ --- ပါ။	da chuh·náw/chuh·má ... ba m/f
boyfriend	ရည်းစား	yì·zà
daughter	သမီး	thuh·mì
father	အဖေ	uh·pay
friend	သူငယ်ချင်း	thuh·nge·jìng
girlfriend	ရည်းစား	yì·zà
husband	အမျိုးသား	uh·myòh·thà
mother	အမေ	uh·may
older brother	အကို	uh·koh
sister (older/younger)	အမ/ညီမ	uh·má/nyi·má
son	သား	thà
younger brother (for man/woman)	ညီ/မောင်လေး	nyi/mowng·làye
wife	အမျိုးသမီး	uh·myòh·thuh·mì

36

Here's my ...	ဒီမှာ ကျနော်/ကျမ	di·hma chuh·náw/chuh·má
	--- ပါ။	... ba m/f
What's your ...?	ခင်ဗျား/ရှင့် ---	kuhng·byà/shíng ...
	က ဘာလဲ။	gá ba·lè m/f
address	လိပ်စာ	lay'·sa
email address	အီးမေးလ်	ì·màyl
home number	အိမ် ဖုန်းနံပါတ်	ayng pòhng·nang·ba'
mobile number	ဆဲလ်ဖုန်းနံပါတ်	şèl·pòhng·nang·ba'

occupations

What's your occupation?	ဘာအလုပ် လုပ်သလဲ။	ba·uh·loh' loh'·thuh·lè
I'm a/an ...	ကျနော်/ကျမ	chuh·náw/chuh·má
	က --- ပါ။	gá ... ba m/f
nurse	သူနာပြု	thu·na·pyú m&f
office worker	ရုံးဝန်ထမ်း	yòhng·wung·dàng m&f
student	ကျောင်းသား/	chòwng·thà/
	ကျောင်းသူ	chòwng·thoo m/f
teacher	ဆရာ/ ဆရာမ	şuh·ya/şuh·ya·má m/f
tradesperson	ကုန်သည်	kohng·the m&f
writer	စာရေးဆရာ/	sa·yày·şuh·ya/
	စာရေးဆရာမ	sa·yày·şuh·ya·má m/f

---

male & female

Burmese equivalents of the personal pronouns 'I', 'we' and 'you' have different forms (male and female), depending on the gender of the person indicated by the pronoun. You'll notice that these forms are marked as m/f in phrases throughout this chapter. Depending on the pronoun (ie 'I/we' or 'you') these abbreviations refer to the speaker or the person addressed. On the other hand, Burmese doesn't distinguish between 'he' and 'she' – both pronouns are translated with the same word – thu (သူ). See also the box **personal & possessive pronouns** on p 31.

background

Where are you from?	ဘယ်က လာသလဲ။	be·gá la·ṭhuh·lè
I'm from ...	--- ကပါ။	... gá·ba
Australia	ဩစတြေးလျ	aw·suh·tray·lyá
Canada	ကနေဒါ	kuh·nay·da
England	အင်္ဂလန်	ing·guh·lang
Ireland	အိုင်ယာလန်	ayng·ya·lang
New Zealand	နယူးဇီလန်	nuh·yòo·zi·lang
Scotland	စကော့တလန်	suh·káw·tuh·lang
the USA	အမေရိကား	uh·may·yí·kà
Wales	ဝေလနိုင်ငံ	way·lá·naing·ngang

Are you married?	အိမ်ထောင် ရှိလားသ။	ayng·downg shí·ṭhuh·là
I'm ...	ကျနေ္တာ်/ကျမ က ---	chuh·náw/chuh·má gá ... m/f
married	အိမ်ထောင် ရှိပါတယ်	ayng·downg shí·ba·de m&f
single	လူပျိုပါ/အပျိုပါ	loo·byoh·ba/uh·pyoh·ba m/f

age

How old ...?	--- အသက်	... uh·the'
	ဘယ်လောက်လဲ။	be·low'·lè
are you	ခင်ဗျား/ရှင်	kuhng·myà/shíng m/f
is your son	ခင်ဗျား/ရှင် သား	kuhng·myà/shíng thà m/f
is your daughter	ခင်ဗျား/ရှင် သမီး	kuhng·myà/shíng thuh·mì m/f

I am ... years old.		
ကျနေ္တာ်/ကျမက --- နှစ် ရှိပြီ။		chuh·náw/chuh·má·gá ... hni' shí·bi m/f
He/She is ... years old.		
သူက --- နှစ် ရှိပြီ။		thu·gá ... hni' shí·bi

classifiers					
animals	ကောင်	kowng	plates (of food)	ပန်းကန်	buh·guhng
clothes	ထည်	te	vehicles	စီး	zì
people	ယောက်	yow'	written things	စောင်	zowng

feelings

I'm ...	ကျနော်/ကျမ --- တယ်။	chuh·náw/chuh·má ... de m/f
I'm not ...	ကျနော်/ကျမ မ --- ဘူး။	chuh·náw/chuh·má muh ... bòo m/f
Are you ...?	--- သလား။	... ţhuh·là
cold	ချမ်း	chàng
happy	ပျော်	pyaw
hot	ပိုက်	ai'
hungry	ဆာ	şa
OK	နေကောင်း	nay·kòwng
thirsty	ရေဆာ	yay·şa
tired	မော	màw

entertainment

beach

Where's the ...	--- ပင်လယ်ကမ်းခြေက	... ping·le·kàng·jay·gá
beach?	ဘယ်မှာလဲ။	be·hma·lè
best	အကောင်းဆုံး	uh·kòwng·zòhng
nearest	အနီးဆုံး	uh·nì·zòhng
public	အများသုံး	uh·myà·thòhng
How much for a/an ...?	--- ဘယ်လောက်လဲ။	... be·low'·lè
chair	ကုလားထိုင် တစ်လုံး	kuh·luh·taing tuh·lòhng
umbrella	ထီးတစ်လက်	tì·tuh·le'

Is it safe to swim/dive here?

ဒီမှာ ရေကူးရင်/ကားမောင်းရင်
အန္တရာယ် ကင်းသလား။

di·hma yay·kòo·yin/kà·mòwng·yin
ang·duh·ye kìng·ţhuh·là

What time is high/low tide?

ဒီရေတက်ချိန်/ဒီရေကျချိန်
ဘယ်တော့လဲ။

di·yay·te'·chayng/di·yay·kyá·jayng
be·dáw·lè

water sports

Can I book a lesson?

သင်တန်းအတွက် ကြိုစာရင်း		thing·dàng·uh·twe' choh·suh·yìng
ပေးလို့ရသလား။		pày·ló·yá·ṭhuh·là

Can I hire (a) ...?	--- ငှားလို့ ရသလား။	... hngà·lóh·yá·ṭhuh·là
canoe	ကနူး	kuh·nòo
diving equipment	ရေငုပ်ကိရိယာ	yay·ngoh'·kuh·ri·ya
guide	ဂိုက်	gai'
life jacket	အသက်ကယ် အင်္ကျီ	uh·the'·ke ìng·ji
motorboat	မော်တော်ဘုတ်	maw·taw·boh'
sailboard	ပင်လယ် လှိုင်းစီး	ping·le hlàing·sì
	ရွက်တပ် ပျဉ်ချပ်	ywe'·ta' pying·ja'
sailing boat	ရွက်လှေ	ywe'·hlay
snorkelling gear	လေပြွန်နဲ့ ရေငုပ်တာ	lay·pyung·né yay·ngoh'·ta
surfboard	လှိုင်းစီးပျဉ်	hlàing·sì·pying

Are there any ...?	--- ရှိသလား။	... shí·ṭhuh·là
reefs	ကျောက်တန်း	chow'·tàng
rips	ရေစီး ကြမ်းတဲ့နေရာ	yay·zì chàng·dé·nay·ya
water hazards	ရေဘေး အန္တရာယ်	yay·bày uhng·duh·ye

going out

Where can I find ...?	--- ဘယ်မှာ ရှိသလဲ။	... be·hma shí·ṭhuh·lè
clubs	ကလပ်တွေ	kuh·la'·tway
pubs	အရက်ဆိုင်တွေ	uh·ye'·ṣaing·dway
restaurants	စားသောက်ဆိုင်တွေ	sà·thow'·ṣaing·dway

I feel like going to a/the ...	--- သွားချင်ပါတယ်။	... thwà·jin·ba·de
concert	စတိတ်ရှိုး	suh·tay'·shòh
folk opera	ပြဇာတ်	pyá·za'
karaoke bar	ကာရာအိုကေဆိုင်	ka·ya·òo·kày·ṣaing
movies	ရုပ်ရှင်	yoh'·shing
party	ပါတီ	pa·ti
performance	ပွဲ	pwè

interests

Do you like ...?	--- ကြိုက်သလား။	... chai'·thuh·là
I like ...	--- ကြိုက်တယ်။	... chai'·te
I don't like ...	--- မကြိုက်ဘူး။	... muh·chai'·pòo
art	အနုပညာ	uh·nú·pying·nya
cooking	အချက်အပြုတ်	uh·che'·uh·pyoh'
movies	ရုပ်ရှင်	yoh'·shing
photography	ဓါတ်ပုံ	da'·pohng
reading	စာဖတ်တာ	sa·pa'·ta
sport	အားကစား	à·guh·zà
surfing the Internet	အင်တာနက် လုပ်တာ	ing·ta·ne' loh'·ta
swimming	ရေကူးတာ	yay·kòo·da
travelling	ခရီးသွားတာ	kuh·yì·thwà·da
watching TV	တီဗွီကြည့်တာ	ti·bi·chí·ta

Do you like to ...?	--- ချင်သလား။	... jing·thuh·là
dance	က	ká
go to concerts	ဂီတပွဲ သွားနားထောင်	gi·tá·pwè thwà·nà·towng
listen to music	သီချင်း နားထောင်	thuh·chìng nà·town

food & drink

finding a place to eat

Can you	--- တစ်ခု	... tuh·kú
recommend a ...?	အကြံပေးနိုင်မလား။	uh·chang·pày·naing·muh·là
bar	အရက်ဆိုင်	uh·ye'·şaing
café	ကော်ဖီဆိုင်	kaw·pi·şaing
restaurant	စားသောက်ဆိုင်	sà·thow'·şaing

I'd like ..., please.	--- လိုချင်ပါတယ်။	... loh·jing·ba·de
a table for (four)	(၄)သောက်စာ စားပွဲ	(làq)·yow'·sa zuh·bwè
the nonsmoking	ဆေးလိပ်	şày·lay'
section	မသောက်ရတဲ့နေရာ	muh·thow'·yá·dé·nay·ya
the smoking	ဆေးလိပ်	şày·lay'
section	သောက်လို့ရတဲ့နေရာ	thow'·lóh·yá·dé·nay·ya

ordering food

breakfast	မနက်စာ	muh·ne'·sa
lunch	နေ့လည်စာ	náy·le·za
dinner	ညစာ	nyá·za
snack	အဆာပြေ စားစရာ	uh·şa·byay sà·zuh·ya
I'd like (the) ..., please.	--- ပေးပါ။	... pày·ba
bill	ဘောက်ချာ	bow'·cha
menu	မီးနူး	mì·nù
that dish	အဲဒီ ဟင်းခွက်	è·di hìng·gwe'
wine list	ဝိုင်စာရင်း	waing·suh·yìng
What would you recommend?	ဘာ အကြံပေးမလဲ။	ba uh·chang·pày·muh·lè
bowl	ပန်းကန်လုံး	buh·gang·lòhng
chopsticks	တူ	too
cloth	လက်သုတ်ပုဝါ	le'·thoh'·puh·wa
cup	ပန်းကန်လုံး	buh·gang·lòhng
fork	ခက်ရင်း	kuh·yìng
glass	ဖန်ခွက်	pang·gwe'
knife	ဓား	dà
plate	ပန်းကန်	buh·gang
spoon	ဇွန်း	zùng
teaspoon	လက်ဖက်ရည်ဇွန်း	luh·pe'·yay·zùng

drinks

(cup of) coffee ...	ကော်ဖီ (၁)ခွက် ---	kaw·pi (tuh·)kwe' ...
(cup of) tea ...	လက်ဖက်ရည် (၁)ခွက် ---	luh·pe'·yay (tuh·)kwe' ...
with milk	နို့နဲ့	nóh·né
without sugar	သကြား မပါဘဲ	ţhuh·jà muh·pa·bè
orange juice	လိမ်မော်ရည်	layng·maw·yay
soft drink	ဖျော်ရည်	pyaw·yay
drinking water	သောက်ရေ	thow'·yay
hot water	ရေနွေး	yay·nwày
mineral water	ရေသန့်ဗူး	yay·ţháng·bòo

in the bar

I'll have …
--- ယူမယ်။ … yoo·me

I'll buy you a drink.
ခင်ဗျား/ရှင့်ကို ကျနော်/ကျမ တိုက်မယ်။ kuhng·myà/shíng·goh chuh·náw/chuh·má tai'·me **m/f**

What would you like?
ဘာမှာမလဲ။ ba·hma·muh·lè

Cheers!
ချီးယား။ chì·yà

gin	ဂျင်	jing
rum	ရမ်	rum
vodka	ဗော့ဒကာ	báw·duh·ka
a bottle/glass of (beer)	(ဘီယာ) ၁ပုလင်း/၁ခွက်	(bi·ya) duh·buh·lìng/tuh·kwe'
a shot of (whisky)	(ဝီစကီ) ၁ပက်	(wi·suh·ki) tuh·pe'
a bottle/glass of … wine	ဝိုင် --- ၁ပုလင်း/၁ခွက်	waing … duh·buh·lìng/tuh·kwe'
red	အနီ	uh·ni
sparkling	စပတ်ကလင်	suh·pa'·kuh·ling
white	အဖြူ	uh·pyu

self-catering

What's the local speciality?
ဒီမြို့က စပယ်ရှယ် အစားအစာက ဘာလဲ။ di·myóh·gá suh·pe·she uh·sà·uh·sa·gá ba·lè

What's that?
အဲဒါ ဘာလဲ။ è·da ba·lè

How much is (a kilo of) …?
--- (တစ်ကီလို) ဘယ်လောက်လဲ။ … (tuh·ki·loh) be·low'·lè

I'd like ...	--- ပေးပါ။	... pày·ba
(100) grams	(တစ်ရာ) ဂရမ်	(tuh·ya)·guh·yang
(two) kilos	(နှစ်) ကီလို	(hnuh)·ki·loh
(three) pieces	(သုံး) ခု	(thòhng)·gú
(six) slices	(ခြောက်) ချပ်	(chow')·cha'

Enough.	တော်ပြီ။	taw·bi
A bit more.	နည်းနည်း	nè·nè
	ထပ်ထည့်ပါဦး။	ta'·té·ba·òhng
Less.	လျှော့လိုက်ပါဦး။	sháw·lai·pa·òhng

special diets & allergies

Is there a vegetarian restaurant near here?

ဒီနားမှာ သက်သတ်လွတ်	di·nà·hma the'·tha·lu'
စားသောက်ဆိုင် ရှိသလား။	sà·thow'·ṣaing shí·ṭhuh·là

Do you have vegetarian food?

သက်သတ်လွတ် စားစရာ	the'·tha·lu' sà·zuh·ya
ရှိသလား။	shí·ṭhuh·là

Could you prepare	--- မပါဘဲ	... muh·pa·bè
a meal without ...?	ပြင်ပေးနိုင်မလား။	pying·pày·naing·muh·là
butter	ထောပတ်	tàw·ba'
eggs	ကြက်ဥ	che'·ú
fish sauce	ငံပြာရည်	ngang·pya·yay
meat	အသား	uh·thà
meat stock	အသားပြွတ်ရည်	uh·thà·pyoh'·yay

I'm allergic to ...	--- နဲ့ မတဲ့ဘူး။	... né muh·té·bòo
cashew	သီဟိုစေ့	thi·hoh·zí
chilli	ငရုတ်သီး	nguh·yoh'·thì
dairy produce	နို့ထွက် အစားအစာ	nóh·dwe' uh·sà·uh·sa
eggs	ကြက်ဥ	che'·ú
MSG	အချိုမှုန့်	uh·choh·hmóhng
peanuts	မြေပဲ	myay·bè
rice	ကောက်ညှင်း	kow'·hnying
seafood	ပင်လယ်စာ	ping·le·za

For other allergies see health, page 48.

menu decoder

bàyng·móhng	ဘိန်းမုန့်	pancakes made from rice flour, coconut, peanuts & poppy seeds
bè·óo·hìng	ဘဲဥဟင်း	duck-egg curry
buh·ya·jaw	ဗယာကြော်	split-pea fritters
buh·zung·hìng	ပုဇွန်ဟင်း	prawns in a tomato & onion curry
chang·yay	ကြံရည်	sugar-cane juice
cha·zang·hìng·gà	ကြာဆံဟင်းခါး	fish soup with rice vermicelli, vegetables & black pepper
cha·zang·ji kow'·şwè	ကြာဆံကြီး ခေါက်ဆွဲ	rice noodles with curry
che'·thà bòo·thì·hìng	ကြက်သား ဘူးသီးဟင်း	chicken & squash simmered in an onion curry sauce
che'·thà·né hmoh·chaw·je'	ကြက်သားနဲ့ မှိုကြော် ချက်	fried mushrooms & chicken
che'·thà şang·byoh'	ကြက်သား ဆန်ပြုတ်	chicken & rice soup
che'·thà uh·sa'·chaw	ကြက်သား အစပ်ကြော်	stir-fried chicken with chilli
ching·bowng·jaw	ချဉ်ပေါင်ကြော်	vegetables sautéed with green chili, prawns & bamboo shoots
chow'·chàw	ကျောက်ကျော	seaweed & coconut jelly
jing·ṭhoh'	ဂျင်းသုပ်	ginger, cabbage & onion salad
kaw·pyáng·jaw	ကော်ပြန့်ကြော်	fried egg roll · fried spring roll
kow'·hnying·bòwng	ကောက်ညှင်းပေါင်း	steamed sticky rice
kuh·luh·bè hìng·joh	ကုလားပဲ ဟင်းချို	split-pea soup
luh·pe'·thoh'	လက်ဖက်သုပ်	salad of peanuts, dried shrimp & lentils
màng·duh·làye móhng·di	မန္တလေး မုန့်တီ	noodles with chicken or fish
móhng·hìng·gà	မုန့်ဟင်းခါး	rice vermicelli in fish sauce
móhng·le'·sòwng	မုန့်လက်ဆောင်း	iced coconut milk with sago

móhng·lòhng·yay·baw	မုန့်လုံးရေပေါ်	sticky-rice dumplings filled with palm sugar
móhng·și·jaw	မုန့်ဆီကြော်	sweet fried rice pancakes
móhng·zàng	မုန့်ဆန်း	sticky-rice cake with jaggery
myay·bè·jaw	မြေပဲကြော်	fried peanuts
nang·byà	နံပြား	dry bread (eaten with beans)
nguh·bòwng·doh'	ငါးပေါင်းထုတ်	steamed fish in banana leaves
nguh·pe·țhoh'	ငါးဖယ်သုပ်	fish salad with coriander, onion & garlic
nwà·mi·hing·gà	နွားမြီးဟင်းခါး	oxtail & watercress
òhng·nóh hing·yay	အုန်းနို့ ဟင်းရည်	chicken in coconut
òhng·nóh kow'·șwè	အုန်းနို့ ခေါက်ဆွဲ	chicken in a coconut soup with noodles & egg
pè·bing·bow' pè·byà·jaw	ပဲပင်ပေါက်ပဲ ပြားကြော်	fried tofu with bean sprouts
pèh·wa·làay hing·joh	ပဲဝါလေး ဟင်းချို	soup of split mung beans
șay'·thà·né pè·hing·joh	ဆိတ်သားနဲ့ ပဲဟင်းချို	lamb soup with green peas
șé·hnuh·myòh hing·joh	ဆယ့်နှစ်မျိုး ဟင်းချို	chicken & vermicelli soup
șuh·nwing·muh·king	ဆနွင်းမကောင်း	semolina pudding
tàng·țhi·móhng	ထန်းသီးမုန့်	palm sugar cake
thìng·bàw·țhi·țhoh'	သဘော်သီးသုပ်	papaya, cabbage & onion salad
thuh·na'·sohng	သနပ်စုံ	salad of mixed vegetables
tóh·hòo·jow'	တို့ဟူးခြောက်	tofu crackers
tuh·muh·nè	ထမနဲ	sticky-rice pudding with sesame
uh·mè·țhà·né a·lòo·hìng	အမဲသားနဲ့ အာလူးဟင်း	beef & potato curry
we'·thà·doh'·tòh	ဝက်သားတုတ်ထိုး	pork kebabs
we'·thà·jow'·hìng	ဝက်သားခြောက်ဟင်း	dry pork curry with tamarind, fish sauce & spices
yuh·kaing móhng·di	ရခိုင် မုန့်တီ	noodles with fish, tamarind & chilli

emergencies

basics

Help!	ကယ်ပါ။	ke·ba
Stop!	ရပ်ပါ။	ya'·pa
Go away!	သွား။	thwà
Thief!	သူခိုး။	thuh·kòh
Fire!	မီး။	mì

Call …	--- ခေါ်ပေးပါ။	… kaw·pày·ba
an ambulance	လူနာတင်ယာဉ်	loo·na·ting·ying
a doctor	ဆရာဝန်	şuh·ya·wung
the police	ပုလိပ်	puh·lay'

It's an emergency!
ဒါ အရေးပေါ် ကိစ္စပါ။ — da uh·yày·baw kay'·sá·ba

Could you help me, please?
ကျေးဇူးပြုပြီး ကူညီပါ။ — chày·zù·pyú·pì koo·nyi·ba

I have to use the phone.
တယ်လီဖုန်း ခဏ ဆက်လို့ရမလား။ — te·li·pòhng kuh·ná şe'·lóh·yá·muh·là

I'm lost.
လမ်းပျောက်နေတယ်။ — làng·pyow'·nay·de

Where are the toilets?
အိမ်သာ ဘယ်မှာလဲ။ — ayng·ţha be·hma·lè

police

Where's the police station?
ရဲစခန်း ဘယ်မှာလဲ။ — yè·suh·kàng be·hma·lè

I want to report an offence.
အမှု ဖွင့်ချင်တယ်။ — uh·hmú pwíng·jing·de

I have insurance.
အာမခံ ရှိတယ်။ — a·má·gang shí·de

I've been assaulted.

ကျနော်/ကျမ ကိုယ်ထိလက်ရောက်
တိုက်ခိုက်ခံရတယ်။

chuh·náw/chuh·má koh·dí·le'·yow'
taí'·kaí'·kang·yá·de m/f

I've been raped.

ကျနော်/ကျမ
မုဒိမ်းကျင့်ခံရတယ်။

chuh·náw/chuh·má
muh·dàyng·chíng·kang·yá·de m/f

I've been robbed.

ကျနော်/ကျမ ခိုးခံရတယ်။

chuh·náw/chuh·má kòh·kang·yá·de m/f

My ... was/were stolen.	ကျနော်/ကျမ --- ခိုးခံရတယ်။	chuh·náw/chuh·má ... kòh·kang·yá·de m/f
I've lost my ...	ကျနော်/ကျမ --- ပျောက်သွားတယ်။	chuh·náw/chuh·má ... pyow'·thwà·de m/f
backpack	ကျောပိုးအိတ်	chàw·bòh·ay'
bags	အိတ်	ay'
credit card	ခရက်ဒစ်ကဒ်	kuh·ye'·dí·ka'
handbag	လက်ဆွဲအိတ်	le'·şwè·ay'
jewellery	လက်ဝတ်ရတနာ	le'·wu'·yuh·duh·na
money	ပိုက်ဆံ	pai'·şang
passport	ပတ်စပို့	pa'·suh·póh
travellers cheques	ခရီးချက်လက်မှတ်	kuh·yì·che'·le'·hma'
wallet	ပိုက်ဆံအိတ်	pai'·şang·ay'
I want to contact my ...	ကျနော်/ကျမ --- ကို ဆက်သွယ်ချင်တယ်။	chuh·náw/chuh·má ... goh şe'·thwe·jing·de m/f
embassy	သံရုံး	thang·yòhng
consulate	ကောင်စစ်ဝန်ရုံး	kown·si'·wung·yòhng

health

medical needs

Where's the nearest ...?	အနီးဆုံး --- က ဘယ်မှာလဲ။	uh·nì·zòhng ... gá be·hma·lè
dentist	သွားဆရာဝန်	thwà·şuh·ya·wung
doctor	ဆရာဝန်	şuh·ya·wung
hospital	ဆေးရုံ	şày·yohng
(night) pharmacist	(ညဖွင့်တဲ့) ဆေးဆိုင်	(nyá·pwíng·dé) şày·zaing

I need a doctor (who speaks English).
(အင်္ဂလိပ်လို တတ်တဲ့)
ဆရာဝန် ခေါ်ပေးပါ။

(ing·guh·lay′·loh ta′·té)
şuh·ya·wung kaw·pày·ba

Could I see a female doctor?
အမျိုးသမီး ဆရာဝန်နဲ့
တွေ့လို့ ရမလား။

uh·myòh·thuh·mì şuh·ya·wung·né
twáy·lóh yá·muh·là

I've run out of my medication.
ဆေးကုန်သွားပြီ။

şày·kohng·thwà·bi

symptoms, conditions & allergies

I'm sick.	နေမကောင်းဘူး။	nay·muh·kòwng·bòo
It hurts here.	ဒီမှာ နာတယ်။	di·hma na·de
ankle	ခြေမျက်စေ့	chay·mye′·sí
arm	လက်မောင်း	le′·mòwng
back	ခါး	kà
chest	ရင်ဘတ်	ying·ba′
ear	နား	nà
eye	မျက်စေ့	mye′·sí
face	မျက်နှာ	mye′·hna
finger	လက်ချောင်း	le′·chòwng
foot	ခြေထောက်	chay·dow′
hand	လက်	le
head	ခေါင်း	gòwng
heart	နှလုံး	hnuh·lòhng
leg	ခြေသလုံး	chay·thuh·lòhng
mouth	ပါးစပ်	buh·za′
neck	လည်ပင်း	le·bìng
nose	နှာခေါင်း	hnuh·kòwng
skin	အရေပြား	uh·yay·byà
stomach	ဗိုက်	bai′
teeth	သွား	thwà
throat	လည်ချောင်း	le·jòwng

I need something for ...

--- အတွက် ဆေးလိုတယ်။   ... uh·twe' şày·loh·de

I have (a) ...

asthma	ပန်းနာရင်ကြပ်နေတယ်။	pàng·na·ying·cha'·nay·de
bronchitis	ချောင်းဆိုး ရင်ကြပ်နေတယ်။	chòwng·şòh ying·cha'·nay·de
constipation	ဝမ်းချုပ်နေတယ်။	wùng·choh'·nay·de
cough	ချောင်းဆိုးနေတယ်။	chòwng·şòh·nay·de
diarrhoea	ဝမ်းလျှောနေတယ်။	wùng·shàw·nay·de
fever	အဖျားရှိတယ်။	uh·pyà·shí·de
headache	ခေါင်းကိုက်နေတယ်။	gòwng·kai'·nay·de
heat stroke	အပူရှပ်တယ်။	uh·poo·sha'·te
nausea	ပျို့ချင်အံချင်တယ်။	pyóh·jing·ang·jing·de
pain	နာတယ်။	na·de
sore throat	လည်ချောင်းနာတယ်။	le·jòwng·na·de
toothache	သွားကိုက်တယ်။	thwà·kai'·te

I'm allergic to ...

--- နဲ့ မတဲ့ဘူး။   ... né muh·té·bòo

antibiotics	အင်တီဘားရောတစ်	ing·ti·bà·yàw·ti'
anti-inflammatories	အယောင်ကျဆေး	uh·yowng·chá·zày
aspirin	အက်စပရင်	e'·suh·puh·ying
bees	ပျား	pyà
codeine	ကိုဒင်	koh·đing
penicillin	ပင်နီစလင်	ping·ni·suh·ling

antimalarial medication	ငှက်ဖျားဆေး	hnge'·pyà·zày
antiseptic	ပိုးသေဆေး	pòh·thay·şày
bandage	ပတ်တီး	pa'·tì
contraceptives	ကိုယ်ဝန်တားဆေး	koh·wung·tà·zày
diarrhoea medicine	ဝမ်းပိတ်ဆေး	wùng·pay'·şày
insect repellent	ပိုးကောင် မလာတဲ့ဆေး	pòh·gowng muh·la·dé·şày
laxatives	ဝမ်းနှုတ်ဆေး	wùng·hnoh'·şày
painkillers	အကိုက်အဘဲ ပျောက်ဆေး	uh·kai'·uh·kè pyow'·şày
rehydration salts	ဓါတ်ဆား	da'·şà
sleeping tablets	အိပ်ဆေး	ay'·şày

See **special diets & allergies**, page 44, for food-related allergies.

The symbols ⓝ, ⓐ and ⓥ (indicating noun, adjective and verb) have been added for clarity where an English term could be either. The symbols ⓜ/ⓕ are used for masculine and feminine forms of a Burmese word. For food terms see the **menu decoder**, page 45.

A

accident မတော်တဆထိခိုက်ဒဏ်ရာမှု muh·taw·tuh·ṣá tí·kaí·dang·ya·yá·hmú

accommodation တည်းစရာ နေရာ tè·zuh·ya nay·ya

adaptor အဒက်တာ uh·de'·ta

address ⓝ လိပ်စာ lay'·sa

after ပြီးတော့ pi·dáw

air-conditioned အဲကွန်းရှိ è·kùng·shí

airplane လေယာဉ်ပျံ lay·ying·byang

airport လေဆိပ် lay·zay'

alcohol အရက် uh·ye'

all အားလုံး à·lòhng

allergy မတ်ဲဘူး။ muh·té·bòo

ambulance လူနာတင်ယာဉ် loo·na·ting·ying

and (between nouns) နဲ့ né

and (between verbs) ပြီးတော့ pi·dáw

arm လက်မောင်း le'·mòwng

B

baby ကလေး kuh·làye

backpack ကျောပိုးအိတ် chàw·bòh·ay'

bad မကောင်းဘူး။ muh·kòwng·bòo

bag အိတ် ay'

bank ဘဏ bang

bank account ဘဏ်စာရင်း bang·suh·ying

bar အရက်ဆိုင် uh·ye'·ṣaing

bathroom အိမ်သာ ayng·tha

battery ဓါတ်ခဲ da'·kè

beach ပင်လယ်ကမ်းခြေ ping·le·kàng·jay

beautiful လှ hlá

bed အိပ်ရာ ay'·ya

beer ဘီယာ bi·ya

before မထိုးခင် muh·tòh·ging

behind နောက်မှာ now'·hma

bicycle စက်ဘီး se'·bàyng

big ကြီး chì

bill ငွေတောင်းလွှာ ngway·tòwng·hlwa

black အမဲ uh·mè

blanket စောင် sowng

blood သွေး thwày

blood group သွေးအုပ်စု thwày·oh'·sú

blue အပြာ uh·pya

book (make a reservation) ⓥ ကြိုတင်လက်မှတ်
ဝယ် choh·ting le'·hma'·we

bottle ပုလင်း puh·ling

bottle opener ပုလင်း ဖောက်တံ
puh·ling pow'·tang

boy ကောင်လေး kowng·làye

brakes (car) ဘရိတ် buh·yay'

breakfast မနက်စာ muh·ne'·sa

broken (faulty) ပျက်နေ pye'·nay

brown အညို uh·nyoh

bus (stop) ဘတ်စ်ကား(ဂိတ်) ba'·suh·kà·(gay')

business (company) လုပ်ငန်း loh'·ngàng

but ဒါပေမဲ့ da·bay·mé

buy ဝယ် we

C

café ကော်ဖီဆိုင် kaw·pi·ṣaing

camera ကင်မရာ king·muh·ya

camp site စခန်း suh·kàng

cancel ဖျက် pye'

can opener ဖောက်တံ pow'·tang

car ကား kà

cash ⓝ ငွေ ngway

cash (a cheque) ⓥ (ချက်ကို)ငွေလဲ (che'-koh)-ngway-lè

cell phone ဆဲလ်ဖုန်း sèl-pòhng

centre ⓝ အလယ် uh-le

change (bus, train) ⓥ ပြောင်း pyòwng

change (clothes, money) ⓥ လဲ lè

change (money) ⓝ အကြွေ uh-chway

cheap ဈေးပေါ zày-pàw

check (bill) ⓝ ငွေတောင်းလွှာ ngway-tòwng-hlwa

check in ⓥ ချက်ကင်လုပ် che'-king-loh'

cheque (bank) ချက်လက်မှတ် che'-le'-hma'

child ⓝ ကလေး kuh-làe

cigarette ဆေးလိပ် sày-lay'

clean ⓥ သန့်ရှင်း tháng-shìn

closed ပိတ် pay'

coffee ကော်ဖီ kaw-pi

coins အကြွေ uh-chway

cold ⓐ အေး ày

cold (illness) ⓝ အအေးမိ uh-ày-mí

come လာ la

compass သံလိုက်အိမ်မြှောင် thang-laì'-ayng-hmyowng

computer ကွန်ပျူတာ kung-pyu-ta

condoms ကွန်ဒုံ kung-dung

contact lenses မျက်ကပ်မှန် mye'-ka'-hmang

cook ⓥ ချက် che'

cost ⓝ ဈေးနှုန်း zày-hnòhng

credit card ခရက်ဒစ်ကဒ် kuh-ye'-dí'-ka'

currency exchange ငွေလဲလှယ်မှု ngway-lè-hle-hmú

customs (immigration) အကောက်ခွန် uh-kow'-kung

D

dangerous ⓐ အန္တရာယ်ရှိ ang-duh-ye shí

date (time) ⓝ ရက်စွဲ ye'-swè

day (general) ရက် ye'

day (of the week) နေ့, နေ့ náy

delay ⓥ နောက်ကျ now'-chá

dentist သွားဆရာဝန် thwà-şuh-ya-wung

departure ထွက်တာ twe'-ta

diaper ကလေးအနှီး kuh-làe uh-hnì

diarrhoea ဝမ်းလျှော wùng-shàw

dictionary အဘိဓာန် uh-bay'-dang

dinner ညစာ nyá-za

direct တိုက်ရိုက် daì'-yaì'

dirty ညစ်ပတ် nyí'-pa'

disabled မသန်မစွမ်းဖြစ် muh-thang-muh-swàn-pyi'

discount ⓝ လျှော့ဈေး sháw-zày

doctor ဆရာဝန် şuh-ya-wung

double bed နှစ်ယောက်အိပ် ခုတင် hnuh-yow'-ay' guh-ding

double room နှစ်ယောက်ခန်း hnuh-yow'-kàng

down အောက် ow'

drink ⓝ သောက်စရာ thow'-suh-ya

drive ⓥ မောင်း mòwng

drivers licence ကားလိုင်စင် kà-laing-sing

drug (illicit) မူးယစ်ဆေးဝါး mòo-yi'-şày-wà

dummy (pacifier) အတု uh-tú

E

ear နား nà

early စော sàw

east အရှေ့ uh-sháy

eat စား sà

economy class ရိုးရိုးတန်း yòo-yòo-dàng

electricity လျှပ်စစ် hlya'-sí'

elevator ဓါတ်လှေကား da'-hlay-gà

email ⓝ အီးမေးလ် ì-màyl

embassy သံရုံး thang-yòhng

emergency အရေးပေါ် uh-yày-baw

empty အလွတ် uh-lu'

English အင်္ဂလိပ် ìng-guh-lay'

enough လောက် low'

entrance အဝင် uh-wing

evening ညနေ nyá-nay

exchange (money) ⓥ လဲလှယ် lè-hle

exchange rate ငွေကြေးလဲလှယ်နှုန်း ngway-chày lè-hle-hnòhng

exit ⓝ အထွက် uh-twe'

expensive ဈေးကြီး zày-chì

express mail အမြန်စာ uh-myang-sa

eye မျက်စေ့ mye'-sí

F

far ဝေး wày
fast မြန် myang
father အဖေ uh·pay
faulty ပျက်နေ pye'·nay
fever အဖျား uh·pyà
film (camera) ဖလင် puh·ling
first ပထမ puh·tuh·má
first-aid kit ရှေးဦးသူနာပြုသေတ္တာ shày·ò·thoo·na·pyú thí'·ta
first-class ပထမတန်း puh·tuh·má·dàng
fish ငါး ngà
fly (a plane) လေယာဉ်ပျံနဲ့သွား lay·ying·byang·né·thwà
food အစားအစာ uh·sà·uh·sa
fork ခရင်း kuh·yìng
free (of charge) အခမဲ့ uh·ká·mé
friend သူငယ်ချင်း thuh·nge·jìng ⑩&ⓕ
fruit အသီးအနှံ uh·thì·uh·hnang
full ပြည့် pyáy
funny ရယ်ရကောင်း yi·zuh·ya·kòwng

G

gift လက်ဆောင် le'·sòwng
girl မိန်းကလေး màyng·kuh·làay
glass (drinking) ဖန်ခွက် pang·gwe'
glasses မျက်မှန် mye'·hmang
go သွား thwà
good ကောင်း kòwng
green အစိမ်း uh·sàyng
guide ဂိုက် gai'

H

half တဝက် tuh·we' ⑩&ⓐ
handbag လက်ဆွဲအိတ် le'·swè·ay'
happy ပျော် pyaw
have ရှိ shí
head ခေါင်း gòwng
headache ခေါင်းကိုက် gòwng·kai'
heart နှလုံး hnuh·lòhng
heart condition နှလုံးရောဂါ hnuh·lòhng yàw·ga

heat အပူ uh·poo
heavy လေး làay
help ⑦ ကူညီ koo·nyi
here ဒီမှာ di·hma
high မြင့် mying
highway အဝေးပြေးလမ်းမကြီး uh·wày·pyày làng·má·jì
hike ⑦ ခြေလျင်ခရီးထွက်ခြင်း chay·lying·kuh·yi twe'·chìng
hospital ဆေးရုံ sàay·yohng
hot ပူ poo
hotel ဟိုတယ် hoo·te
hungry ဆာ şa
husband အမျိုးသား uh·myòo·thà

I

identification (card) သက်သေခံကတ်ပြား the'·thay·gang ka'·pyà
ill နေမကောင်းဘူး nay·muh·kòwng·bòo
important အရေးကြီး uh·yàay·chì
included ပါ pa
injury ဒဏ်ရာ dang·ya
insurance အာမခံ a·má·gang
Internet အင်တာနက် ing·ta·ne'
interpreter ဘာသာပြန် ba·tha·byang

J

jewellery လက်ဝတ်ရတနာ le'·wu'·yuh·duh·na
job အလုပ် uh·lo'

K

key သော့ tháw
kilogram ကီလိုဂရမ် ki·loh·guh·yang
kitchen မီးဖိုချောင် mi·boh·jowng
knife ဓား dà

L

late နောက်ကျ now'·chá
laundry (place) ပင်းမင်းဆိုင် ping·ming·şaing
lawyer ရှေ့နေ sháy·nay

left luggage အပ်နှံထားတဲ့ ပစ္စည်းတွေ a'·hnang·tà·dé pyí·sì·dway

leg ခြေသလုံး chay·thuh·lòhng

less ပိုနဲ့ poh·nè

letter စာ sa

lift (elevator) ဓါတ်လှေကား da'·hlay·gà

light ⓐ အလင်းရောင် uh·ling·yowng

like ⓥ ကြိုက် chai'

lock ⓝ သော့ခလောက် tháw·guh·low'

long ရှည် shay

lost ပျောက် pyow'

love ⓥ ချစ် chi'

luggage သေတ္တာ thi'·ta

lunch နေ့လယ်စာ náy·le·za

M

mail ⓝ စာ sa

man အမျိုးသား uh·myòh·thà

map မြေပုံ myay·bohng

market ဈေး zày

matches မီးခြစ် mì·ji'

meat အသား uh·thà

medicine ဆေး şày

menu စားသောက်ဖွယ်စာရင်း sà·thow'·pwe suh·ying

message သတင်း ţhuh·ding

milk နို့ nóh

minute မိနစ် mí·ni'

mobile phone ဆဲလ်ဖုန်း şèl·pòhng

money ပိုက်ဆံ pai'·şang

month လ lá

morning မနက် muh·ne'

mother အမေ uh·may

motorcycle မော်တော်ဆိုင်ကယ် maw·taw·şaing·ke

motorway ကားလမ်းမကြီး kà·làng·má·ji

mountain တောင် towng

music သီချင်း thuh·chìng

N

name ⓝ နာမည် nang·me

nappy (diaper) ကလေးအနှီး kuh·làye uh·hnì

nausea ပျို့ချင်အန်ချင် pyòh·jing·ang·jing

near နားမှာ nà·hma

new အသစ် uh·thi'

news သတင်း ţhuh·ding

newspaper သတင်းစာ ţhuh·ding·za

next နောက် now'

night ည nyá

no ဟင့်အင် híng·ing

noisy ဆူညံ şoo·nyang

nonsmoking ဆေးလိပ်မသောက်ရ။ şày·lay' muh·thow'·yá

north မြောက်ဘက် myow'·pe'

nose နှာခေါင်း hnuh·kòwng

now အခု uh·gú

number နံပါတ် nang·ba'

O

oil (engine) ဆီ şi

old (animals/people) အသက်ကြီး uh·the'·chì

old (objects) ဟောင်း hòwng

on အပေါ်မှာ uh·paw·hma

one-way ticket အသွားလက်မှတ် uh·thwà·le'·hma'

open ⓐ ဖွင့် pwing

other တခြား tuh·chà

outside အပြင်မှာ uh·pying·hma

P

pacifier (dummy) အတု uh·tú

package အထုပ် uh·toh'

pain ဝေဒနာ way·duh·na

painkillers အကိုက်အခဲပျောက်ဆေး uh·kai'·uh·kè pyow'·şày

paper စက္ကူ se'·koo

park (car) ⓥ ကားရပ် kà·ya'

passport ပတ်စပို့ pa'·suh·póh

pay ပေး pày

pen ဘောပင် bàw·ping

petrol ဓါတ်ဆီ da'·şi

pharmacy ဆေးဆိုင် şày·zaing

phonecard ဖုန်းကတ် pòhng·ka'

photo ဓါတ်ပုံ da'·pohng

plate ပန်းကန် buh·gang

police ပုလိပ် puh·lay'

postcard ပို့စကတ် póh·suh·ka'
post office စာတိုက် sa·daî'
pregnant ကိုယ်ဝန်ရှိ koh·wung·shí
price ဈေး-နှုန်း zàyး·hnòhng

Q

quiet အေးအေး àyး· şàyး

R

rain ⓝ မိုး mòh
razor မုတ်ဆိတ်ရိတ်ဓား moh'·şay'·yay'·dà
receipt ပြေစာ pyay·za
recommend အကြံပေး uh·chang·pàyး
red အနီ uh·ni
refund ⓥ ပြန်အမ်း pyang·àng
registered mail မှတ်ပုံတင်ပြီးပို့တဲ့စာ hma'·pohng·ting·pyì póh·dé·sa
rent ⓝ ငှားခ hngà·gá
repair ⓥ ပြင် pying
reservation ဘွတ်ကင် bu'·king
restaurant စားသောက်ဆိုင် sà·thow'·şaing
return ⓥ ပြန် pyang
return ticket အသွားအပြန် လက်မှတ် uh·thwà·uh·pyang le'·hma'
right (correct) မှန် hmang
right (direction) ညာဘက် nya·be'
road လမ်း làng
room အခန်း uh·kàng
rope ကြိုး chòh

S

safe ⓐ ဘေးကင်း bàyး·king
sanitary napkins အမျိုးသမီးလစဉ်သုံးပစ္စည်း uh·myòh·thuh·mì lá·zing·thòhng pyî'·si
sea ပင်လယ် ping·le
seat ထိုင်ခုံ tain'·gohng
send ပို့ póh
service station ဆါဗစ်ဆိုင် da'·şi·zaing
sex လိင် layng
shaving cream မုတ်ဆိတ်ရိတ်ဆပ်ပြာ moh'·şay'·yay' şa'·pya

sheet (bed) အိပ်ရာခင်း ay'·yuh·ğing
shirt အင်္ကျီ ing·ji
shoes ဖိနပ် puh·na'
shop ⓝ ဆိုင် şaing
short (height) ပု póo
short (length) တို toh
shower ⓝ ရေပန်း yay·bàng
single room တစ်ယောက်ခန်း tuh·yow'·kàng
size (clothes) ဆိုက် şaî'
skirt စကတ် suh·ka'
sleep ⓥ အိပ် ay'
slowly ဖြည်းဖြည်း pyàyး·byàyး
small ငယ် nge
smoke ⓥ ဆေးလိပ်သောက် şàyး·lay'·thow'
soap ဆပ်ပြာ şa'·pya
some တချို့ tuh·chóh
soon မကြာခင် muh·cha·ging
south တောင်ဘက် towng·be'
souvenir shop အမှတ်တရ ပစ္စည်းဆိုင် uh·hma'·tuh·yá pyî'·si·zaing
speak ပြော pyàw
spoon ဇွန်း zùng
stamp တံဆိပ်ခေါင်း duh·zay'·gòwng
standby ticket အစောင့်လေယာဉ်လက်မှတ် uh·sowng lay·ying·le'·hma'
station (train) ဘူတာ boo·da
stomachache ဗိုက်နာ baî'·na
stop (bus) ⓝ မှတ်တိုင် hma'·taing
stop ⓥ ရပ် ya'
street လမ်း làng
student ကျောင်းသား/ကျောင်းသူ chòwng·thà/chòwng·thoo ⓜ/ⓕ
sun နေ nay
supermarket ဆူပါမားကက် şoo·pa·mà·ke'
sweet (taste) ⓐ ချို choh
swim ⓥ ရေကူး yay·kòo

T

taxi တက္ကစီ te'·kuh·si
telephone တယ်လီဖုန်း te·li·pòhng
television တီဗွီ ti·bi
temperature (weather) အပူချိန် uh·poo·jayng
tent မိုးကာတဲ mòh·ga·tè

that ⓐ အဲဒီ è-di
thirsty ရေဆာ yay-ṣa
this ⓐ ဒီ di
ticket လက်မှတ် le'-hma'
time ⓝ အချိန် uh-chayng
tired မော màw
tissues တစ်ရှူး tí-shòo
today ဒီနေ့ di-náy
toilet အိမ်သာ ayng-tha
tomorrow မနက်ဖြန် muh-ne'-pang
tonight ဒီည di-nyá
toothache သွားကိုက် thwà-kai'
toothbrush သွားပွတ်တံ thuh-bu'-tang
toothpaste သွားတိုက်ဆေး thwà-dai'-ṣày
torch (flashlight) လက်နှိပ်ဓါတ်မီး le'-hnay'-da'-mì
tour ⓥ ခရီးသွား kuh-yì-thwà
tourist ⓝ တိုးရစ် tòh-yi'
tourist office ကမ္ဘာလှည့်ခရီးသည်ရုံး guh-ba-hlé kuh-yì-the-yòhng
towel မျက်နှာသုတ်ပုဝါ mye'-hnuh-thoh'-puh-wa
town မြို့ myóh
train ရထား yuh-tà
translate ဘာသာပြန် ba-tha-byang
travel agency ခရီးသွားလုပ်ငန်း kuh-yì-thwà loh'-ngàng
travellers cheque ခရီးချက်လက်မှတ် kuh-yì che'-le'-hma'
trousers ဘောင်းဘီ bòwng-bi
twin beds တစ်ယောက်အိပ် ခုတင်နှစ်လုံး tuh-yow'-ay' guh-ding hnuh-lòhng
tyre ဘီး bàyng

U

underwear အတွင်းခံ uh-twìng-gang
up အပေါ် uh-paw
urgent အရေးပေါ် uh-yày-baw

V

vacant အား à
vacation အားလပ်ရက် à-la'-ye'
vegetable ⓝ ဟင်းသီးဟင်းရွက် hìng-thì-hìng-ywe'

vegetarian သက်သတ်လွတ် the'-tha'-lu'
visa ဗီဇာ bi-za

W

waiter စားပွဲထိုး zuh-bwè-dòh
walk ⓥ လမ်းလျှောက် làng-show'
wallet ပိုက်ဆံအိတ် pai'-ṣang-ay'
warm ⓐ နွေး nwày
wash (clothes/hair) လျှော် shaw
wash (body/dishes) ဆေး ṣày
watch ⓝ လက်ပတ်နာရီ le'-pa'-na-yi
watch ⓥ ကြည့် chí
water ရေ yay
weekend စနေ့ တနင်္ဂနွေ suh-náy tuh-ning-guh-nway
west အနောက်ဘက် uh-now'-pe'
wheelchair ဘီးတပ်ကုလားထိုင် bàyng-ta' kuh-luh-taing
when (future) ဘယ်တော့ --- လဲ be-dáw ... lè
when (past) ဘယ်တုန်းက --- လဲ be-dòhng-gá ... lè
where ဘယ်မှာ --- လဲ be-hma ... lè
white အဖြူ uh-pyoo
who ဘယ်သူ --- လဲ be-thoo ... lè
why ဘာဖြစ်လို့ --- လဲ baa-pyí'-lóh ... lè
wife အမျိုးသမီး uh-myòh-thuh-mì
window ပြတင်းပေါက် buh-dìng-bow'
wine ဝိုင်အရက် waing-uh-ye'
with နဲ့ né
without မပါဘဲ muh-pa-bè
woman အမျိုးသမီး uh-myòh-thuh-mì
write ရေး yày

Y

yellow အဝါ uh-wa
yes ဟုတ်ကဲ့ hoh'-ké
yesterday မနေ့က muh-náy-gá

Z

zipper ဇစ် zí'

Khmer

consonants

ក	ខ	គ	ឃ	ង
gaw	kaw	gow	kow	ngow
ច	ឆ	ជ	ឈ	ញ
jaw	chaw	jow	chow	nyow
ដ	ឋ	ឌ	ឍ	ណ
daw	taw	dow	tow	naw
ត	ថ	ទ	ធ	ន
daw	taw	dow	tow	now
ប	ផ	ព	ភ	ម
baw	paw	bow	pow	mow
យ	រ	ល	វ	ស
yow	row	low	wow	saw
ហ	ឡ	អ		
haw	law	aw		

independent vowels

ឥ	ឦ	ឧ	ឩ	ឫ
ei	ei (long)	oh	euw	reu
ឬ	ឭ	ឮ	ឯ	ឰ
reu (long)	leu	leu (long)	ai	ao
ឱ				
ao·y				

dependent vowels (the letter ក is used as the consonant base)

កា	កិ	កី	កឹ	កឺ
gaa/gee·a	gayh/gih	gei/gee	gerh/geuh	ger/geu
កុ	កូ	កួ	កើ	កឿ
goh/gooh	gow/goo	goo·a	gaar/ger	geu·a
កៀ	កេ	កែ	កៃ	កោ
gee·a	gay	gai/gae	gai/gei	gao/gow
កៅ	កុំ	កំ	កាំ	កះ
gaa·ew/geuw	gohm	guhm/gohm	guhm/gay·uhm	gah/gay·uh
កិះ	កុះ	កេះ	កោះ	
gayh/gih	goh/gooh	gayh	gawh/goo·uh	

introduction

Khmer, which is part of the Mon-Khmer language family, is spoken by approximately 9 million people in the Kingdom of Cambodia and is understood by many in neighbouring countries. Although distinct from its Thai, Lao and Burmese neighbours, Khmer shares with them the common roots of Sanskrit and Pali – a heritage of centuries of linguistic and cultural interaction and of their shared faith in Theravada Buddhism. Written Khmer is based on the ancient Brahmi script of southern India. Khmer inscriptions have been dated back to the 7th century AD.

The Khmer language as spoken in Phnom Penh is generally intelligible to Khmers nationwide. There are, however, several distinct dialects in other areas of the country. Most notably, the Khmers of Takeo province (south of Phnom Penh) tend to modify or slur hard consonant combinations, especially those that contain the sound r, eg bruhm (five) becomes pay·uhm, and sraa (alcohol) becomes say·aa. In Siem Reap, sharp-eared travellers will notice a very Lao-sounding lilt to the local speech. Here, certain vowels are modified, such as in bo·an (thousand), which becomes beu·an, and kuh·see·aa (smoking pipe), which becomes kuh·seu·aa.

Although English is fast becoming Cambodia's second language, the Khmer still cling to the Francophone pronunciation of the Roman alphabet and most foreign words. This is helpful to remember when spelling Western words and names aloud – 'ay-bee-cee' becomes 'ah-bey-sey', and so on. French speakers will have an advantage when addressing the older generation, as most educated Khmers studied French at some point during their schooling. Many household items, medical and technical terms retain their French names as well, especially those which were introduced to Cambodia by the French during the colonial period, such as *robinet* (tap/faucet) and *ampoule* (light bulb).

Khmer has 33 consonants and 35 vowels and diphthongs (vowel sound combinations). Unlike Burmese, Lao, Thai and Vietnamese, Khmer doesn't have tones. The haphazard transliteration system left over from the days of French rule has been simplified in this chapter for the purpose of basic communication – you'll be understood just fine if you follow the coloured pronunciation guides provided next to each phrase. The best way to improve your pronunciation is to listen carefully to native speakers. The full Khmer alphabet is included on the page opposite. Khmer grammar is very simple – there are no endings for singular or plural, masculine or feminine. The basic grammar rules are included in this chapter, to help you build your own phrases.

pronunciation

vowel sounds

symbol	english equivalent	khmer example	symbol	english equivalent	khmer example
a	**calm** (short)	baht	eh	**may** (short and hard)	jeh
aa	**calm** (lengthened)	laan	ei	uh followed by ee	bei
aar	aa followed by er	daar	er	**jerk** (soft, open)	lerk
aay	**bite** (lengthened)	muh-**daay**	eu	like the 'u' in 'Luke' but with lips spread as for the 'i' in 'pin'	cheu
ae	**cat**	baet	eu-uh	eu followed by uh	reu-uhng
ai	**bite** (short)	dai	euw	a very nasal eu	deuw
ao	**down**	maong	ih	a short and hard ee	jih
aw	**law**	sawk	oh	**hose** (short and hard)	jraw-moh
ay	**may**	mayk	oo	**boot**	joo
e	**bang**	beng	ooh	a short and hard ow	nooh
ee	**feet**	mee	ow	**glow** (long)	dow
ee-aa	ee followed by aa	jee-aa	u	**Luke**	mun
ee-uh	ee followed by uh	ree-uhn	uh	**but**	kuht

consonant sounds

There are two types of consonant sounds in Khmer – those that have an inherent 'a' vowel and those with an 'o'. There's also a difference between the aspirated sounds (pronounced with a puff of air after the sound) and the unaspirated ones. Watch out for the b̖ sound, which is halfway between a 'b' and a 'p', and the đ sound, which is halfway between a 'd' and a 't'.

Some consonant combinations can be a bit difficult for English speakers to produce, such as j-r in j-rook (pig) or ch-ng in ch-ngain (delicious). For ease of pronunciation, we've separated these clusters into syllables with a dot in our pronunciation guides.

symbol	english equivalent	khmer example
b	**bit**	baan
b̖	**puppy** (hard, unaspirated)	b̖ehl
ch	**cheese**	chuh-ngain
d	**dog**	duhm
đ	**stand** (hard, unaspirated)	đoh
g	**get**	go-uht
h	**hot**	haang
j	**jump**	juy
k	**kind**	kai
l	**love**	layk
m	**mix**	mee-uhn
n	**no**	neung
ng	**sing**	ngee-ay
ny	**onion**	nyuhm
p	**please**	howp
r	**rum** (hard and rolled)	rung
s	**sun**	sohm
t	**take**	tuh-lai
w	**would**	wee-uhl
y	**yes**	yohp

pronunciation – ការបញ្ចេញសំឡេង

phrasebuilder

be

The verb used between nouns or pronouns is jee·aa ជា (be):

I'm a doctor.	ខ្ញុំជាគ្រូពេទ្យ	kuh·nyohm jee·aa kru baet
		(lit: I be doctor)

counters/classifiers

Nouns have the same form for the singular and the plural. When counting, however, every noun takes a classifier (a word which defines the category that an item belongs to). Classifiers go after the noun and the number. For some common classifiers and the categories of items they refer to, see the box on page 86.

three houses	ផ្ទះបីខ្នង	puh·day·uh bei kuh·nawng
		(lit: house three structure)

have

The word for 'have' is mee·uhn មាន, which can also be used as 'there is/are'.

I have insurance.	ខ្ញុំមានអ៊ិនស៊ូរ៉ង	kuh·nyohm mee·uhn ihn·su·rahng
		(lit: I have insurance)

negatives

Verbs are negated by placing muhn មិន before the verb, and đay ទេ (no) at the end of the sentence.

I don't eat meat.	ខ្ញុំមិនហ្ញបសាច់ទេ	kuh·nyohm muhn howp sait đay
		(lit: I muhn eat meat no)

pronouns

Khmer pronouns reflect the person's age, gender and social standing. For a list of the easiest and most general pronouns, see the box on page 79.

questions

To form a yes/no question, place đay ទេ (no) at the end of a statement. For 'yes', men say baat បាទ and women say jaa ចាស. For 'no' they both say đay ទេ.

Is this seat free?	កៅអីនេះទំនេរទេ?	gao ei nih đohm-nay đay
		(lit: seat this free no)
Yes.	បាទ/ចាស	baat/jaa m/f
No.	ទេ	đay

requests

To make a polite request, use sohm សូម (please) before the verb.

Take me to this address, please.

សូមជូនខ្ញុំទៅអាសយដ្ឋាននេះ   sohm joon kuh-nyohm đeuw aa-sai-yah-tahn nih
(lit: please take me go address this)

verbs

Khmer verbs don't change according to tense – often the context will indicate when an action happened. You can use the verb alone for the present tense, but to specify a future or a completed action, add a particle in front the verb: nuhng និង (lit: will) for the future, and hao-y ហើយ (lit: already) for the past tense.

I'm learning Khmer.

ខ្ញុំរៀនភាសាខ្មែរ   kuh-nyohm ree-uhn pee-aa-saa kuh-mai
(lit: I learn language Khmer)

We'll leave next week.

យើងនឹងទៅអាទិត្យក្រោយ   yerng nuhng đeuw aa-đuht krao-y
(lit: we will go week after)

He took my bags.

គាត់យកក្របូបខ្ញុំហើយ   go-uht yohk graw-bowp kuh-nyohm hao-y
(lit: he take bag my already)

basics

language difficulties

Do you speak English?
អ្នកចេះភាសាអង់គ្លេសទេ?　　　nay·uhk jes phi·a·saa awn·glay đay

Do you understand?
អ្នកយល់ទេ?　　　nay·uhk yuhl đay

I understand.
ខ្ញុំយល់ហើយ　　　kuh·nyohm yuhl hao·y

I don't understand.
ខ្ញុំមិនយល់ទេ　　　kuh·nyohm muhn yuhl đay

What does (អរគុណ) **mean?**
(អរគុណ) មាននិយ័យថាម៉េច?　　　(aw gohn) mee·uhn nuh·ee taa mait

How do you ...?	តើអ្នក ...?	đaa·er nay·uhk ...
pronounce this	និយាយពាក្យនេះ	ni·yay ƀi·uhk nih
	ថាម៉េច	taa mait
write (thank you)	សរសេរយ៉ាងម៉េច	saw·say yahng mait
	ពាក្យថា (អរគុណ)	ƀee·uhk taa (aw·gohn)

Could you please ...?	សូម ...	sohm ...
repeat that	និយាយម្ដងទៀត	ni·yay muh·dawng đee·iht
speak more slowly	និយាយយឺតៗ	ni·yay yeut yeut
write it down	សរសេរ ឲ្យខ្ញុំ	saw·say ao·y kuh·nyohm

essentials

Yes. (said by a man)	បាទ	baat
Yes. (said by a woman)	ចាំស	jaa
No.	ទេ	đay
Please.	សូម	sohm
Thank you (very much).	អរគុណ (ច្រើន)	aw gohn (juh·rarn)
You're welcome.	មិនអីទេ	muhn ei đay
Excuse me.	សុំទោស	sohm đoh
Sorry.	សុំទោស	sohm đoh

numbers

0	សូន្យ	sohn	17	ដប់ប្រាំពីរ	dawp bruhm ʾbee
1	មួយ	muy	18	ដប់ប្រាំបី	dawp bruhm bei
2	ពីរ	ʾbee	19	ដប់ប្រាំបួន	dawp bruhm boo·uhn
3	បី	bei	20	ម្ភៃ	muh·pei
4	បួន	boo·uhn	21	ម្ភៃមួយ	muh·pei muy
5	ប្រាំ	bruhm	22	ម្ភៃពីរ	muh·pei ʾbee
6	ប្រាំមួយ	bruhm muy	30	សាមសិប	saam suhp
7	ប្រាំពីរ	bruhm ʾbee	40	សែសិប	sai suhp
8	ប្រាំបី	bruhm bei	50	ហាសិប	haa suhp
9	ប្រាំបួន	bruhm boo·uhn	60	ហុកសិប	hohk suhp
10	ដប់	dawp	70	ចិតសិប	jet suhp
11	ដប់មួយ	dawp muy	80	ប៉ែតសិប	ʾbaet suhp
12	ដប់ពីរ	dawp ʾbee	90	កៅសិប	kao suhp
13	ដប់បី	dawp bei	91	កៅសិបមួយ	kao suhp muy
14	ដប់បួន	dawp boo·uhn	100	មួយរយ	muy roy
15	ដប់ប្រាំ	dawp bruhm	1000	មួយពាន់	muy ʾbo·an
16	ដប់ប្រាំមួយ	dawp bruhm muy	1,000,000	មួយលាន	muy lee·an

numerals									
0	1	2	3	4	5	6	7	8	9
០	១	២	៣	៤	៥	៦	៧	៨	៩

time & dates

What time is it?
ឥឡូវនេះម៉ោងប៉ុន្មាន?   ei·leuw nih maong ʾbohn·maan

It's (one) o'clock.
ម៉ោង (មួយ)   maong (muy)

It's (two) o'clock.
ម៉ោង (ពីរ)   maong (ʾbee)

Quarter past (one).
ម៉ោង (មួយ) ដប់ប្រាំមីនុត   maong (muy) dawp bruhm mi·nut

Half past (one).

ម៉ោង (មួយ) សាមសិប   maong (muy) saam suhp

Quarter to (eight).

ម៉ោង (ប្រាំពីរ) សែសិបប្រាំ   maong (bruhm bee) sai suhp bruhm
                                    (lit: hour (seven) forty five)

At what time ...?	... នៅម៉ោងប៉ុន្មាន?	... neuw maong bohn·maan
At ...	នៅម៉ោង ...	neuw maong ...
am (morning)	ព្រឹក	bruhk
pm (evening/night)	យប់	yohp
Monday	ថ្ងៃចន្ទ	tuh·ngai juhn
Tuesday	ថ្ងៃអង្គារ	tuh·ngai awng·gee·a
Wednesday	ថ្ងៃពុធ	tuh·ngai boht
Thursday	ថ្ងៃព្រហស្បតិ៍	tuh·ngai bro·ho·ah
Friday	ថ្ងៃសុក្រ	tuh·ngai sohk
Saturday	ថ្ងៃសៅរ៍	tuh·ngai saa·ew
Sunday	ថ្ងៃអាទិត្យ	tuh·ngai aa·duht
January	ខែមករា	kai mohk·ah·raa
February	ខែកុម្ភៈ	kai gohm·pe·ah
March	ខែមីនា	kai mee·naa
April	ខែមេសា	kai may·saa
May	ខែឧសភា	kai oh·sa·pee·aa
June	ខែមិថុនា	kai mee·toh·naa
July	ខែកក្កដា	kai gahk·ga·daa
August	ខែសីហា	kai sei·haa
September	ខែកញ្ញា	kai gan·nyaa
October	ខែតុលា	kai đoh·laa
November	ខែវិច្ឆិកា	kai wich·ih·gaa
December	ខែធ្នូ	kai tuh·noo
since (May)	តាំងពី (ខែឧសភា)	đuhng bee (kai oh·sa·pee·aa)
until (June)	រហូតដល់ (ខែមិថុនា)	ruh·howt dahl (kai mee·toh·naa)

What date is it today?

ថ្ងៃនេះជាថ្ងៃអ្វី?   tuh·ngai nih jee·aa tuh·ngai ei

It's (15 December).

ថ្ងៃទី (ដប់ប្រាំ ខែធ្នូ)   tuh·ngai đee (dawp bruhm kai tuh·noo)

last ...	... មិញ	... mein
next ...	... ក្រោយ	... krao·ee
night	យប់	yohp
week	អាទិត្យ	aa·đuht
month	ខែ	kai
year	ឆ្នាំ	chuh·nuhm
yesterday ...	... ម្សិលមិញ	... muh·suhl mein
tomorrow ...	... ថ្ងៃស្អែក	... tuh·ngai sah·aik
morning	ព្រឹក	bruhk
afternoon	រសៀល	ruh·seal
evening	ល្ងាច	luh·ngee·ihk

weather

What's the weather like?

ធាតុអាកាសយ៉ាងម៉េចទៅ?   tee·uht·aa·kah yahng mait đeuw

It's ...	វា ...	wee·aa ...
cold	ត្រជាក់	đraw·jay·uhk
(very) hot	ក្ដៅ (ណាស់)	guh·daa·ew (nah)
rainy	ភ្លៀង	plee·uhng
warm	កក់ក្ដៅ	gawk guh·daa·ew
windy	មានខ្យល់ខ្លាំង	mee·uhn kuh·shahl kluhng
cool season	ខែត្រជាក់	kai đraw·jay·uhk
dry season	ខែប្រាំង	kai bruhng
hot season	ខែក្ដៅ	kai guh·daa·ew
rainy season	ខែភ្លៀង	kai plee·uhng

border crossing

I'm ...	ខ្ញុំ ...	kuh·nyohm ...
in transit	ធ្វើដំណើរឆ្លង	twuhr duhm·naar
	ព្រំដែន	chuh·lawng brohm dain
on business	ធ្វើដំណើរជា	twuhr duhm·naar jee·aa
	ផ្លូវការ	pleuw gaa
on holiday	ដើរលេងវិកក់	daar leng waa·gawng

I'm here for ...　　　　　　ខ្ញុំមករយៈពេល ...　　kuh·nyohm mao ruh·yay·uh ɓehl ...
　(10) days　　　　　　　　(ដប់) ថ្ងៃ　　　　　(dawp) tuh·ngai
　(two) months　　　　　　(ពីរ) ខែ　　　　　　(ɓee) kai
　(three) weeks　　　　　　(បី) អាទិត្យ　　　　(bei) aa·ɗuht

I'm going to (Phnom Penh).
　　ខ្ញុំទៅ (ភ្នំពេញ)　　　　　　kuh·nyohm ɗeuw (puh·nohm ɓein)

I'm staying at the (Siem Reap Hotel).
　　ខ្ញុំស្នាក់នៅ
　　(អូតែលសៀមរាប)　　　　(oh·tail see·uhm ree·uhp)

I have nothing to declare.
　　គ្មានអ្វីរាយការទេ　　　　　kuh·mee·uhn ah·wei ree·ay gaa ɗay

I have something to declare.
　　មានអ្វីរាំង់ត្រូវរាយការ　　mee·uhn ei·wuhn ɗrow ree·ay gaa

That's (not) mine.
　　នោះ (មិនមែន)　　　　　　nooh (muhn maen)
　　ជារបស់ខ្ញុំ (ទេ)　　　　　jee·aa ruh·bawh kuh·nyohm (ɗay)

I didn't know I had to declare it.
　　ខ្ញុំមិនដឹងថាត្រូវរាយ　　kuh·nyohm muhn duhng taa ɗrow ree·ay
　　ការវាទេ　　　　　　　　gaa wee·aa ɗay

transport

tickets & luggage

Where can I buy a ticket?
　　ខ្ញុំត្រូវទិញបុបុរទៅឯណា?　　kuh·nyohm ɗrow ɗeen suhm·boht neuw ei naa

Do I need to book?
　　តើខ្ញុំត្រូវកក់កៅអីទេ?　　ɗaar kuh·nyohm ɗrow gawk gao ei ɗay

One ... ticket to　　　　　សុំសំបុត្រ ...　　　sohm suhm·boht ...
(Battambang), please.　　មួយទៅ (បាត់ដំបង)　muy ɗeuw (baht·duhm·bawng)
　one-way　　　　　　　　តែទៅទេ　　　　　ɗai ɗeuw ɗay
　return　　　　　　　　　ទៅមក　　　　　　ɗeuw mao

I'd like to ... my ticket, please.	សុំ ... សំបុត្ររបស់ខ្ញុំ	sohm ... suhm-boht ruh-bawh kuh-nyohm
cancel	លប់ចោលឈប់	lohp jaowl chohp
change	ផ្លាស់ផ្តូរ	plah puh-dow
collect	ទទួល	đuh-đool
confirm	បញ្ជាក់	buhn-jay-uhk

I'd like a ... seat, please.	ខ្ញុំចង់បានកៅអីនៅកន្លែង ...	kuh-nyohm jawng baan gao ei neuw guhn-laing ...
nonsmoking	មិនជក់បារី	muhn joo-uhk baa-rei
smoking	ជក់បារី	joo-uhk baa-rei

How much is it?
តំលៃប៉ុន្មាន? duhm-lai bohn-maan

Is there air conditioning?
មានម៉ាស៊ីនត្រជាក់ទេ? mee-uhn ma-suhn đraw-jay-uhk đay

Is there a toilet?
មានបង្គន់ទេ? mee-uhn bawng-gohn đay

How long does the trip take?
ធ្វើដំណើរអស់រយៈ twer duhm-naar awh ruh-yay-uh
ពេលប៉ុន្មាន? behl bohn-maan

Is it a direct route?
មានផ្លូវទៅត្រង់តែម្តងទេ? mee-uhn pleuw đeuw đrawng đai muh-dawng đay

My luggage has been ...	វ៉ាលីសរបស់ខ្ញុំត្រូវ ...	waa-lih ruh-bawh kuh-nyohm đrow ...
damaged	ខូចខាត	kow-iht kaat
lost	បាត់	baht
stolen	គេលួច	gay loo-iht

getting around

Where does flight (TG 132) arrive?
ជើងហោះ (ទីជី ១៣២) jerng hawh (đee jee muy bei bee)
មកដល់ម៉ោងប៉ុន្មាន? mao dahl maong bohn-maan

Where does flight (TG 132) depart?
ជើងហោះ (ទីជី ១៣២) jerng hawh (đee jee muy bei bee)
ចេញម៉ោងប៉ុន្មាន? jain maong bohn-maan

Where's (the) ...?	... នៅឯណា?	... neuw ei naa
arrivals hall	កន្លែងធ្វើដំណើរ	guhn-laing twuhr duhm-naar
	ចូលស្រុក	johl srawk
departures hall	កន្លែងធ្វើដំណើរ	guhn-laing twuhr duhm-naar
	ចេញពីស្រុក	jain bee srawk
duty-free shop	ហាងលក់មិន	haag lu-uhk muhn
	បង់ពន្ធ	bawng tuh-lai bohn
gate (12)	ទ្វារលេខទី (ដប់ពីរ)	đweu-uh layk đee (dawp bee)

Is this the ... to	នេះជា ... ទៅ	nih jee-aa ... đeuw
(Siem Reap)?	(សៀមរាប) ទេ?	(see-uhm ree-uhp) đay
boat	ទូក	đook
bus	ឡានឈ្នួល	laan chuh-nool
plane	យន្តហោះ	yohn hawh
train	រថភ្លើង	rah-teh plerng

At what time's	ឡានឈ្នួល ...	laan chuh-nool ...
the ... bus?	ចេញទៅម៉ោងប៉ុន្មាន?	jain đeuw maong bohn-maan
first	មុនគេបង្អស់	mun gay bawng-awh
last	ចុងក្រោយបង្អស់	johng krao-y bawng-awh
next	ជើងក្រោយ	jerng krao-y

What time does it leave?
វាចេញទៅម៉ោងប៉ុន្មាន?　　wee-aa jain đeuw maong bohn-maan

How long will it be delayed?
ត្រូវរង់ចាំរយៈពេលប៉ុន្មាន?　　đrow rohng jaam ruh-yay-uh bel bohn-maan

What station is this?
ស្ថានីយនេះឈ្មោះអ្វី?　　suh-taa-nee nih chuh-mu-uh ei

What's the next stop?
បន្ទាប់ពីនេះគេឈប់នៅឯណា?　　bawn-đo-uhp bee nih gay chohp neuw ei naa

Does it stop at (Siem Reap)?
វាឈប់នៅ (សៀមរាប) ទេ?　　wee-aa chohp neuw (see-uhm ree-uhp) đay

Please tell me when we get to (Kampong Saom).
សូមប្រាប់ខ្ញុំនៅពេល　　sohm brahp kuh-nyohm pawng neuw bel
យើងទៅដល់ (កំពង់សោម)　　yerng đeuw dahl (kahm-bohng saom)

How long do we stop here?
យើងត្រូវឈប់នៅទីនេះយូរទេ?　　yerng đrow chohp neuw đee nih yoo đay

Is this seat available?

កៅអីនេះទំនេរឬទេ?   gao ei nih đohm-nay reu đay

That's my seat.

នេះជាកៅអីរបស់ខ្ញុំ   nih jee-aa gao ei ruh-bawh kuh-nyohm

I'd like a taxi …	ខ្ញុំត្រូវការឡ្យាន	kuh-nyohm đrow gaa laan
	តាក់ស៊ី …	đahk-see …
at (9am)	នៅម៉ោង	neuw maong
	(ប្រាំបួនព្រឹក)	(bruhm boo-uhn bruhk)
now	ឥឡូវនេះ	ei-leuw nih
tomorrow	ថ្ងៃស្អែក	tuh-ngai suh-aik

Is this … available?	… ទំនេរទេ?	… đohm-nay đay
cyclo	ស៊ីក្លូ	see-klow
motorcycle-taxi	ម៉ូតូឌុប	mow-đow dohp
tuk-tuk	ទុកទុក	đuk đuk

Is this taxi free?

ឡ្យានតាក់ស៊ីនេះទំនេរទេ?   laan đahk-see nih đohm-nay đay

How much is it to …?

ទៅ … យកថ្លៃប៉ុន្មាន?   đeuw … yohk tuh-lai bohn-maan

Please put the meter on.

សូមប្រើមីទ័រផង   sohm braar mee-đer pawng

Please take me to (this address).

សូមជូនខ្ញុំទៅ   sohm jun kuh-nyohm đeuw
(អាសយដ្ឋាននេះ)   (aa-sai-yah-tahn nih)

Please …	សូម …	sohm …
slow down	ជិះយឺតៗ	jih yeut yeut
stop here	ឈប់នៅទីនេះ	chohp neuw đee nih
wait here	ចាំខ្ញុំនៅទីនេះ	jaam kuh-nyohm neuw đee nih

car, motorbike & bicycle hire

I'd like to hire a ...	ខ្ញុំចង់ជួល ...	kuh·nyohm jawng jool ...
bicycle	កង់	gawng
car	ឡាន	laan
motorbike	ម៉ូតូ	mow·đow

with ...	ដែលមាន ...	dail mee·uhn ...
air conditioning	ម៉ាស៊ីនត្រជាក់	ma·suhn đraw·jay·uhk
a driver	អ្នកបើកបរ	nay·uhk baok baw

How much for	គិតជួលជា ...	guht jool jee·aa ...
... hire?	ថ្ងៃប៉ុន្មាន?	tuh·lai bohn·maan
hourly	ម៉ោង	maong
daily	ថ្ងៃ	tuh·ngai
weekly	អាទិត្យ	aa·đuht

air	ខ្យល់	kuh·shahl
oil	ប្រេងកាត	preng gaat
petrol	ប្រេងសាំង	preng sahng
tyres	កង់ឡាន	gawng laan

I need a mechanic.
ខ្ញុំត្រូវការជាងឡាន   kuh·nyohm đrow gaa jee·ahng laan

I've run out of petrol.
អស់សាំង   awh sahng

I have a flat tyre.
បែកកង់   baik gawng

directions

Where's a/the ...?	... នៅឯណា?	... neuw ei naa
city centre	មជ្ឈមណ្ឌលក្រុង	mah·chay·uh mahn·dahl grohng
market	ផ្សារ	puh·saa
police station	ប៉ុស្តិ៍ប៉ូលិស	boh bow·lih
post office	ប្រៃសណីយ៍	prai·suh·nee
public toilet	បង្គន់សាធារណៈ	bawng·gohn saa·tee·ah·rah·nah
tourist office	ការិយាល័យទេសចរ	gaa·ree·yaa·lai đeh·sah·jaw

Is this the road to (Angkor Wat)?

ផ្លូវនេះទៅ (អង្គរវត្ត) ឬ? — pleuw nih đeuw (ahn-go waht) reu

Can you show me (on the map)?

សុំបង្ហាញខ្ញុំ (លើផែនទី) — sohm bawng-hain kuh-nyohm (ler pain-đee)

What's the address?

សុំអាស័យដ្ឋាន? — sohm aa-say-yah-taan

How far is it?

វាទៅឆ្ងាយប៉ុន្មាន? — wee-aa neuw chuh-ngay bohn-mahn

How do I get there?

ទៅដល់តាមផ្លូវណា? — đeuw dahl đaam pleuw naa

Turn ...	បត់ ...	bawt ...
at the corner	នៅកាច់ជ្រុង	neuw gait juh-rohng
at the traffic lights	នៅភ្លើងស្តុប	neuw plerng stohp
left/right	ឆ្វេង/ស្តាំ	chuh-weng/suh-duhm

It's ...	វាទៅ ...	wee-aa neuw ...
behind ...	ខាងក្រោយ ...	kang krao-y ...
far away	ឆ្ងាយ	chuh-ngay
here	ទីនេះ	đee nih
in front of ...	ខាងមុខ ...	kang mohk ...
left	ខាងឆ្វេង	kang chuh-weng
near	ជិត	juht
next to ...	ជាប់ ...	jo-ahp ...
opposite ...	ទល់មុខ ...	đohl mohk ...
right	ខាងស្តាំ	kang suh-duhm
straight ahead	ត្រង់	đrawng
there	ទីនោះហើយ	đee nooh hao-y

by bus	ជិះឡានឈ្នួល	jih laan chuh-nool
by taxi	ជិះតាក់ស៊ី	jih đahk-see
by train	ជិះរថភ្លើង	jih ruh-teh plerng
on foot	ដើរ	daar

north	ខាងជើង	kang jerng
south	ខាងត្បូង	kang duh-bowng
east	ខាងកើត	kang gaot
west	ខាងលិច	kang leit

signs

ផ្លូវចូល/ផ្លូវចេញ	pleuw johl/pleuw jain	**Entrance/Exit**
បើក/បិត	baok/buht	**Open/Closed**
មានបន្ទប់ផួល	mee-uhn bahn-đohp jool	**Vacancies**
គ្មានបន្ទប់ផួល	kuh-mee-uhn bahn-đohp jool	**No Vacancies**
កន្លែងពត៌មាន	guhn-laing bo-rah-mee-uhn	**Information**
ប៉ុស្តប៉ូលិស	boh bow-lih	**Police Station**
ហាម	haam	**Prohibited**
បង្គន់	bawng-gohn	**Toilets**
ប្រុស/ស្រី	brawh/srei	**Men/Women**
ក្ដៅ/ត្រជាក់	guh-daa-ew/draw-jay-uhk	**Hot/Cold**

accommodation

finding accommodation

Where's a ...?	... នៅឯណា?	... neuw ei naa
camping ground	កន្លែងបោះជំរំ	guhn-laing bawh johm rohm
guesthouse	ផ្ទះសំណាក់	puh-đay-uh suhm-nahk
hotel	សណ្ឋាគារ	suhn-taa-gee-aa

Can you recommend somewhere ...?	មានស្គាល់កន្លែង ... ណាទេ?	mee-uhn sko-ahl guhn-laing ... naa đay
cheap	ថោក	taok
good	ល្អ	luh-aw
nearby	ជិតៗនេះ	juht juht nih

Do you have a ... room?	មានបន្ទប់ ... ទេ?	mee-uhn bawn-đohp ... đay
double	ដែលមានគ្រែធំ	dail mee-uhn krae tohm
single	ដែលមានគ្រែ	dail mee-uhn krae
	តែមួយ	đai muy
twin	ដែលមានគ្រែពីរ	dail mee-uhn krae bee

I'd like to book a room, please.
ខ្ញុំចង់កក់បន្ទប់មួយ — kuh·nyohm jawng gawk bawn·đohp muy

I have a reservation.
ខ្ញុំបានកក់បន្ទប់ទុកជាមុន — kuh·nyohm baan gawk bawn·đohp đohk jee·aa mun

My name is ...
ខ្ញុំឈ្មោះ ... — kuh·nyohm chuh·moo·uh ...

How much is it per night/person?
មួយយប់/នាក់តម្លៃប៉ុន្មាន? — muy yohp/nay·uhk duhm·lai ɓohn·maan

I'd like to stay for (two) nights.
ខ្ញុំចង់ស្នាក់នៅ (ពីរ) យប់ — kuh·nyohm jawng snahk neuw (ɓee) yohp

From (July 2) to (July 6).
ពី (ថ្ងៃទី២ខែកក្កដា) — ɓee (tuh·ngay đee ɓee kai gahk·ga·daa)
ដល់ (ថ្ងៃទី៦ខែកក្កដា) — dahl (tuh·ngay đee bruhm muy kai gahk·ga·daa)

Can I see it?
ខ្ញុំសុំមើលបន្ទប់បានទេ? — kuh·nyohm sohm muhl bawn·đohp baan đay

Am I allowed to camp here?
ខ្ញុំអាចបោះជំរំនៅទីនេះបានទេ? — kuh·nyohm aait bawh johm rohm neuw đee nih baan đay

Can I pay ...?	សុំបង់ជា ... បានទេ?	sohm bawng jee·aa ... baan đay
by credit card	ប័ត្រក្រេឌិត	baht kre·diht
with a travellers cheque	សែកទេសចរ	saik đeh·sah·jaw

requests & queries

When's breakfast served?
គេញ៉ាំម្ហូបពេលព្រឹកអង្កាល់? — gay nyuhm muh·howp ɓehl ɓruhk ang·kahl

Where's breakfast served?
គេញ៉ាំម្ហូបពេលព្រឹកនៅឯណា? — gay nyuhm muh·howp ɓehl ɓruk neuw ei naa

Please wake me at (seven).
សូមដាស់ខ្ញុំនៅ (ម៉ោងប្រាំពីរ) — sohm dah kuh·nyohm neuw (maong bruhm ɓee)

Could I have my key, please?
សុំកូនសោបន្ទប់ — sohm gown sao bawn·đohp

Do you have a ...?	តើអ្នកមាន ... ទេ?	đaar nay·uhk mee·uhn ... đay
mosquito net	មុង	mung
safe	ទូដែក	đoo daik

The room is too ...	បន្ទប់នេះ ... ពេក	bawn·đohp nih ... ʰayk
expensive	ថ្លៃ	tuh·lai
noisy	ថ្ងង់	tuh·lawng
small	តូច	đow·iht

The ... doesn't work.	... ខូចហើយ	... kow·iht hao·y
air conditioner	ម៉ាស៊ីនត្រជាក់	ma·suhn đraw·jay·uhk
fan	កង្ហារ	gawng·hahl
toilet	បង្គន់	bawn·gohn

This ... isn't clean.	... មិនស្អាតទេ	... muhn sah·aat đay
pillow	ខ្នើយ	kuh·nao·y
sheet	ក្រមាពូក	guhm·raal pook
towel	កន្សែង	guhn·saing

checking out

What time is checkout?
ត្រូវចាកចេញនៅម៉ោងប៉ុន្មាន?   đrow jaak jain neuw maong ʰohn·maan

Can I leave my luggage here?
ខ្ញុំផ្ញើទុកក្របូបនៅ   kuh·nyohm puh·nyaar đohk gra·bohp
ទីនេះបានទេ?   neuw đee nih baan đay

Could I have my ...,
please?
សុំ ... មកវិញ   sohm ... mao wein

deposit	លុយកក់	luy gawk
passport	លិខិតឆ្លងដែន	lih·kuht chuh·lawng dain
valuables	របស់មានតម្លៃ	ruh·bawh mee·uhn duhm·lai

communications & banking

the internet

Where's the local Internet café?
មានកន្លែងប្រើអ៊ីនធើ
ណេតនៅឯណា?
mee·uhn guhn·laing braar
in·ter·net neuw ei naa

How much is it per hour?
ប្រើមួយម៉ោងគិតថ្លៃប៉ុន្មាន?
braar muy maong kuht tuh·lai bohn·maan

I'd like to ... ខ្ញុំចង់ ... kuh·nyohm jawng ...
  check my email ឆែកអ៊ីម៉ែល chaik ee·mail
  get Internet access ប្រើកុំព្យូទ័រមើល braar gohm·byu·tor
   អ៊ីនធើនេត muhl in·ter·net
  use a printer ប្រើម៉ាស៊ីនបោះពុម្ព braar ma·suhn bawh bum
  use a scanner ប្រើម៉ាស៊ុនស្កេនធើ braar ma·suhn skan·ner

mobile/cell phone

I'd like a mobile/cell phone for hire.
ខ្ញុំចង់បានទូរស័ព្ទដៃជួល
kuh·nyohm jawng baan đu·rah·sahp dai jool

I'd like a SIM card for your network.
ខ្ញុំចង់បានស៊ីមកាតសំរាប់ប្រើ
នៅស្រុកខ្មែរ
kuh·nyohm jawng baan sim·kaad
suhm·rahp braar neuw srawk kuh·mai

What are the rates?
ថ្លៃប្រើវាគិតថ្លៃប៉ុន្មាន?
tuh·lai braar wee·aa kuht tuh·lai bohn·maan

telephone

What's your phone number?
សុំលេខទូរស័ព្ទរបស់អ្នក?
sohm layk đu·rah·sahp ruh·bawh nay·uhk

The number is ...
លេខទូរស័ព្ទគឺ ...
layk đu·rah·sahp keu ...

Where's the nearest public phone?
ទូរស័ព្ទសាធារណៈ
ជិតនេះនៅឯណា?
đu·rah·sahp saa·tee·aa·rah·nah
juht nih neuw ei naa

I'd like to buy a phonecard.

ខ្ញុំចង់ទិញកាតទូរស័ព្ទ   kuh·nyohm jawng đeen kaad đu·rah·sahp

I want to ...	ខ្ញុំចង់ ...	kuh·nyohm jawng ...
call (Singapore)	ទូរស័ព្ទទៅ (សិង្ហបុរី)	đu·rah·sahp đeuw (suhng·hah·bo·rei)
make a local call	ទូរស័ព្ទក្នុងស្រុក	đu·rah·sahp kuh·nohng srawk
reverse the charges	ឱ្យអ្នកទទួលបង់លុយ	ao·y nay·uhk đoh·đool bawng luy

How much does ... cost?	ទូរស័ព្ទ ... គិតថ្លៃប៉ុន្មាន?	đu·rah·sahp ... kuht tuh·lai bohn·maan
a (three)-minute call	(បី) មិនុត	(bei) mee·nut
each extra minute	រាល់មិនុតលើស កំណត់	rahl mee·nut lerh guhm·nawt

(1 dollar) per (minute).	តំលៃ (មួយដុល្លារ) សំរាប់ (មួយមិនុត)	duhm·lai (muy do·laa) suhm·rahp (muy mee·nut)

post office

I want to send a ...	ខ្ញុំចង់ផ្ញើ ...	kuh·nyohm jawng puh·nyaar ...
fax	ហ្វាក់	fahk
letter	សបុត្រ	suhm·boht
parcel	ប្រអប់	pruh·awp
postcard	កាតប៉ុស្តាល់	kaad boh·staal

I want to buy a/an ...	ខ្ញុំចង់ទិញ ...	kuh·nyohm jawng đeen ...
envelope	ស្រោមសបុត្រ	sraom suhm·boht
stamp	តែម	đaim

Please send it (to Australia) by ...	សូមផ្ញើវារទៅ (អូស្ត្រាលី) តាម ...	sohm puh·nyaar wee·aa đeuw (oh·straa·lee) đaam ...
airmail	យន្តហោះ	yohn hawh
express mail	ប៉ុស្តអ៊ីមេស្រេស	boh ee·em·eh
regular mail	បញ្ជើរធម្មតា	buhn·yaar to·ah·mah·daa
sea mail	តាមកប៉ាល់សមុទ្រ	đaam kuh·paal sah·moht

Is there any mail for me?

មានសបុត្រមកសំរាប់ខ្ញុំទេ?   mee·uhn suhm·boht mao suhm·rahp kuh·nyohm đay

bank

Where's a foreign exchange office?

មានកន្លែងប្តូរលុយបរទេស
នៅឯណា?

mee-uhn guhn-laing dow luy bo-ra-đeh
neuw ei naa

Where can I ...?	ខ្ញុំអាច ... បានៅឯណា?	kuh-nyohm aait ... baan neuw ei naa
cash a cheque	ប្តូរសែក	dow saik
change money	ប្តូរលុយ	dow luy
change a travellers cheque	ប្តូរសែកទេសចរ	dow saik đeh-sah-jaw
get a cash advance	យកលុយពីកាត ក្រេឌិត	yohk luy bee kaad kre-dit
withdraw money	ដកលុយ	dawk luy

What's the ...?	... ប៉ុន្មាន?	... bohn-maan
charge for that	ថ្លៃ	tuh-lai
exchange rate	អត្រាប្តូរលុយ	ah-traa dow luy

It's ...	គឺលេខី ...	duhm-lai keu ...
(12) riel	(ដប់ពីរ) រៀល	(dawp bee) riel
free	អត់គិតថ្លៃទេ	awt kuht tuh-lai đay

personal pronouns		
I	ខ្ញុំ	kuh-nyohm
you	អ្នក	nay-uhk
he/she/they pol/inf	គាត់/គេ	go-uht/gay
it	វា	wee-aa
we	យើង	yerng

possessive pronouns		
my	របស់ខ្ញុំ	ruh-bawh kuh-nyohm
your	របស់អ្នក	ruh-bawh nay-uhk
his/her/their pol/inf	របស់គាត់/គេ	ruh-bawh go-uht/gay
our	របស់យើង	ruh-bawh yerng

sightseeing

getting in

What time does it open/close?
កន្លែងនេះបើក/បិតម៉ោងប៉ុន្មាន?   guhn·laing nih baok/buht maong ʔbohn·maan

What's the admission charge?
តំលៃចូលថ្ងៃប៉ុន្មាន?   duhm·lai johl tuh·lai ʔbohn·maan

Is there a discount for children/students?
មានចុះតំលៃឲ្យ   mee·uhn joh duhm·lai ao·y
កូនក្មេង/សិស្សទេ?   gown kuh·meng/suh ɗay

I'd like a ...   ខ្ញុំសុំ ...   kuh·nyohm sohm ...
  guide   សៀវភៅនាំណែនាំ   see·iw peuw nai no·uhm
  local map   ផែនទីស្រុក   pain·ɗee srawk

I'd like to see ...   ខ្ញុំចង់មើល ...   kuh·nyohm jawng muhl ...
Can I take a photo?   ថតរូបបានទេ?   tawt roop baan ɗay

tours

When's the next ...?	... ទៅអង្កាល់?	... ɗeuw ahng·kahl
boat trip	ទូកទេសចរ	ɗook ɗeh·sah·jaw
tour	ដើរទេស្សនា	daar ɗoh·sah·naa
Is (the) ... included?	តំលៃនេះគិតទាំង	duhm·lai nih kuht ɗe·ahng
	... ដែរឬទេ?	... dai reu ɗay
accommodation	ការស្នាក់	gaa snahk
admission charge	ថ្លៃចូល	tuh·lai johl
food	អ្នប	moh·howp
transport	ការដឹកជញ្ជូន	gaa duhk juhn·joon
museum	សារមន្ទីរ	saa·rah·mohn·ɗee
palace	វាំង	way·ahng
statues	រូបចម្លាក់	roop juhm·luhk
temple	វត្ត	waht

shopping

enquiries

Where's a … ?	… ទៅណា?	… neuw ei naa
bank	ធនាគារ	tuh·nee·ah·gee·aa
bookshop	ហាងលក់សៀវភៅ	haang lu·uhk see·iw peuw
camera shop	ហាងលក់កាម៉ារ៉ា	haang lu·uhk ka·ma·raa
department store	ហាងលក់ផំៗ	haang lu·uhk tohm tohm
market	ផ្សារ	puh·saa

Where can I buy (a padlock)?
ខ្ញុំទិញ (មេសោ)
បានទៅណា?
kuh·nyohm đeen (may sao) baan neuw ei naa

Can I look at it?
សុំមើលវាបានទេ?
sohm muhl wee·aa baan đay

Do you have any others?
មានទៀតទេ?
mee·uhn đee·uht đay

Can I have it sent overseas?
ផ្ញើរវាទៅក្រៅស្រុក
ឲ្យខ្ញុំបានទេ?
puh·nyaar wee·aa đeuw kraa·ew srawk ao·y kuh·nyohm baan đay

Can I have my … repaired?
ខ្ញុំចង់ផ្សុផ្សុល …
kuh·nyohm jawng joo·ah juhl …

It's faulty.
វាខូចហើយ
wee·aa ko·iht hao·y

I'd like (a) …, please.	ខ្ញុំសុំ …	kuh·nyohm sohm …
bag	ក្របូប	gra·bowp
refund	ឲ្យអ្នកសង	ao·y nay·uhk sawng
	ពីលុយវិញ	duhm·lai wee·aa wein
to return this	សងអីវ៉ាន់នេះវិញ	sawng ei·wuhn nih wein

paying

How much is it?
ថ្លៃប៉ុន្មាន?   tuh·lai bohn·maan

Can you write down the price?
សូមសរសេរពីលៃឲ្យខ្ញុំ   sohm saw·say duhm·lai ao·y kuh·nyohm

That's too expensive.
ថ្លៃពេក   tuh·lai bayk

What's your lowest price?
តំលៃថោកបំផុតថ្លៃប៉ុន្មាន?   duhm·lai taok buhm·poht tuh·lai bohn·maan

I'll give you (12) riel.
ខ្ញុំឲ្យ (ដប់ពីរ) រៀល   kuh·nyohm ao·y (dawp bee) riel

There's a mistake in the bill.
គិតលុយខុសហើយ   kuht luy koh hao·y

Do you accept ...?   អ្នកទទួល ... បានទេ?   nay·uhk đoh·đool ... baan đay
    credit cards   ប័ត្រក្រេឌីត   baht kre·điht
    travellers cheques សែកទេសចរ   saik đeh·sah·jaw

I'd like ..., please. ខ្ញុំសុំ ...   kuh·nyohm sohm ...
    my change   លុយអាប់របស់ខ្ញុំ   luy ahp ruh·bawh kuh·nyohm
    a receipt   បង្កាន់ដៃ   bawng·guhn dai

clothes & shoes

Can I try it on?
ខ្ញុំសុំពាក់វាសាក   kuh·nyohm sohm bay·uhk wee·aa
មើលបានទេ?   saak muhl baan đay

My size is (42).
ពាក់លេខ (សែសិបពីរ)   kuh·nyohm bay·uhk layk (sai suhp bee)

It doesn't fit.
ពាក់មិនត្រូវទេ   bay·uhk muhn đrow đay

small   ruច   đow·iht
medium   កណ្ដាល   kuhn·đahl
large   ធំ   tohm

books & music

I'd like a ...	ខ្ញុំសុំ ...	kuh·nyohm sohm ...
newspaper	កាសែត (ជាភាសា	gaa·sait (jee·aa
(in English)	អង់គ្លេស)	pee·aa·saa awng·glay)
pen	ប៊ិច	bihk

Is there an English-language bookshop?

មានហាងលក់សៀវភៅ
ជាភាសាអង់គ្លេសទេ?

mee·uhn haang lu·uhk see·iw peuw
jee·aa pee·aa·saa awng·glay đay

Can I listen to this?

សុំស្តាប់សាកមើលបានទេ?

sohm suh·dahp saak muhl baan đay

photography

Can you ...?	សុំជួយ ... បានទេ?	sohm juy ... baan đay
develop this film	ល្បិសួបថតហ្វិល	puh·duht roop tawđ fil
load my film	ដាក់ហ្វិលចូល	dahk fil johl
	កាម៉ារ៉ា	kaa·maa·raa

I need a/an ... film	ខ្ញុំត្រូវការហ្វិល ...	kuh·nyohm đrow kaa fil ...
for this camera.	សំរាប់កាម៉ារ៉ានេះ	suhm·rahp kaa·maa·raa nih
APS	អេ ពី អេស	ay bee eh
B&W	ស ខ្មៅ	saw kuh·maw
colour	ពណ៌	bo·uh
(200) speed	ស្ពីត (ពីររយ)	speed (bee roy)

When will it be ready?

ល្បិតវាហើយអង្កាល់?

puh·duht wee·aa hao·y awng·kahl

toiletries

conditioner	សាប៊ូកក់សក់	saa·boo kawk sawk
condoms	ស្រោមអនាម័យ	sraom ah·naa·mai
deodorant	ថ្នាំលាបក្លៀក	tuh·nuhm lee·uhp klee·uhk
insect repellent	ថ្នាំការពារមុស	tuh·nuhm gaa ៦ee·aa muh
razor blades	ឡាមកោរពុកមាត់	laam gao ៦ohk mo·uht
sanitary napkins	សំម្លីអនាម័យស្ត្រី	suhm·lei ah·naa·mai sah·drei
shampoo	សាប៊ូកក់សក់	saa·boo kawk sawk
shaving cream	ក្រែមកោរពុកមាត់	kraim gao ៦ohk mo·uht
soap	សាប៊ូដុំ	saa·boo dohm
toilet paper	ក្រដាស់អនាម័យ	gra·dah ah·naa·mai
toothbrush	ប្រាសដុសធ្មេញ	j·rah doh tuh·mein
toothpaste	ថ្នាំដុសធ្មេញ	tuh·nuhm doh tuh·mein

meeting people

greetings, goodbyes & introductions

Hello.	ជំរាបសួរ	johm ree·uhp soo·uh
Hi.	សួស្ដី	soo·uh suh·dei
Goodbye.	លាសិនហើយ	lee·aa suhn hao·y
Good night.	រាត្រីសួស្ដី	ree·aa drei soo·uh suh·dei

Mr/Sir	លោក	lohk
Mrs/Madam	លោកស្រី	lohk srei
Miss/Ms	នាង	nee·uhng

How are you?	សុខសប្បាយទេ?	sohk sa·baay day
Fine. And you?	ខ្ញុំសុខសប្បាយ ចុះអ្នក?	kuh·nyohm sohk sa·baay joh nay·uhk
What's your name?	អ្នកឈ្មោះអ្វី?	nay·uhk chuh·mu·ah ei
My name is ...	ខ្ញុំឈ្មោះ ...	kuh·nyohm chuh·mu·ah ...
I'm pleased to meet you.	ខ្ញុំរីករាយដោយបាន ជួបអ្នក	kuh·nyohm reek ree·ay dao·y baan ju·uhp nay·uhk

This is my ...	នេះគឺជា ... របស់ខ្ញុំ	nih keu ... ruh-bawh kuh-nyohm
boyfriend	សង្សារ	sawng-saa
brother (older)	បងប្រុស	bawng brawh
brother (younger)	ប្អូនប្រុស	buh-own brawh
daughter	កូនស្រី	gown srei
father	ឪពុក	euw-bohk
friend	ពួកម៉ាក	'bu-uhk maak
girlfriend	សង្សារ	sawng-saa
husband	ប្តី	buh-dei
mother	ម្តាយ	muh-daay
partner (intimate)	គូស្នេហ៍	goo suhm-lain
sister (older)	បងស្រី	bawng srei
sister (younger)	ប្អូនស្រី	buh-own srei
son	កូនប្រុស	gown brawh
wife	ប្រពន្ធ	pruh-bohn

Here's my ...	នេះជា ...	nih jee-aa ...
What's your ...?	សុំ ... របស់អ្នក	sohm ... ruh-bawh nay-uhk
address	អាសយដ្ឋាន	aa-sai-yah-taan
email address	អាត្រេសអ៊ីមែល	aa-dreh ee-mail
fax number	លេខហ្វាក់	layk fahk
home number	លេខផ្ទះ	layk puh-day-uh
mobile number	លេខទូរស័ព្ទដៃ	layk đoo-rah-sahp dai

occupations

What's your occupation?	តើអ្នកធ្វើការអ្វី?	đaar nay-uhk twer gaa ah-wei
I'm a/an ...	ខ្ញុំធ្វើការជា ...	kuh-nyohm twer gaa jee-aa ...
carpenter	ជាងឈើ	jee-ahng cher
electrician	ជាងភ្លើង	jee-ahng plerng
mechanic	ជាងម៉ាស៊ីន	jee-ahng laan
nurse	អាហ្វីមីញ៉ៃ	ahng-fee-mee-nyai
office worker	បុគ្គលិកនៅ	bohk-ga-lerk neuw
	ការិយាល័យ	gaa-ree-aa-lai
student	និស្សិត	ni-suht
teacher	គ្រូបង្រៀន	kroo bawng-ree-uhn
writer	អ្នកនិពន្ធ	nay-uhk ni-'bohn

background

Where are you from?	អ្នកមកពីណា?	nay·uhk mao bee naa
I'm from ...	ខ្ញុំមកពី ...	kuh·nyohm mao bee ...
Australia	អូស្ត្រាលី	ow·straa·lee
Canada	កាណាដា	kaa·naa·daa
England	អង់គ្លេស	awng·glay
Ireland	ប្រទេសអៀរឡង់	prah·teh ee·ah lawng
New Zealand	នីវស៊ីឡង់	niw see·lawng
Scotland	ស្កុត	skawt
the USA	សហរដ្ឋអាមេរិក	sah·hah·rawt aa·me·rihk
Wales	វែល	wehl

Are you married?	អ្នកមានគ្រួសារ ហើយឬនៅ?	nay·uhk mee·uhn kru·ah saa hao·y reu neuw
I'm ...	ខ្ញុំ ...	kuh·nyohm ...
married	មានគ្រួសារហើយ	mee·uhn kru·ah saa hao·y
single	នៅលីវ	neuw liw

age

How old ...?	... អាយុប៉ុន្មាន?	... aa·yuh bohn·maan
are you	អ្នក	nay·uhk
is your daughter	កូនស្រីអ្នក	gown srei nay·uhk
is your son	កូនប្រុសអ្នក	gown brawh nay·uhk

I am ... years old.
ខ្ញុំអាយុ ... ឆ្នាំ   kuh·nyohm aa·yooh ... chuh·nuhm

He/She is ... years old.
គាត់អាយុ ... ឆ្នាំ   go·uht aa·yooh ... chuh·nuhm

classifiers					
animals	ក្បាល	guh·baal	people	នាក់	nay·uhk
clothes	សម្រាប់	suhm·raap	plates (of food)	ចាន	jaan
houses	ខ្នង	kuh·nawng	vehicles	គ្រឿង	kreu·uhng

feelings

I'm (not) ...	ខ្ញុំ (មិន) ...	kuh·nyohm (muhn) ...
Are you ...?	អ្នកមានអារម្មណ៍	nay·uhk mee·uhn aa·rahm
	... ទេ?	... đay
cold	រងា	ruh·ngee·aa
embarrassed	ខ្មាស់គេ	kuh·mah gay
happy	សប្បាយចិត្ត	suh·baay juht
hot	ក្តៅ	guh·daw
hungry	ឃ្លានបាយ	klee·uhn baay
thirsty	ស្រេកទឹក	srayk đuhk
tired	ហត់	hawt
OK	សប្បាយ	suh·baay

entertainment

beach

Where's the ...	ឆ្នេរសមុទ្រ ...	chuh·nay suh·moht ...
beach?	នៅឯណា?	neuw ei naa
best	ស្អាតជាងគេ	sah·aat jee·uhng gay
nearest	ជិតជាងគេ	juht jee·uhng gay
public	សាធារណៈ	saa·tee·aa·rah·nah

How much for a/an ...?	... មួយថ្លៃប៉ុន្មាន?	... muy tuh·lai bohn·maan
chair	កៅអី	gao ei
umbrella	ឆត្រ	chaht

Is it safe to swim here?
ហែលទឹកនៅទីនេះមាន
គ្រោះថ្នាក់ទេ?
hail đuhk neuw đee nih mee·uhn
kru·ah tuh·nahk đay

Is it safe to dive here?
មុជទឹកនៅទីនេះមាន
គ្រោះថ្នាក់ទេ?
mu·iht đuhk neuw đee nih mee·uhn
kru·ah tuh·nahk đay

What time is high/low tide?
ទឹកឡើង/ ចុះនៅម៉ោងប៉ុន្មាន?
đeuk laong/joh neuw maong bohn·maan

water sports

Can I book a lesson?	ខ្ញុំចូលរៀន បានទេ?	kuh·nyohm johl ree·uhn baan đay
Can I hire (a) ...?	ខ្ញុំជួល ... បានទេ?	kuh·nyohm jool ... baan đay
canoe	ទូកចែវមួយ	đook jaiw muy
diving equipment	អ៊ីវ៉ាន់សំរាប់	ei·wuhn suhm·rahp
	មុជទឹក	mu·iht đeuk
guide	អ្នកនាំផ្លូវ	nay·uhk no·uhm pleuw
life jacket	អាវសង្គ្រោះ	aaw sawng·kru·ah
motorboat	ទូកមានម៉ាស៊ីន	đook mee·uhn ma·suhn
sailing boat	ទូកក្ដោង	đook guh·daong
Are there any ...?	មាន ... ទេ?	mee·uhn ... đay
reefs	ថ្មប៉ិប្រេះទឹក	tuh·maw bawh·brah đeuk
rips	ចរន្តទឹកខ្លាំង	juh·rawn đeuk kluhng
water hazards	គ្រោះថ្នាក់ក្នុងទឹក	kru·ah tuh·nahk kuh·nohng đeuk

going out

Where can I find ...?	មាន ... នៅឯណា?	mee·uhn ... neuw ei naa
bars	បារ	baa
clubs	កន្លែងដិស្គ	guhn·laing dis·kow
gay venues	បារសំរាប់មនុស្ស	baa suhm·rahp ma·nooh
	ខ្ទើយ	guh·đeuy
nightclubs	ទៅលេងដិស្គ	đeuw leng dis·kow
restaurants	ភោជនីយដ្ឋាន	pow·chuh·nee·yuh·taan
I feel like going to a/the ...	ខ្ញុំចង់ទៅដើរ លេង ...	kuh·nyohm jawng đeuw daar leng ...
concert	កុងសេីស្ដាប់ភ្លេង	gawng·sert suh·dahp pleng
folk opera	ល្ខោន	luh·kaon
karaoke bar	បារការ៉ាអូកេ	baa kaa·raa·ow·kay
movies	កុន	gohn
party	ជួបលាង	ju·uhp lee·ahng
performance	ល្ខោនសិល្ប	luh·kaon sil·a·pah

interests

Do you like ...?	តើអ្នកចូលចិត្ត ... ទេ?	đaar nay·uhk johl juht ... đay
I like ...	ខ្ញុំចូលចិត្ត ...	kuh·nyohm johl juht ...
I don't like ...	ខ្ញុំមិនចូលចិត្ត ... ទេ	kuh·nyohm muhn johl juht ... đay
art	សិល្បៈ	sil·a·bah
cooking	ធ្វើម្ហូប	twer muh·howp
movies	មើលកុន	muhl gohn
photography	ថតរូប	tawt roop
reading	អានសៀវភៅ	aan siew·peuw
sport	កីឡា	gei·laa
surfing the Internet	មើលអិនទើនេត	muhl in·ter·net
swimming	ហែលទឹក	hail đeuk
travelling	ធ្វើដំណើរ	twer duhm·naar
Do you like to ...?	តើអ្នកចូលចិត្ត ... ទេ?	đaar nay·uhk johl juht ... đay
dance	រាំ	ro·uhm
go to concerts	ទៅកង់ស្បិតស្ដាប់ភ្លេង	đeuw gawng·sert suh·dahp pleng
listen to music	ស្ដាប់ភ្លេង	suh·dahp pleng

food & drink

finding a place to eat

Can you recommend a ...?	អ្នកមានស្គាល់ ... ល្អទេ?	nay·uhk mee·uhn sko·uhl ... luh·aw đay
bar	បារ	baa
café	ហាងបាយ	haang baay
restaurant	ភោជនីយដ្ឋាន	pow·chuh·nee·yuh·taan
I'd like ..., please.	ខ្ញុំសុំ ...	kuh·nyohm sohm ...
a table for (four)	តុសំរាប់ (បួន)	đohk suhm·rahp (boo·uhn)
	នាក	nay·uhk
the (non)smoking section	តុទៅកន្លែង (មិន) ឲ្យជក់បារី	đohk neuw guhn·laing (muhn) ao·y joo·uhk baa·rei

ordering food

breakfast	អ្នកពេលព្រឹក	muh·howp ɓehl ɓruhk
lunch	អ្នកថ្ងៃត្រង់	muh·howp tuh·ngai drawng
dinner	អ្នកពេលល្ងាច	muh·howp ɓehl luh·ngee·ihk
snack	អ្នកញ៉ាំលេង	muh·howp nyuhm leng

I'd like (the) ..., please.	សុំ ...	sohm ...
bill	គិតលុយ	kuht luy
menu	ម៉ឺនុយ	me·nuy
that dish	មុខអ្នកនោះ	mohk muh·howp nuh

What would you recommend?	មានមុខអ្នកអ្វី ញ្ញាំពិសេសទេ?	mee·uhn mohk muh·howp ah·wei chuh·ngain ɓi·seh ɗay

bowl	ចានគោម	jaan gowm
chopsticks	ចង្កឹះ	jawng·kah
cloth	កន្សែង	guhn·saing
cup	ពែង	ɓeng
fork	សម	sawm
glass	កែវ	gaiw
knife	កាំបិត	guhm·buht
plate	ចាន	jaan
spoon	ស្លាបព្រា	slahp·ɓree·uh
teaspoon	ស្លាបព្រាតូច	slahp·ɓree·uh ɗow·iht

drinks

(cup of) coffee ...	កាហ្វេ (មួយពែង) ...	gaa·fay (muy ɓeng) ...
(cup of) tea ...	តែ (មួយពែង) ...	ɗai (muy ɓeng) ...
with milk	ដាក់ទឹកដោះគោ	dahk ɗeuk dawh gow
without sugar	កុំដាក់ស្ករ	gohm dahk skaw saw

boiled water	ទឹកឆ្អិន	ɗuhk chuh·uhn
hot water	ទឹកក្ដៅ	ɗuhk guh·daa·ew
orange juice	ទឹកក្រូចពោធិសាត់	ɗeuk krow·iht ɓow·saht
soft drink	ទឹកក្រូច	ɗeuk krow·iht
sparkling mineral water	ទឹកមានពពុះ	ɗuhk mee·uhn ɓo·ɓuh

in the bar

I'll have ...	ខ្ញុំសំ ...	kuh·nyohm sohm ...
I'll buy you a drink.	ខ្ញុំទិញទឹកដឹកឲ្យអ្នក	kuh·nyohm đihn đuhk puhk ao·y nay·uhk
What would you like?	អ្នកចង់ពិសាអ្វីខ្លះ?	nay·uhk jawng ʼbi·saa ah·wei klah
Cheers!	ជយោ!	chuh·yow
gin	ស្រាជិន	sraa jin
rum	ស្រារ៉ម	sraa rum
vodka	ស្រាវ៉ុតកា	sraa woht·gaa
a bottle/glass of (beer)	(បៀរ) មួយដប/កែវ	(bee·ah) muy dawp/gaiw
a shot of (whisky)	ស្រា (វិស្គី)	sraa (wis·kee)
	មួយកែវតូច	muy gaiw đow·iht
a bottle/glass	ស្រាទំពាំងបាយជូរ	sraa đohm·ʼbay·uhng baay joo
of ... wine	... មួយដប/កែវ	... muy dawp/gaiw
red	ក្រហម	kruh·hawm
sparkling	មានពពុះ	mee·uhn ʼbo·ʼbuh
white	ស	saw

self-catering

What's the local speciality?
មានមុខម្ហូបឆ្ងាញ់ពិ
សេសអ្វីខ្លះ?
mee·uhn mohk muh·howp chuh·ngain ʼbi·seh ah·wei klah

What's that?
នោះជាអ្វី?
nooh jee·aa ah·wei

How much is (a kilo of) ...?
... (មួយគីឡូ) ថ្លៃប៉ុន្មាន?
... (muy kee·low) tuh·lai ʼbohn·maan

I'd like ...	សុំ ...	sohm ...
(100) grams	(មួយរយ) ក្រាម	(muy roy) kraam
(two) kilos	(ពីរ) គីឡូ	(bee) kee·low
(three) pieces	(បី) ដុំ	(bei) dohm
(six) slices	(ប្រាំមួយ) កំណាត់	(bruhm muy) guhm·naht

Enough.	បានហើយ	baan hao·y
A bit more.	សុំថែមបន្តិច	sohm taim buhn·điht
Less.	ច្រើនពេក	juh·rarn bayk

special diets & allergies

Is there a vegetarian restaurant near here?

មានហាងបាយបួស
នៅជិតនេះទេ?

mee·uhn haang baay muh·howp bu·uh
neuw juht nih đay

Do you have vegetarian food?

ទីនេះមានលក់អូប
បួសទេ?

đee nih mee·uhn lu·uhk
muh·howp bu·uh đay

Could you prepare a meal without ...?	សុំធ្វើអូបដែលមិន ដាក់ ... បានទេ?	sohm twer muh·howp muhn dahk ... baan đay
butter	ប៊ឺរ	beur
eggs	ពង	bohng
fish sauce	ទឹកត្រី	đeuk đrei
meat	សាច់	sait
meat stock	ជាតិសាច់	jee·uht sait

I'm allergic to ...	ខ្ញុំមិនត្រូវជាតុ ឯង ...	kuh·nyohm muhn đrow tee·uht nuhng ...
cashews	គ្រាប់ស្វាយចន្ទី	kro·uhp swaay juhn·đee
chilli	ម្ទេស	muh·đeh
dairy produce	អូបធ្វើអំពីទឹក ផោះគោ	muh·howp twer uhm·bee đeuk dawh gow
eggs	ពង	bohng
MSG	ប៊ីចេង	bee·jeng
nuts	គ្រាប់ផ្លែឈើ	kro·uhp plai cher
peanuts	សណ្តែកដី	suhn·daik dei
seafood	គ្រឿងសមុទ្រ	kreu·uhng suh·moht

menu decoder

aa·mohk	អាម៉ុក	fish in a thick coconut milk curry, wrapped in banana leaves & steamed
ahn·sawm juh·rook	អន្សមជ្រូក	rice cake filled with pork & mung-bean paste & wrapped in banana leaves
awn·tohng	អន្ទង់	eel
bain chaiw	បាញ់ចែវ	rice-flour crepe filled with bean sprouts & meat
baw baw	បបរ	congee or rice porridge, usually with chicken or pork
bawng·kee·aa	បង្គា	shrimp
bohk luh·hohng	បុកល្ហុង	green papaya salad with a lime juice & fish sauce dressing
chaa·yaw	ឆាយ៉	fried spring rolls
chuh·nuhng puh·nohm plerng	ឆ្នាំងភ្នំភ្លើង	marinated beef mixed with eggs & accompanied by rice & vegetables
đee·uhp	ទៀប	custard apple
downg	ដូង	coconut
draw·yowng jayk mee·uhn snool	ត្រយ៉ូងចេកមានស្នូល	chicken & pork sausages wrapped in banana leaves & deep-fried
drei buhm·bohng	ត្រីបំពង	fried fish with lettuce, carrot & tomato in a spicy sauce
drei ngee·iht	ត្រីង៉ៀត	dried fish
đuhk đrei	ទឹកត្រី	fish sauce
đuhk see·iw	ទឹកស៊ីអ៊ីវ	soy sauce
gaa·ree	ការី	curry
gawng·gaip	កង្កែប	frog
guh·daam	ក្ដាម	crab

guy đee·ow	គុយទាវ	rice noodles
guy đee·ow buhn·lai	គុយទាវបន្លែ	noodle soup with vegetables
guy đee·ow sait gow	គុយទាវសាច់គោ	beef noodle soup
kuh·yawng	ខ្យង	snails
lohk·lahk	ឡុកឡាក់	beef chunks in gravy topped with a fried egg
mee	មី	egg noodles
meuk	មឹក	squid
muh·đeh	ម្ទេស	chilli
muh·joo kreu·uhng sait mo·uhn	ម្សូរគ្រឿងសាច់មាន់	chicken in a coconut soup with water spinach & pickled fish
naim	ណែម	fresh spring rolls
nguhm ngeuw	ង៉ាំង៉ើវ	chicken soup flavoured with preserved lemons
nohm ahn·sawm jayk	នំអន្សមចេក	rice cake filled with bananas & wrapped in banana leaves
nohm buhn·johk sait gow chaa·yaw	នំបញ្ចុកសាច់គោឆាយ	cold noodles with lemon grass, braised beef & spring rolls
nyo·uhm sait gow	ញាំសាច់គោ	cold marinated beef with a salad of rice vermicelli, carrot, onions, cabbage & cucumber
pra·hohk	ប្រហុក	fermented fish paste
sait gow chaa muh·no·ah	សាច់គោឆាម្នាស់	stir-fried beef with pineapple, cabbage, tomato & peppers
sait grawk gow	សាច់ក្រកគោ	beef sausages
sait mo·uhn chaa đrawp	សាច់មាន់ឆាត្រប់	chicken & eggplant stir-fry
slaap mo·uhn chaa gaa·ree	ស្លាបមាន់ឆាការី	stir-fried chicken wings with curry sauce
suhm·law gaa·ree saap	សម្លការីសាប	vegetarian coconut curry with tofu, eggplant & potato
suhm·law muh·joo	សម្លម្សូរ	sour tamarind soup with chicken or fish, pineapple, tomato & herbs

emergencies

basics

Help!	ជួយផង!	joo·y pawng
Stop!	ឈប់!	chohp
Go away!	ទៅអោយឆ្ងាយ!	đeuw ao·y chuh·ngaay
Thief!	ចោរ!	jao
Fire!	ភ្លើងឆេះ!	plerng cheh
Call ...	ជួយហៅ ... មក	joo·y haa·ew ... mao
a doctor	គ្រូពេទ្យ	kru baet
an ambulance	ឡានពេទ្យ	laan baet
the police	ប៉ូលិស	bow·lih

It's an emergency!
នេះជារឿងបន្ទាន់!
nih jee·aa reu·uhng bawn·đo·uhn

Could you help me, please?
ជួយខ្ញុំផងបានទេ?
joo·y kuh·nyohm pawng baan đay

I have to use the phone.
ខ្ញុំត្រូវប្រើទូរស័ព្ទ
kuh·nyohm đrow braar đu·rah·sahp

I'm lost.
ខ្ញុំវង្វេងផ្លូវ
kuh·nyohm wohng·weng pleuw

Where are the toilets?
បង្គន់នៅឯណា?
bawng·gohn neuw ei naa

police

Where's the police station?
ប៉ុស្តិ៍ប៉ូលិសនៅឯណា?
boh bow·lih neuw ei naa

I want to report an offence.
ខ្ញុំចង់រាយការអំពី
បទឧក្រិដ្ឋ
kuh·nyohm jawng ree·ay gaa uhm bee bawt oh·kruht

I have insurance.
ខ្ញុំមានអ៊ីសុីរ៉ង់
kuh·nyohm mee·ihn uhn·su·rahng

I've been raped.

ខ្ញុំត្រូវគេចាប់រំលោភ   kuh·nyohm đrow gay jahp rohm·lohp

I've been assaulted.

ខ្ញុំត្រូវគេវាយ   kuh·nyohm đrow gay waay

I've been robbed.

ខ្ញុំត្រូវចោរប្លន់   kuh·nyohm đrow jao plawn

My ... was/were stolen.	... ត្រូវគេលួច	... đrow gay loo·iht
I've lost my ...	ខ្ញុំបាត់ ...	kuh·nyohm baht ...
	របស់ខ្ញុំ	ruh·bawh kuh·nyohm
backpack	ក្របូបស្ពាយ	gra·bowp spee·ay
bags	វ៉ាលីស	waa·lih
credit card	ប័ត្រក្រេឌីត	baht kre·diht
handbag	ក្របូបដៃ	gra·bowp dai
jewellery	គ្រឿងអលង្ការ	kreu·uhng ah·lahng·kaa
money	លុយ	luy
passport	លិខិតឆ្លងដែន	lih·kuht chuh·lawng dain
travellers cheques	សែកទេសចរ	saik đeh·sah·jaw
wallet	ក្របូបលុយ	gra·bowp luy

I want to contact	ខ្ញុំចង់ហៅ ...	kuh·nyohm jawng haa·ew ...
my ...	របស់ប្រទេសខ្ញុំ	ruh·bawh pra·đeh kuh·nyohm
consulate	កុងស៊ុល	kohng·sul
embassy	ស្ថានទូត	suh·taan đoot

health

medical needs

Where's the	មាន ...	mee·uhn ...
nearest ...?	នៅជិតនេះ?	neuw ei naa juht nih
dentist	ពេទ្យធ្មេញ	baet đuh·mein
doctor	គ្រូពេទ្យ	kru baet
hospital	មន្ទីរពេទ្យ	mohn·đee baet
(night)	កន្លែងលក់ថ្នាំ	guhn·laing lu·uhk tuh·nuhm
pharmacist	ពេទ្យ (ពេលយប់)	baet (behl yohp)

I need a doctor (who speaks English).

ខ្ញុំចង់ជួបគ្រូពេទ្យ   kuh·nyohm jawng joo·uhp kru baet

(ដែលចេះភាសាអង់គ្លេស)   (dail jeh pee·aa·saa awng·glay)

Could I see a female doctor?

សុំជួបគ្រូពេទ្យស្រី   sohm joo·uhp kru baet srei

I've run out of my medication.

ថ្នាំរបស់ខ្ញុំអស់ហើយ   tuh·nuhm ruh·bawh kuh·nyohm awh hao·y

symptoms, conditions & allergies

I'm sick.

ខ្ញុំមិនស្រួលខ្លួន   kuh·nyohm muhn sru·uhl klu·uhn

It hurts here.

ខ្ញុំឈឺកន្លែងនេះ   kuh·nyohm cheu guhn·laing nih

ankle	កជើង	kaw jerng
arm	ដៃ	dai
back	ខ្នង	kuh·nawng
chest	ទ្រូង	droong
ear	ត្រចៀក	draw·jee·uhk
eye	ភ្នែក	puh·naik
face	មុខ	mohk
finger	ម្រាមដៃ	muh·ree·uhm dai
foot	ជើង	jerng
hand	ដៃ	dai
head	ក្បាល	guh·baal
heart	បេះដូង	beh downg
leg	ជើង	jerng
mouth	មាត់	mo·uht
neck	ក	kaw
nose	ច្រមុះ	jruh·moh
skin	ស្បែក	suh·baik
stomach	ពោះ	boo·uh
teeth	ធ្មេញ	tuh·mein
throat	បំពង់ក	buhm·bohng kaw

I have (a) ...	ខ្ញុំកើត ...	kuh·nyohm gaot ...
asthma	រោគហឺត	rowk hert
bronchitis	រោគរលាក	rowk ruh·lee·uhk
	ទងសួត	đohng soo·uht
constipation	ទល់លាមក	đohl lee·aa mohk
cough	ក្អក	guh·awk
diarrhoea	ជំងឺរាគ	jooh ree·uhk
fever	គ្រៅខ្លួន	guh·đaa·ew kluʔuhn
headache	ឈឺក្បាល	cheu guh·baal
heat stroke	ចាញ់គ្រៅ	jaʔihn guh·đaa·ew
nausea	វិលមុខចង់ក្អួត	wuhl mohk jawng guh·oo·uht
pain	ឈឺ	cheu
sore throat	ឈឺក	cheu kaw
toothache	ឈឺធ្មេញ	cheu tuh·mein

I'm allergic to ...	ខ្ញុំមិនត្រូវជាតុ នឹង ...	kuh·nyohm muhn đrow tee·uht nuhng ...
antibiotics	ថ្នាំអង់ទីប៊ីអូតិច	tuh·nuhm awng·đee·bee·ow·đik
anti-inflammatories	ថ្នាំបំបាត់ហើម	tuh·nuhm buhm·baht haom
aspirin	ប៉ារ៉ាសេតាម៉ុល	paa·raa·se·đaa·mohl
bees	ឃ្មុំ	kuh·mohm
codeine	ថ្នាំកូឌីន	tuh·nuhm gow·deen
penicillin	ប៉េនីស៊ីលីន	pay·nee·see·leen

antimalarial medication	ថ្នាំការពារ ជម្ងឺគ្រុនចាញ់	tuh·nuhm gaa ẞee·aa johm·ngeu krohn jaʔihn
antiseptic	ថ្នាំសលាប់មេរោគ	tuh·nuhm suhm·lahp may rowk
bandage	បង់ស៊ីមង	bawng see·mawng
contraceptives	ថ្នាំការពារ កុំឲ្យមានកូន	tuh·nuhm gaa ẞee·aa gohm ao·y mee·uhn gown
diarrhoea medicine	ថ្នាំសារប់ រោគជំងឺរាគ	tuh·nuhm suhm·rahp rowk jooh ree·uhk
insect repellent	ថ្នាំការពារមូស	tuh·nuhm gaa ẞee·aa muh
laxatives	ថ្នាំសំរាប់ ទល់លាមក	tuh·nuhm suhm·rahp đohl lee·aa mohk
painkillers	ថ្នាំសំរាប់ ការឈឺចុក	tuh·nuhm suhm·rahp gaa cheu johk
sleeping tablets	ថ្នាំធ្វើងងុយដេក	tuh·nuhm twer nguh·nguy dayk

The symbols ⓝ, ⓐ, ⓥ and adv (indicating noun, adjective, verb and adverb) have been added for clarity where an English term could be either. For food terms see the **menu decoder**, page 93.

A

accident ការគ្រោះថ្នាក់ gaa kru-ah tuh-nahk
accommodation ទីកន្លែងស្នាក់ dee guhn-laing snahk
address ⓝ អាសយដ្ឋាន aa-sah-yah-taan
after បន្ទាប់ពី bawn-do-uhp bee
air-conditioned មានម៉ាស៊ីនត្រជាក់ mee-uhn maa-suhn draw-jay-uhk
airplane យន្តហោះ yohn hawh
airport វាលយន្តហោះ wee-uhl yohn hawh
alcohol ស្រា sraa
all ទាំងអស់ day-uhng awh
allergy រោគមិនត្រូវជាតុអ្វីមួយ rowk muhn drow tee-uht ah-wei muy
ambulance ឡានពេទ្យ laan baet
and នឹង nuhng
arm ដៃ dai

B

baby កូនង៉ែត gown ngait
backpack ក្របូបស្ពាយ gra-bowp spee-ay
bad អាក្រក់ aa-krawk
bag វិលីស waa-lih
baggage claim កន្លែងទទួលវិលីស guhn-laing doh-dool waa-lih
bank ធនាគារ duh-nee-aa-gee-aa
bank account កុងធនាគារ gohng tuh-nee-aa-gee-aa
bar បារ baa
bathroom បន្ទប់ទឹក bawn-dohp duhk
battery ថ្មពិល tuh-maw buhl
beach ឆ្នេរសមុទ្រ chuh-nay suh-moht
beautiful ស្អាត sah-aat

bed គ្រែ krae
beer បៀរ bee-uh
before មុន mun
behind ខាងក្រោយ kang krao-y
bicycle កង់ gawng
big ធំ tohm
bill ប័ណ្ណកិលលុយ buhn kuht luy
black ពណ៌ខ្មៅ bo-uh kuh-maa-ew
blanket ភួយ puy
blood ឈាម chee-uhm
blood group ក្រុបឈាម grup chee-uhm
blue ពណ៌ខៀវ bo-uh kee-iw
book (make a reservation) ⓥ កក់ទុកជាមុន gawk dohk jee-aa mun
both ទាំងពីរ day-uhng bee
bottle ដប dawp
bottle opener ប្រដាប់បើកដប pra-dahp baok dawp
boy ក្មេងប្រុស kuh-meng brawh
brakes (car) ប្រ៊ាំង fruhng
breakfast អ្វារពេលព្រឹក muh-howp behl bruhk
broken (faulty) ខូច kow-iht
brown ពណ៌ត្នោត bo-aa tuh-naot
bus ឡានក្រុង laan grohng
bus stop កន្លែងឡានក្រុងឈប់ guh-laing laan grohng chohp
business កិច្ចការ gait-gaa
but ប៉ុន្តែ bohn-dai
buy ទិញ dihn

C

café ហាងបាយ haang baay
camera កាម៉េរ៉ា kaa-ma-raa

camp site កន្លែងបោះជំរុំ
guhn-laing bawh johm rohm

cancel លប់ចោល lohp jaowl

can opener ប្រដាប់បើកកំប៉ុង
brah-dahp baok guhm-bohng

car ឡាន laan

cash ⓝ លុយ luy

cash (a cheque) ⓥ ផ្ដូរ (សែក) dow (saik)

cell phone ទូរស័ព្ទដៃ du-rah-sahp dai

centre ⓝ មជ្ឈមណ្ឌល mah-chay-uh mahn-dohl

change ⓥ ផ្ដូរ dow

cheap ថោក taok

check (bill) ⓝ ប័ណ្ណគិតលុយ buhn kuht luy

check in ⓥ ចូលចុះឈ្មោះ johl joh chuh-mu-uh

cheque (bank) សែក (ធនាគារ)
saik (tuh-nee-aa-gee-aa)

child ក្មេង gown kuh-meng

cigarette បារី baa-rei

clean ស្អាត sah-aat

closed បិទ buht

coffee កាហ្វេ gaa-fay

coins លុយកាក់ luy kahk

cold ⓐ រងា ruh-ngee-aa

cold (illness) ⓝ ផ្ដាសាយ puh-daa saay

collect call អ្នកទទួលបង់លុយឲ្យ
nay-uhk doh-dool bawng luy ao-y

come មក mao

compass គ្រឿងសំដៅ drei wih-sai

computer កុំព្យូទ័រ gohm-byu-dor

condoms ស្រោមអនាម័យ sraom ah-naa-mai

cook ⓥ ធ្វើម្ហូប twer muh-howp

cost ⓝ តម្លៃ duhm-lai

credit card ប័ត្រក្រេឌីត baht kre-diht

currency exchange ការប្ដូរលុយបរទេស
gaa dow luy baw-ruh-deh

customs (immigration) គយ goy

D

dangerous គ្រោះថ្នាក់ kru-ah tuh-nahk

date (time) ⓝ ថ្ងៃខែ tuh-ngai kai

day ថ្ងៃ tuh-ngai

delay ⓥ ធ្វើឲ្យយឺតពេល twer ao-y yeut behl

dentist ពេទ្យធ្មេញ baet tuh-mein

departure ការចេញដំណើរ gaa jain duhm-naar

diaper កន្ទប់ហ្គោនក្មេង guhn-dohp gown kuh-meng

diarrhoea ហោះចុះរាក rowk joh ree-uhk

dictionary វចនានុក្រម wah-jah-naa-nu-grawm

dinner អាហារពេលល្ងាច
muh-howp behl luh-ngee-ihk

direct ផ្ដួយទៅត្រង់ខែម្ដង
pleuw deuw drawng dai muh-dawng

dirty ក្រខ្វក់ graw-kwuhk

disabled ពិការ bi-gaa

discount ⓥ ចុះថ្លៃ joh tuh-lai

doctor គ្រូពេទ្យ kru baet

double bed ត្រែគម្ krae tohm

double room បន្ទប់សំរាប់ពីរនាក់
bawn-dohp suhm-rahp bee nay-uhk

down ចុះក្រោម joh kraom

drink ⓝ គ្រឿងផឹក kreu-uhng puhk

drive ⓥ បើកឡាន baok laan

drivers licence លិខិតបើករថ lih-kuht baok baw

drug (illicit) គ្រឿងញៀន kreu-uhng nyee-ahn

dummy (pacifier) ចណ្ណុចដោះសំរាប់ក្មេងរៀម
juhn-dawng dawh suhm-rahp kuh-meng
bee-uhm

E

early ពីព្រលឹម bee bruh-luhm

east ខាងកើត kang gaot

eat ហ្ញាម howp

electricity ភ្លើងអគ្គិសនី plerng ah-kis-suh-nee

elevator លើក lerk

email អ៊ីមែល ee-mail

embassy ស្ថានទូត suh-taan doot

emergency ភាពបន្ទាន់ pee-ahp bawn-do-uhn

empty ទទេ do-day

English ភាសាអង់គ្លេស bee-aa-saa awng-glay

enough បានហើយ baan hao-y

entrance ផ្លូវចូល pleuw johl

evening ពេលល្ងាច behl luh-ngee-ihk

exchange (money) ⓥ ផ្ដូរ (លុយ) dow (luy)

exchange rate អត្រាផ្ដូរលុយ ah-draa dow luy

exit ⓝ ផ្លូវចេញ pleuw jain

expensive ថ្លៃ tuh-lai

express mail ប៉ុស្ដិ៍អ៊ីមែមរេស boh ee-em-eh

DICTIONARY

100

F

far ឆ្ងាយ chuh-ngaay
fast លឿន leu-uhn
father ឪពុក euw-bohk
faulty ខូច kow-iht
fever គ្រុនខ្ដៅ guh-daa-ew klu-uhn
film (camera) ហ្វីល fil
first មុនដំបូង mun duhm-bowng
first-aid kit គ្រឿងពេទ្យបម្រើ
kreu-uhng baet byee-aa-baal
first-class ⓐ ថ្នាក់ទីមួយ tuh-nahk đee muy
fish ⓝ ត្រី đrei
fly (a plane) ⓥ ហោះ hawh
food អាហារ muh-howp
fork សម sawm
free (of charge) អត់គិតលុយ awt kuht luy
friend ពួកម៉ាក bu-uhk maak
fruit ផ្លែឈើ plai cher
full ពេញ bein
funny គួរឱ្យចង់សើច goo-uh ao-y jawng sao-iht

G

gift អំណោយ uhm-nao-y
girl ក្មេងស្រី kuh-meng srei
glass (drinking) កែវ gaiw
glasses វែនតា waen-đaa
go ទៅ đeuw
good ល្អ luh-aw
green ពណ៌បៃតង bo-uh bai dawng
guide ⓝ អ្នកនាំផ្លូវ nay-uhk no-uhm pleuw

H

half ⓐ ពាក់កណ្ដាល bay-ahk guhn-daal
handbag ក្របូបដៃ graw-bowp dai
happy សប្បាយចិត្ត suh-baay juht
have មាន mee-uhn
head ក្បាល guh-baal
headache ឈឺក្បាល cheu guh-baal
heart បេះដូង beh downg

heart condition បញ្ហាបេះដូង
buhn-nya-haa beh downg
heat ⓝ កំដៅ guhm-daa-ew
heavy ធ្ងន់ tuh-ngun
help ⓥ ជួយ juy
here ទីនេះ đee-nih
high ខ្ពស់ kuh-bu-uh
highway ផ្លូវជាតិ pleuw tuh-nahl
hike ⓥ ដើរលេងព្រៃ daar leng brey puh-nohm
homosexual ⓝ មនុស្សខ្ទើយ ma-nooh kuh-đuhy
hospital មន្ទីរពេទ្យ mohn-đee baet
hot ក្ដៅ guh-daa-ew
hotel សណ្ឋាគារ suhn-taa-gee-aa
hungry ឃ្លាន klee-uhn
husband ប្ដី buh-dei

I

identification (card) លិខិតសំគាល់ខ្លួន
lih-kuht suhm-go-uhl klu-uhn
ill ឈឺ cheu
important សំខាន់ suhm-kuhn
included រួមជាមួយ ru-uhm jee-aa muy
injury របួស ruh-bu-uh
insurance អិនស៊ូរ៉ង់ ihn-su-rahng
Internet អិនធើនេត in-der-net
interpreter អ្នកបកប្រែ nay-uhk bawk brai

J

jewellery គ្រឿងអលង្ការ kreu-uhng ah-lahng-kaa
job ការងារ gaa ngee-aa

K

key កូនសោ gown sao
kilogram គីឡូក្រាម kee-low-graam
kitchen ផ្ទះបាយ puh-đay-uh baay
knife កាំបិត guhm-buht

L

late ⓐ យប់ជ្រៅ yohp j-reuw
late adv មកយឹត mao yeut

laundry (n) ខោអាវក្រខ្វក់ត្រូវបោកអ៊ុត
kao aa·ew graw·kwuhk đrow baok ut
lawyer មេធាវី may tee·aa wee
left luggage វ៉ាលិសដែលផ្ញើរទុក
waa·lih dail puh·nyaar đohk
leg ជើង jerng
lesbian (n) មនុស្សខ្ទើយស្រី
ma·nooh guh·đeuy srei
less តិចជាង điht jee·ahng
letter សំបុត្រ suhm·boht
lift (elevator) លើក lerk
light (n) ភ្លើង plerng
lock (n) មេសោ may sao
long វែង weng
lost វង្វេងផ្លូវ wohng·weng pleuw
love (n) ការស្រឡាញ់ gaa sraw·lain
luggage វ៉ាលិស waa·lih
lunch ម្ហូបថ្ងៃត្រង់ muh·howp tuh·ngai đrawng

M

mail (n) សំបុត្រប៉ុស្ត suhm·boht ɓoh
man ប្រុស brawh
map ផែនទី pain·đee
market ផ្សារ puh·saa
matches ឈើគូស cher gooh
meat សាច់ sait
medicine ថ្នាំពេទ្យ tuh·nuhm ɓaet
menu ម៉ឺនុយ me·nuy
message សារ saa
milk ទឹកដោះគោ đuhk dawh gow
minute មីនុត mee·nut
mobile phone ទូរសព្ទដៃ đu·rah·sahp dai
money លុយ luy
month ខែ kai
morning ពេលព្រឹក ɓehl ɓruhk
mother ម្តាយ muh·daay
motorcycle ម៉ូតូ mow·đow
motorway ផ្លូវថ្នល់ pleuw tuh·nahl
mountain ភ្នំ puh·nohm
music ភ្លេង pleng

N

name ឈ្មោះ chuh·mu·uh
nappy កន្ទបកូនក្មេង guhn·đohp gown kuh·meng
nausea វិលមុខចង់ក្អួត
wuhl mohk jawng guh·oo·uht
near ជិត juht
new ថ្មី tuh·mei
news ពត៌មាន ɓo·ruh·mee·uhn
newspaper កាសែត gaa·sait
next ក្រោយ krao·y
night ពេលយប់ ɓehl yohp
no ទេ đay
noisy ថ្លង់ tuh·lawng
nonsmoking មិនអោយជក់បារី
muhn ao·y ju·uhk baa·rei
north ខាងជើង kang jerng
nose ច្រមុះ jruh·moh
now ឥឡូវនេះ ei·leuw nih
number លេខ layk

O

oil (engine) ប្រេងកាត preng gaat
old ចាស់ jah
on នៅលើ neuw ler
one-way ticket សំបុត្រតែទៅទេ
suhm·boht đai đeuw đay
open (a) បើក baok
other ទៀត đee·iht
outside ខាងក្រៅ kang kraa·ew

P

package ប្រអប់ pra·awp
pain ការឈឺចុក gaa cheu johk
painkillers ថ្នាំសំរាប់ការឈឺចុក
tuh·nuhm suhm·rahp gaa cheu johk
paper ក្រដាស graw·dah
park (car) (v) ចត (ឡាន) jawt (laan)
passport លិខិតឆ្លងដែន lih·kuht chuh·lawng dain
pay (v) បង់លុយ bawng luy
pen ប៊ិច bihk
petrol ប្រេងសាំង preng sahng

pharmacy ហាងលក់ឪ្សថពេញ្យ
haang lu-uhk tuh-nuhm baet

phonecard ការកទូរសព្ទ kaad du-rah-sahp

photo រូបថត roop tawt

plate ចាន jaan

police ប៉ូលិស bow-lih

postcard ការប៉ុស្តាល់ kaat bos-dahl

post office ប្រៃសណីយ៍ prai-suh-nee

pregnant មានផ្ទៃពោះ mee-uhn puh-day bu-ah

price តំលៃ duhm-lai

Q

quiet ស្ងាត់ sgnuht

R

rain ⓝ ភ្លៀង plee-uhng

razor ឡាមកោរពុកមាត់ laam gao bohk mo-uht

receipt បង្កាន់ដៃ bawng-guhn dai

red ពណ៌ក្រហម bo-uh graw-hawm

refund ⓥ សងលុយមកវិញ sawng luy mao wein

rent ⓥ ជួល jool

repair ⓥ ជួសជុល ju-uh johl

reservation កក់ទុកជាមុន kawk dohk jee-aa mun

restaurant ភោជនីយដ្ឋាន pow-chuh-nee-yah-taan

return ⓥ មកវិញ mao wein

return ticket សំបុត្រទៅមក suhm-boht deuw mao

right (direction) ខាងស្តាំ kang sa-duhm

road ផ្លូវ pleuw

room បន្ទប់ bawn-dohp

rope ខ្សែ bu-aa

S

safe ⓐ ពពេ្រាះថ្នាក់ uht kru-ah tuh-nahk

sanitary napkins សម្ភើអនាម័យស្រ្តី
suhm-lei ah-naa-mai sah-drei

sea សមុទ្រ suh-moht

seat កៅអី gao ei

send ផ្ញើ puh-nyaar

service station កន្លែងចាក់សាំង
guh-laing jahk sahng

sex ការរួមដំណេក gaa ru-uhm duhm-nayk

shaving cream ក្រែមកោរពុកមាត់
kraim gao bohk mo-uht

sheet (bed) កម្រាល (ព្រៃ) guhm-raal (bok)

shirt អាវ aa-ew

shoes ស្បែកជើង suh-baik jerng

shop ⓝ ហាង haang

short ទាប dee-uhp

shower ⓥ ងូតទឹក ngoot duhk

single room បន្ទប់សំរាប់មួយនាក់
bawn-dohp suhm-rahp muy nay-uhk

size (clothes) ទំហំ (នៅអាវ)
dohm hohm (kao aa-ew)

skirt សំពត់ suhm-boht

sleep ⓥ ដេក dayk

slowly យឺតៗ yeut yeut

small តូច dow-iht

smoke ⓥ ជក់បារី ju-uhk baa-rei

soap សាប៊ូ saa-boo

some ខ្លះ klah

soon នៅពេលបន្តិចទៀត
neuw behl buhn-diht dee-iht

south ខាងត្បូង kang duh-bowng

souvenir shop ហាងលក់វត្ថុអនុស្សាវរីយ៍
haang lu-uhk waht-toh ah-nu-saa-wah-ree

speak និយាយ nih-yay

spoon ស្លាបព្រា slaap-bree-aa

stamp តែម daim

station (train) ស្ថានីយ៍ suh-taa-nee

stomachache ឈឺពោះ cheu bu-ah

stop ⓥ ឈប់ chohp

stop (bus) ⓝ កន្លែងឡានក្រុងឈប់
guh-laing laan grohng chohp

street ផ្លូវ pleuw

student និស្សិត ni-suht

sun ព្រះអាទិត្យ bre-ah aa-duht

sunblock ថ្នាំការពារពន្លឺថ្ងៃ
tuh-nuhm gaa-bee-aa bohn-leu tuh-ngai

surname នាមត្រកូល nee-ahm draw-gohl

sweet ⓐ ផ្អែម puh-aim

swim ⓥ ហែលទឹក hail duhk

103

T

taxi ឡានពាក់ស៊ី laan dahk-see
telephone ទូរស័ព្ទ du-rah-sahp
television ទូរទស្សន៍ du-rah-dooh
temperature (weather) សីតុណ្ហភាព sei-dohn-hah-pee-ahp
tent តង់ dawng
thirsty ស្រេកទឹក srayk duhk
this នេះ nih
ticket សំបុត្រ suhm-boht
time ⓝ ពេលវេលា behl way-lee-aa
tired ហត់ hawt
tissues ក្រដាសជូត graw-dah joot
today ថ្ងៃនេះ tuh-ngai nih
toilet បង្គន់ bawng-gohn
tomorrow ថ្ងៃស្អែក tuh-ngai sah-aik
tonight យប់នេះ yohp nih
toothache ឈឺធ្មេញ cheu tuh-mein
toothbrush ច្រាសដុសធ្មេញ jrah doh tuh-mein
toothpaste ថ្នាំដុសធ្មេញ duh-nuhm doh tuh-mein
torch (flashlight) ពិល buhl
tour ⓝ ដើរទស្សនា daar doh-sah-naa
tourist អ្នកទេសចរ nay-uhk des-sah-jaw
tourist office ការិយាល័យទេសចរ gaa-ree-aa-lai deh-sah-jaw
towel កន្សែង guhn-saing
town ទីក្រុង dee grohng
train រថភ្លើង rah-teh blerng
translate បកប្រែ bawk brai
travel agency ហាងលក់សំបុត្រសំរាប់ទេសចរ haang lu-uhk suhm-boht suhm-rahp deh-sah-jaw
travellers cheque សែកទេសចរ saik deh-sah-jaw
trousers ខោ kao
twin beds គ្រែគូ krae dow-iht
tyre កង់ gawng

U

underwear ខោទ្រនាប់ kao dro-no-ahp
up ឡើងលើ laong ler
urgent បន្ទាន់ bawn-do-uhn

V

vacant ទំនេរ dohm-nay
vacation វិកង waa-gawng
vegetable ⓝ បន្លែ buhn-lai
vegetarian ⓝ មនុស្សតមសាច់ ma-nooh dawm sait
visa វីហ្សា wee-saa

W

waiter អ្នកបម្រើ nay-uhk buhm-raar
walk ⓥ ដើរ daar
wallet ក្របូបលុយ graw-bowp luy
warm ⓐ កក់ក្ដៅ gawk guh-daa-ew
wash (clothes) បោក (ខោអាវ) baok (kao aa-ew)
wash (hands) លាង lee-ahng
watch ⓝ នាឡិកា nee-aa-lih-gaa
water ទឹក duhk
weekend ថ្ងៃសៅរ៍អាទិត្យ tuh-ngai saa-ew aa-đuht
west ខាងលិច kang leit
wheelchair រទេះអ្នកពិការ ruh-đeh nay-uhk bi-gaa
when នៅពេលណា neuw behl naa
where នៅឯណា neuw ei naa
white ពណ៌ស bo-uh saw
who អ្នកណា nay-uhk naa
why ហេតុអ្វី het ei
wife ប្រពន្ធ pruh-bohn
window បង្អួច bawng-oo-iht
wine ស្រាទំពាំងបាយជូរ sraa dohm-bay-uhng baay joo
with ជាមួយ jee-aa muy
without អត់មាន awt mee-uhn
woman ស្រី srei
write សរសេរ saw-say

Y

yellow ពណ៌លឿង bo-uh leu-uhng
yes (said by man/woman) បាទ/ចាស baat/jaa
yesterday ម្សិលមិញ muh-suhl mein

Lao

consonants

ກ gor gai	ຂ kŏr kai	ຄ kor kwai	ງ ngor ngúa	ຈ jor jork
ສ sŏr sĕu·a	ຊ sor sáng	ຍ nyor nyóong	ດ dor dek	ຕ dor đah
ຖ tŏr tŏng	ທ tor tung	ນ nor nok	ບ bor bae	ປ bor 'bah
ຜ pŏr pèung	ຝ fŏr fŏn	ພ pór póo	ຟ for fái	ມ mor mah
ຢ yor yah	ລ lor leeng	ວ wŏr wee	ຫ hŏr hăhn	ອ or o
ຮ hor heu·an				

vowels (the symbol 'x' is used as the consonant base)

xະ a	x̂ i	x̧ u	x̂ eu	xາ ah
x̂ ee	x̱ oo	x̂ eu	ເxະ e	ໂxະ o
ເx air	ແx aa	ໄx oh	ໃx̂ eu	ເxຍ ee·a
x̂ວ u·a	ເx̂ຍ ee·a	x̊ or	ເx̂ eu	ເx̂ອ eu·a
ເx̂າ ow	ໄx ai	ໄx ai	xຳ am	

introduction

The official language of Laos is the Vientiane dialect, which has become the lingua franca between all Lao and non-Lao ethnic groups in the country. Of course, Lao is spoken with different accents and with slightly different vocabularies as you move from one part of the country to the next, especially in a north-to-south direction – but it's the Vientiane dialect that's most widely understood. The other main dialects within the country are: Northern, North-Eastern, Central and Southern Lao.

All Lao dialects are members of the Thai-Kadai language family and are closely related to languages spoken in Thailand, northern Myanmar and China's Yunnan Province. Standard Lao is indeed close enough to Standard Thai that, for native speakers, the two are mutually intelligible. In fact, virtually all speakers of Lao living in the Mekong River valley can easily understand spoken Thai, since the bulk of the television and radio they listen to is broadcast from Thailand. Even closer to Standard Lao are Thailand's Northern and North-Eastern Thai dialects. If you're travelling to Laos after a spell in Thailand (especially the north-east), you should be able to put whatever you learned in Thailand to good use in Laos. It doesn't work as well in the opposite direction – native Thais can't always understand Lao since they've had less exposure to the language.

Among educated Lao, written Thai is also easily understood, in spite of the fact that the two scripts differ considerably. This is because many of the textbooks used at college and university level in Laos are actually in Thai. Lao script is based on an early alphabet devised by the Thais, which was later extensively revised. The current spelling system has been highly simplified and uses only the letters actually pronounced. The vowel symbols are used in varying combinations and can be written above, below, before or after the consonants. The Lao alphabet is shown on the page opposite.

As the writing system is fairly complex and there's no official method of transliterating Lao (the most common methods follow the colonial French system of transliteration), we've created a system that will make it easy for you to use this chapter. Just follow our coloured pronunciation guides provided next to the script.

The basics of Lao grammar are outlined on the following pages for those interested to go beyond the phrases in this chapter. If you're inspired to create your own sentences and would like to learn more about this aspect of the language, it will point you in the right direction.

introduction – ລາວ

pronunciation

vowel sounds

For the Lao pronunciation guides we've used hyphens to separate syllables from each other – the word àng-gít (meaning 'English') is made up of two distinct syllables: àng and gít. In some words we've divided the diphthongs (ie vowel sound combinations) further with a dot (·) to help you separate vowel sounds and avoid mispronunciation – the word kĕe·an (write) is actually pronounced as one syllable with two separate vowel sounds. Accents above vowels (like à, é and ô) relate to the tones (see below).

symbol	english equivalent	lao example	symbol	english equivalent	lao example
a	**run**	lăng	i	**bit**	àh-tít
aa	**bad**	maa	o	**hot**	jót-măi
aa-ou	**aa** followed by **u**	lâa-ou	oo	**moon**	la-doo
ah	**father**	pàhk	oh	**note**	lôhk
ai	**aisle**	săi	or	**for**	bor
air	**flair**	lot máir	ow	**cow**	đorn sŏw
e	**bed**	pén	oy	**boy**	kòy
ee	**see**	èek	u	**put**	ga-lú-náh
eu	**her**	seu			

tones

Many syllables in Lao are differentiated by tone only. There are five distinct tones in Lao – two of those are level (low and high) while two follow pitch inclines (rising and falling). The accent marks above the vowel remind you which one to use. Note that the mid tone has no accent.

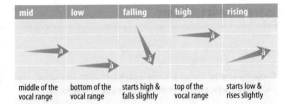

mid	low	falling	high	rising
a	à	â	á	ǎ
middle of the vocal range	bottom of the vocal range	starts high & falls slightly	top of the vocal range	starts low & rises slightly

consonant sounds

Watch out for the b̖ sound, which is halfway between a 'b' and a 'p', and the d̖ sound, which is halfway between a 'd' and a 't'.

symbol	english equivalent	lao example
b	**big**	bor
b̖	**spin**	b̖en
d	**dog**	dek
d̖	**stop**	d̖ôrng
f	**full**	fáhk
g	**get**	gôw
h	**hat**	hàh
j	**junk**	jôw
k	**kite**	kòy
l	**like**	lâa-ou
m	**mat**	maan
n	**nut**	naa-ou
ng	**sing**	neung
ny	**canyon**	nyǎng
p	**push**	péh
s	**sit**	síp
t	**tap**	tow
w	**watch**	wan
y	**yes**	yàhk

phrasebuilder

be

The two forms of 'be' – maan ແມ່ນ (for objects) and ben ເປັນ (for people) – join nouns and pronouns, but aren't necessary between nouns and adjectives.

This is a pedicab.	ອັນນີ້ແມ່ນສາມລໍ້	an nêe maan sǎhm lôr
		(lit: this is pedicab)
I'm a musician.	ຂ້ອຍເປັນນັກດົນຕີ	kòy ben nak don-đee
		(lit: I am musician)
This food is delicious.	ອາຫານນີ້ແຊບ	ah-hǎhn nêe sàap
		(lit: food this delicious)

counters/classifiers

Nouns have the same form for the singular and the plural. When counting, however, every noun takes a classifier (a word which defines the category that an item belongs to). Classifiers go after the noun and the number. The box on page 134 lists some common classifiers referring to certain categories of items.

| four dogs | ໝາສີ່ໂຕ | mǎh see đoh |
| | | (lit: dogs four đoh) |

have

The word for 'have' is mée ມີ, which can also be used to mean 'there is/are'.

I have a bicycle.
ຂ້ອຍມີລົດຖີບ

kòy mée lot tèep
(lit: I have vehicle pedal)

negatives

Any verb or adjective can be negated by inserting bor ບໍ່ (no) before it.

I don't have any cash.
ຂ້ອຍບໍ່ມີເງິນ

kòy bor mée ngéun
(lit: I no have money)

pronouns

Some pronouns in Lao have different forms which vary in the level of formality. Both 'he' and 'she' are translated with the same word. The pronouns that will be suitable for most situations you're likely to encounter are listed in the box on page 136.

questions

To ask a yes/no question, the word bor ບໍ່ (no) is used at the end of the sentence, like the English 'isn't it'. To answer questions, just repeat the verb for 'yes' and add bor ບ before it for 'no'.

Do you want to drink tea?	ຍາກກິນນ້ຳຊາບໍ່	yàhk gin nâm sáh bor
		(lit: want eat water tea no)
Yes.	ຍາກກິນ	yàhk gin
		(lit: want eat)
No.	ບໍ່ຍາກກິນ	bor yàhk gin
		(lit: no want eat)

requests

The word kŏr ຂໍ (roughly equivalent to 'please give me') is used at the beginning of the sentence to make polite requests – often the word daa ແດ່ (please) is added to the end of the sentence.

Please pass some rice.	ຂໍເຂົ້າແດ່	kŏr kòw daa
		(lit: please-give-me rice please)

verbs

Verbs don't change form to express tense. Out of context and in the absence of time markers (such as 'yesterday' and 'tomorrow'), they normally express the present. The word làa·ou ແລ້ວ (already) used after the verb indicates past tense, whereas já ຈະ (will) or see ຊິ (no literal meaning) used before the verb mark a future action.

I spent the money.	ຂ້ອຍຈ່າຍເງິນແລ້ວ	kòy jai ngéun làa·ou
		(lit: I spend money already)
He/She will buy rice.	ລາວຈະຊື້ເຂົ້າ	lów já sêu kòw
		(lit: he/she will buy rice)

basics

language difficulties

Can you speak English?
ເຈົ້າເວົ້າພາສາອັງກິດໄດ້ບໍ່?   jôw wôw páh-sǎa àng-gít dâi bor

Do you understand?
ເຈົ້າເຂົ້າໃຈບໍ່?   jôw kôw jai bor

I (don't) understand.
ຂ້ອຍ (ບໍ່) ເຂົ້າໃຈ   kòy (bor) kôw-jai

What does (sa-bai dee) **mean?**
ຄຳວ່າ (ສະບາຍດີ)   kam wáh (sa-bai dee)
ໝາຍຄວາມວ່າຈັ່ງໃດ?   mǎi kwáhm wáh jàng dai

How do you ...?   ເຈົ້າ ... ແນວໃດ?   jôw ... naa-ou dai
   pronounce this   ອອກສຽງຄຳນີ້ວ່າ   òrk-sěe-ang kam nêe wah
   write (Vientiane)   ຂຽນ (ວຽງຈັນ)   kěe-an (wée-ang-jan)

Please ...   ກະລຸນາ ...   ga-lu-náh ...
   repeat that   ເວົ້າຄືນໃໝ່   wôw kéun mai
   speak slowly   ເວົ້າຊ້າໆ   wôw sǎh sǎh
   write it down   ຂຽນໃສ່   kěe-an sai

essentials

Yes.	ແມ່ນ	maan
No.	ບໍ່	bor
Please.	ກະລຸນາ	ga-lú-náh
Thank you.	ຂອບໃຈ	kòrp jai
You're welcome.	ດ້ວຍຄວາມຍິນດີ	doo-ay kwáhm nyeen dée
Excuse me.	ຂໍໂທດ	kǒr-tôht
Sorry.	ຂໍໂທດ	kǒr-tôht

numbers

0	ສູນ	sŏon		17	ສິບເຈັດ	síp-jét
1	ໜຶ່ງ	neung		18	ສິບແປດ	síp-bàat
2	ສອງ	sŏrng		19	ສິບເກົ້າ	síp-gòw
3	ສາມ	sähm		20	ຊາວ	sów
4	ສີ່	see		21	ຊາວເອັດ	sów-ét
5	ຫ້າ	hàh		22	ຊາວສອງ	sów-sŏrng
6	ຫົກ	hók		30	ສາມສິບ	sähm-síp
7	ເຈັດ	jét		40	ສີ່ສິບ	see-síp
8	ແປດ	bàat		50	ຫ້າສິບ	hàh-síp
9	ເກົ້າ	gòw		60	ຫົກສິບ	hók-síp
10	ສິບ	síp		70	ເຈັດສິບ	jét-síp
11	ສິບເອັດ	síp-ét		80	ແປດສິບ	bàat-síp
12	ສິບສອງ	síp-sŏrng		90	ເກົ້າສິບ	gòw-síp
13	ສິບສາມ	síp-sähm		91	ເກົ້າສິບເອັດ	gòw-síp-ét
14	ສິບສີ່	síp-see		100	ໜຶ່ງຮ້ອຍ	neung-hòy
15	ສິບຫ້າ	síp-hàh		1000	ໜຶ່ງພັນ	neung-pán
16	ສິບຫົກ	síp-hók		1,000,000	ໜຶ່ງລ້ານ	neung-lâhn

numerals									
0	1	2	3	4	5	6	7	8	9
໐	໑	໒	໓	໔	໕	໖	໗	໘	໙

time & dates

What time is it?
ເວລາຈັກໂມງ?   wáir-láh ják móhng

It's (one) o'clock.
ເວລາ (ໜຶ່ງ) ໂມງ   wáir-láh (neung) móhng

It's (two) o'clock.
ເວລາ (ສອງ) ໂມງ   wáir-láh (sŏrng) móhng

Quarter past (eight).
ເວລາ (ແປດ) ໂມງສິບຫ້ານາທີ   wáir-láh (bàat) móhng síp hàh náh-tée

Half past (eight).

ເວລາ (ແປດ) ໂມງເຄິ່ງ   wáir·láh (bàat) móhng kèung

Quarter to (eight).

ອີກສິບຫ້ານາທີ (ແປດ) ໂມງ   eek síp hàh náh·tée (bàat) móhng

At what time?	ຕອນຈັກໂມງ?	đorn ják móhng
At ...	ຕອນ ...	đorn ...

Monday	ວັນຈັນ	wan jan
Tuesday	ວັນອ້າງຄານ	wan ang·káhn
Wednesday	ວັນພຸດ	wan pùt
Thursday	ວັນພະຫັດ	wan pa·hát
Friday	ວັນສຸກ	wan súk
Saturday	ວັນເສົາ	wan sŏw
Sunday	ວັນອາທິດ	wan àh·tít

January	ເດືອນມັງກອນ	deu·an máng·gorn
February	ເດືອນກຸມພາ	deu·an gum·páh
March	ເດືອນມີນາ	deu·an mí·náh
April	ເດືອນເມສາ	deu·an máir·sáh
May	ເດືອນພຶດສະພາ	deu·an peut·sá·páh
June	ເດືອນມິຖຸນາ	deu·an mi·tú·náh
July	ເດືອນກໍລະກົດ	deu·an gor·la·gót
August	ເດືອນສິງຫາ	deu·an sing·hăh
September	ເດືອນກັນຍາ	deu·an gan·yáh
October	ເດືອນຕຸລາ	deu·an đú·láh
November	ເດືອນພະຈິກ	deu·an pa·jík
December	ເດືອນທັນວາ	deu·an tan·wáh

What date is it today?

ວັນທີເທົ່າໃດ?   wan tee tòw·dai

It's (13 January).

ວັນທີ (ສິບສາມເດືອນມັງກອນ)   wan tee (síp·săhm deu·an máng·gorn)

since (May)	ຕັ້ງແຕ່ (ເດືອນຫ້າ)	đàng đáa (deu·an hàh)
until (June)	ຈົນເຖິງ (ເດືອນຫົກ)	jòn tĕung (deu·an hók)
last night	ກາງຄືນກອນ	gahng kéun górn
today	ມື້ນີ້	mêu·nêe

last ...	... ກ່ອນ	... gorn
next ...	... ຕໍ່ໄປ	... đor bai
week	ອາທິດ	àh-tít
month	ເດືອນ	deu-an
year	ປີ	bee
yesterday ...	ມື້ວານນີ້ ...	mêu wàhn nêe ...
tomorrow ...	ມື້ອື່ນ ...	mêu eun ...
morning	ຕອນເຊົ້າ	đorn sôw
afternoon	ຕອນສວຍ	đorn sôo-ay
evening	ຕອນແລງ	đorn láang

weather

What's the weather like?	ອາກາດເປັນຈັ່ງໃດ?	àh-gaht bèn jáng dai
It's ...	ມັນ ...	mán ...
(very) cold	ໜາວ (ຫລາຍ)	nŏw (lăi)
(very) hot	ຮ້ອນ (ຫລາຍ)	hórn (lăi)
windy	ລົມພັດ	lóm pat

spring	ລະດູໃບໄມ້ປົ່ງ	la-doo bai mâi bong
summer	ລະດູຮ້ອນ	la-doo hôrn
autumn	ລະດູໃບໄມ້ຫລົ່ນ	la-doo bai mâi lon
winter	ລະດູໜາວ	la-doo nŏw

dry season	ລະດູແລ້ງ	la-doo láang
hot season	ລະດູຮ້ອນ	la-doo hôrn
rainy season	ລະດູຝົນ	la-doo fŏn

border crossing

I'm ...	ຂ້ອຍ ...	kòy ...
in transit	ກຳລັງຢູ່ໃນຊ່ວງ	gam-láng yoo nai sŭang
	ປ່ຽນຍົນ	bèe-an nyón
on business	ມາເຮັດທຸລະກິດ	máh hèt tù-là-gít
on holiday	ມາທ່ຽວ	máh têe-o

I'm here for ...	ຂ້ອຍມາຢູ່ນີ້ ...	kòy máh yoo nêe ...
(10) days	(ສິບ) ມື້	(síp) mêu
(two) months	(ສອງ) ເດືອນ	(sòrng) deu·an
(three) weeks	(ສາມ) ອາທິດ	(sǎhm) àh-tít

I'm going to (Champasak).
ຂ້ອຍກຳລັງຈະໄປ (ຈຳປາສັກ) kòy gam-láng ja bai (jam-bah-sak)

I'm staying at the ...
ຂ້ອຍພັກຢູ່ທີ່ໂຮງແຮມ ... kòy pák yoo tee hóhng háam ...

I have nothing to declare.
ຂ້ອຍບໍ່ມີເຄື່ອງຕ້ອງແຈ້ງ kòy bor mée keu·ang đôrng jáang

That's (not) mine.
ອັນນັ້ນ (ບໍ່) ແມ່ນເຄື່ອງຂ້ອຍ an nán (bor) maan keu·ang kòy

I didn't know I had to declare it.
ຂ້ອຍບໍ່ຮູ້ວ່າຕ້ອງໄດ້ແຈ້ງ kòy bor hoo wàh đôrng dâi jáang

transport

tickets & luggage

Where can I buy a ticket?
ຂ້ອຍຊື້ປີ້ຢູ່ໃສ? kòy sêu bêe yoo săi

Do I need to book?
ຂ້ອຍຕ້ອງຈອງບໍ່? kòy đôrng jorng bor

One ... ticket to	ປີ້ ... ນຶ່ງໄປ	bêe ... neung bai
(Khammuan), please.	(ຄຳມ່ວນ) ແດ່	(kàm-muan) dáa
one-way	ປີ້ຖ້ຽວດຽວ	bêe tèe·o dèe·o
return	ປີ້ໄປກັບ	bêe bài gáp

I'd like to ... my	ຂ້ອຍຢາກ ...	kòy yàhk ...
ticket, please.	ປີ້ຂອງຂ້ອຍ	bêe kŏrng kòy
cancel	ຍົກເລີກ	nyôk lêuk
change	ປ່ຽນ	bee·an
confirm	ຢືນຢັນ	yéun yán

I'd like a ... seat,	ຂ້ອຍຕ້ອງການ ...	kòy đôrng gahn ...
please.	ບ່ອນນຶ່ງ	born neung
nonsmoking	ບ່ອນປອດຢາສູບ	born bòrt yáh soop
smoking	ບ່ອນສູບຢາ	born soop yáh

How much is it?
ບ່ອນລະເທົ່າໃດ?   born la tow dài

Is there air conditioning?
ມີແອປັບອາກາດບໍ່?   mee àa bap àh-gaht bor

Is there a toilet?
ມີຫ້ອງນ້ຳບໍ່?   mee hòrng nám bor

How long does the trip take?
ຈະໃຊ້ເວລາເດີນທາງດິນປານໃດ?   ja sài wáir-láh deun táhng don bahn dai

Is it a direct route?
ມັນເປັນທາງສາຍຕົງບໍ່?   mán bèn táhng sǎi đông bor

I'd like a luggage locker.
ຂ້ອຍຕ້ອງການ   kòy đôrng gahn
ຕູ້ມ້ຽບເຄື່ອງທີ່ມີ ກຸນແຈ   đôo mêe·an keu·ang tèe mée goon-jaa

My luggage	ກະເປົາເຄື່ອງຍຸ້ງ	ga-bow keu·ang noong
has been ...	ຂອງຂ້ອຍ ...	kõrng kòy ...
damaged	ເປເພ	bàir páir
lost	ເສຍ	sée·a
stolen	ຖຶກລັກ	teuk lák

getting around

Where does flight (TG 132) arrive/depart?
ບ່ອນຂຶ້ນ/ລົງຍົນ   born kèun/lóng nyón
(ທີ່ຈີຊຶ່ງສາມສອງ) ຢູ່ໃສ?   (tee-jee neung sǎhm sõrng) yoo sǎi

Where's (the) ...?	... ຢູ່ໃສ?	... yoo sǎi
arrivals hall	ບ່ອນລົງຍົນ	born lóng nyón
departures hall	ບ່ອນຂຶ້ນຍົນ	born kèun nyón
duty-free shop	ຮ້ານຂາຍເຄື່ອງ	hãhn kǎi keu·ang
	ປອດພາສີ	bòrt pah-sěe
gate (12)	ປະຕູເລກທີ (ສິບສອງ)	bá-đoo lék tee (síp-sõrng)

Is this the ...	ນີ້ແມ່ນໄປ ...	nêe maan bai ...
to (Luang Nam Tha)?	(ຫຼວງນ້ຳທາ) ບໍ່?	(lúang nâm tâh) bor
boat	ເຮືອ	héu·a
bus	ລົດເມ	lot·máir
plane	ເຮືອບິນ	héu·a·bin

At what time's	ຈັກໂມງ ລົດເມ	ják móhng lot máir
the ... bus?	... ອອກ?	... ork
first	ຄັນທີ່ໜຶ່ງ	kán tee neung
last	ຄັນສຸດທ້າຍ	kán sút tâi
next	ຄັນຕໍ່ໄປ	kán đor bai

At what time does it leave?
ລົດເມອອກເດີນທາງຈັກໂມງ? lot máir ork deun táhng ják móhng

How long will it be delayed?
ລົດເມຈະອອກຊ້າປານໃດ? lot máir já ork sâh bahn dai

What (station) is this?
ນີ້ແມ່ນ (ສະຖານີ) ໃດ? nêe maan (sa-tăh-née) dai

What's the next (stop)?
(ປ້າຍຈອດ) ຕໍ່ໄປແມ່ນຫຍັງ? (bâi jort) đor bai maan nyăng

Does it stop at (Pakse)?
ມັນຈອດທີ່ (ປາກເຊ) ບໍ່? mán jórt tee (bàhk-sáir) bor

Can you tell me when we get to (Savannakhet)?
ເຈົ້າຊ່ວຍບອກຂ້ອຍໄດ້ບໍ່ jôw soo-ay bórk kòy dâi bor
ເວລາໄປธອດ (ສະຫວັນນະເຂດ)? wáir-láh bai hórt (sa-wăn-na-két)

How long do we stop here?
ລົດจอดຢູ່ນີ້ດົນปานໃด? lot jort yoo nêe don bahn dai

I want to get off.
ຂ້อยຢາກລົງ kòy yàhk lóng

Is this seat taken?
ມີໃผนั่งຢູ່ນี้ບໍ່? mée pǎi nàng yoo nêe bor

That's my seat.
ນີ້ແມ່ນບ່ອນນັ່ງຂອງຂ້อย nêe maan born nàng kŏrng kòy

I'd like a taxi ...	ຂ້ອຍຢາກຂໍ້ລົດ	kòy yàhk kee lót
	ແທກຊີ່ອອກ ...	táak-sée ork ...
at (9am)	ເວລາ	wáir-láh
	(ເກົ້າໂມງເຊົ້າ)	(gòw móhng sôw)
now	ດງວນີ້	dèe-o nêe
tomorrow	ມື້ອື່ນ	méu eun

Is this ... available?	ບ່ອນ ... ນີ້ຫວ່າງບໍ່?	born ... nàng nêe wàhng bor
bicycle rickshaw	ລົດຖີບສາມລໍ້	lot tèep sähm lôr
motorcycle-taxi	ລົດຈັກຮັບຈ້າງ	lot jáhk hàp jähng
tuk-tuk	ຕຸກໆ	đuk-đuk

How much is it to (Vientiane)?
ໄປ (ວຽງຈັນ) ເທົ່າໃດ?   bài (wée-ang-jan) tow dai

Please put the meter on.
ກະລຸນາເປີດມິເຕີ້ແດ່   gá-lu-náh béut mi-đèu dáa

Please take me to (this address).
ກະລຸນາພາຂ້ອຍໄປ (ທີ່ຢູ່ນີ້) ແດ່   gá-lu-náh páh kòy bài (tee yoo nêe) dáa

Please drive slowly.	ກະລຸນາຂັບຊ້າໆແດ່	gá-lu-náh káp sâh-sâh dáa
Please stop here.	ກະລຸນາຈອດຢູ່ນີ້	gá-lu-náh jort yoo nêe
Please wait here.	ກະລຸນາຖ້າຢູ່ນີ້	gá-lu-náh tâh yoo nêe

car, motorbike & bicycle hire

I'd like to hire a ...	ຂ້ອຍຢາກເຊົ່າ ...	kòy yàhk sôw ...
bicycle	ລົດຖີບ	lot tèep
car	ລົດໃຫຍ່	lot nyai
motorbike	ລົດຈັກ	lot jáhk

with ...	ທີ່ມີ ...	tee mée ...
air conditioning	ແອປັບອາກາດ	àa bàp àh-gaht
a driver	ຄົນຂັບລົດ	kón káp lot

How much for ... hire?	ຄ່າເຊົ່າ ... ເທົ່າໃດ?	káh-sôw ... tów dai
hourly	ຊົ່ວໂມງລະ	sua móhng la
daily	ມື້ລະ	méu la
weekly	ອາທິດລະ	àh-tít la

Where's the next petrol station?

ບໍ່ນໍ້ມັນຕໍ່ໄປຢູ່ໃສ?   bǎm nàm mán đòr bài yoo sǎi

I've run out of petrol.

ນໍ້ມັນລົດຂ້ອຍໝົດ   nàm mán lot kòy mót

I have a flat tyre.

ຍາງລົດຂ້ອຍຮົ່ວ   yáhng lot kòy hua

I need a mechanic.

ຂ້ອຍຕ້ອງການຊ່າງແປງ   kòy đôrng gahn sahng bàang

air	ລົມ	lóm
oil	ນໍ້ມັນເຄື່ອງ	nàm-mán-keu-ang
petrol	ນໍ້ມັນ	nàm-mán
tyre	ຍາງລົດ	yáhng lot

directions

Where's a/the ...?	... ຢູ່ໃສ?	... yòo sǎi
bank	ທະນາຄານ	ta-náh-káhn
city centre	ສູນກາງເມືອງ	sǒon gahng méu-ang
hotel	ໂຮງແຮມ	hóhng háam
market	ຕະຫລາດ	đa-làht
police station	ຕຳຫລວດ	đàm-lùat
post office	ຫ້ອງການໄປສະນີ	hòrng gahn bai-sá-née
public toilet	ຫ້ອງນໍ້ສາຫາລະບະ	hòrng nàm sǎh-tah-là-nà

Is this the road to (Vientiane)?

ທາງນີ້ໄປ (ວຽງຈັນ) ບໍ່?   táhng nêe bai (wée-ang jan) bor

Can you show me (on the map)?

ເຈົ້າບອກທາງຂ້ອຍ   jôw bork táhng kòy
(ຢູ່ໃນແຜນທີ່) ໄດ້ບໍ່?   (yoo nai pǎan tee) dài bor

What's the address?

ທີ່ຢູ່ແມ່ນຫຍັງ?   tee yòo maan nyǎng

How far is it?

ມັນໄກປານໃດ?   mán gài bahn dai

How do I get there?

ຂ້ອຍໄປຮອດພຸ້ນຈັ້ງໃດ?   kòy bai hôrt pûn jàng dai

Turn ...	ລ້ຽວ ...	lêe-o ...
at the corner	ຢູ່ແຈທາງ	yoo jàa táhng
at the traffic lights	ຢູ່ໄຟແດງ	yoo fái dàang
left/right	ຊ້າຍ/ຂວາ	sâi/kŭa

It's ...	ມັນຢູ່ ...	mán yoo ...
behind ...	ທາງຫລັງ ...	táhng lăng ...
far	ໄກ	gai
here	ຢູ່ນີ້	yoo nêe
in front of ...	ທາງໜ້າ ...	táhng nâh ...
near	ໄກ້	gâi
next to ...	ຂ້າງກັບ ...	káhng gap ...
opposite ...	ກົງກັນຂ້າມ ...	gong gan kâhm ...
there	ຢູ່ນັ້ນ	yoo hân

| Go straight ahead. | ໄປຊື່ໆ | bai seu·seu |

by bus	ຂີ່ລົດເມ	kee lot máir
by taxi	ຂີ່ລົດແທກຊີ່	kee lot táak-sée
on foot	ຍ່າງໄປ	nyáhng bai

north	ທິດເໜືອ	tit nĕu·a
south	ທິດໃຕ້	tit đâi
east	ທິດຕາເວັນອອກ	tit đah-wén ork
west	ທິດຕາເວັນຕົກ	tit đah-wén đók

signs

ທາງເຂົ້າ/ອອກ	táhng kôw/ork	Entrance/Exit
ເປີດ/ອັດ	béut/át	Open/Closed
ຫວ້າງ	wâhng	Vacancies
ບໍ່ຫວ້າງ	bor wâhng	No Vacancies
ຂໍ້ມູນ	kòr moon	Information
ສະຖານີຕຳຫລວດ	sá-tăh-née đam-luat	Police Station
ຫ້າມ	hàhm	Prohibited
ຫ້ອງນ້ຳ	hòrng nàm	Toilets
ຊາຍ/ຍິງ	sái/nyíng	Men/Women
ຮ້ອນ/ເຢັນ	hôrn/yen	Hot/Cold

accommodation

finding accommodation

Where's a ...?	... ຢູ່ໃສ?	... yoo săi
camping ground	ບ່ອນຕັ້ງເຕັ້ນ	born đăng kêm
guesthouse	ເຮືອນພັກ	héu-an pak
hotel	ໂຮງແຮມ	hóhng háam

Can you recommend	ເຈົ້າຊ່ວຍແນະນຳ	jôw soo-ay naa-nám
somewhere ...?	ບ່ອນທີ່... ໄດ້ບໍ?	born tee ... dâi bor
cheap	ຖຶກ	tèuk
good	ດີ	dee
nearby	ຢູ່ໃກ້	yoo gâi

Do you have a ...?	ເຈົ້າມີ ... ທ່າງບໍ?	jôw mée ... wâhng bor
double room	ຫ້ອງນອນຕຽງຄູ່	hòrng nórn đee-ang koo
single room	ຫ້ອງນອນຕຽງດ່ຽວ	hòrng nórn đee-ang dee-o

How much is it per ...?	... ເທົ່າໃດ?	... tów dai
night	ຄືນລະ	kéun-la
person	ຄົນລະ	kón-la

I'd like to book a room, please.
ຂ້ອຍຢາກຈອງ
ຫ້ອງນອນຫ້ອງນຶ່ງ
kòy yahk jorng
hòrng nórn hòrng neung

I have a reservation.
ຂ້ອຍໄດ້ຈອງຫ້ອງແລ້ວ
kòy dâi jorng hòrng lâa-ou

My name is ...
ຂ້ອຍຊື່ ...
kòy seu ...

I'll stay for (two) nights.

ຂ້ອຍຈະພັກ (ສອງ) ຄືນ   kòy jà pak (sŏrng) kéun

From (July 2) to (July 6).

ຈາກ (ວັນທີສອງ ເດືອນເຈັດ)   jahk (wán tee sŏrng deu·an jét)

ຫາ (ວັນທີຫົກ ເດືອນເຈັດ)   hah (wán tee hók deu·an jét)

Can I see the room?

ຂ້ອຍຈະຂໍເບິ່ງຫ້ອງໄດ້ບໍ່?   kòy jà kŏr beung hòrng dâi bor

Can I camp here?

ຂ້ອຍຕັ້ງຕູບຜ້າຢູ່ນີ້ໄດ້ບໍ່?   kòy đáng đòop·pàh yoo nêe dâi bor

Is there a camp site nearby?

ຢູ່ໃກ້ນີ້ມີບ່ອນຕັ້ງແຄ້ມບໍ່?   yoo gâi nêe mée born đáng kêm bor

Can I pay ...?	ຂ້ອຍຈ່າຍ ... ໄດ້ບໍ່?	kòy jai ... dâi bor
by credit card	ດ້ວຍບັດເຄຣດິດ	dôo·ay bát·kláir·dít
with a travellers cheque	ເຊັກເດີນທາງໆ	sék·deun·táhng

requests & queries

When's breakfast served?

ອາຫານເຊົ້າເສີບຕອນຈັກໂມງ?   ah·hăhn sôw séup đorn ják móhng

Where's breakfast served?

ອາຫານເຊົ້າເສີບຢູ່ໃສ?   ah·hăhn sôw séup yoo săi

Please wake me at (seven).

ກະລຸນາ ປຸກຂ້ອຍເວລາ (ເຈັດ) ໂມງ   ga·lú·náh búk kòy wáir·láh (jét) móhng

Could I have my key, please?

ເອົາກຸນແຈຂອງຂ້ອຍໃຫ້ແດ່?   ow gun·jàa kŏrng kòy hâi dàa

Do you have a ...?	ເຈົ້າມີ ... ບໍ່?	jôw mée ... bor
mosquito net	ມຸ້ງກາງຍຸງ	múng gang nyúng
safe	ຕູ້ເຊັຟ	đôo sép

I'd like a ...	ຂ້ອຍຕ້ອງການຫ້ອງ	kòy đôrng gahn hòrng
room.	... ນີ້	... nêe
cheaper	ລາຄາຖືກກວ່າ	láh·káh téuk gwah
larger	ໃຫຍ່ກວ່າ	nyai gwah
quieter	ມິດກວ່າ	mit gwah

The ... doesn't work.	... ใช้บ่ได้	... sâi bor dâi
air conditioning	แอเย็น	aa yén
fan	พัดลม	pat lóhm
toilet	ห้องน้ำ	hòrng nàm

This ... isn't clean.	... นี่บ่สะอาด	... nêe bor sá·aht
pillow	หมอน	mörn
sheet	ผ้าปูบ่อน	pàh·boo·born
towel	ผ้าเซ็ดโต	pàh sét đoh

checking out

What time is checkout?
เวลาเช็กออกโรงแรมจักโมง? wáir·láh sék ork hóhng háam ják móhng

Can I leave my luggage here?
ຂ້ອຍຈະຝາກເຄື່ອງຢູ່ນີ້ໄດ້ບໍ່? kòy jà fáhk keu·ang yoo nêe dâi bor

Could I have	เอา ... ຂອງຂ້ອຍ	ow ... körng kòy
my ..., please?	ใຫ້ຂ້ອຍແດ່ໄດ້ບໍ່?	hài kòy dàa dâi bor
deposit	ເງິນມັດຈຳ	ngéun mát jám
passport	ໜັງສືຜ່ານແດນ	năng·sĕu pahn daan

communications & banking

the internet

Is there a local Internet café?
ມີຮ້ານອິນເຕີແນັດບໍ່? mee hàhn in·đéu·naat bor

How much is it per hour?
ຊົ່ວໂມງລະເທົ່າໃດ? sua·móhng la tow dai

I'd like to ...	ຂ້ອຍຢາກ ...	kòy yahk ...
check my email	กวดอิเมวຂອງຂ້ອຍ	guat ée·máa·ou körng kòy
get Internet access	ใช้อินเตີແນັດ	sâi in·đéu·naat
use a printer	จักพิม	sâi jak pím
use a scanner	ใช้สะแกนเบิ้	sâi sà·gaan·néu

mobile/cell phone

I'd like a mobile/cell phone for hire.
ຂ້ອຍຕ້ອງການເຊົ່າ ໂທລະສັບມືຖືອັນນຶ່ງ
kòy đôrng gahn sòw
toh-lá-sáp méu tĕu an neung

I'd like a SIM card for your network.
ຂ້ອຍຕ້ອງການເຊົ່າ ຊິມກາດ ສຳລັບເຜືອຄ່າຍຂອງເຈົ້າ
kòy đôrng gahn sòw
sím-kaht săm-làp kéu-a kai kŏrng jôw

What are the rates?
ອັດຕາຄ່າໂທເທົ່າໃດ?
àt-đah káh tóh tòw dai

telephone

What's your phone number?
ເບີໂທລະສັບຂອງເຈົ້າແມ່ນຫຍັງ?
beu toh-lá-sáp kŏrng jôw màan nyăng

The number is ...
ເບີໂທລະສັບແມ່ນ ...
beu toh-lá-sàp maan ...

I'm looking for a public phone.
ຂ້ອຍຊອກຫາໂທລະສັບ ສາທາລະນະ
kòy sórk hăh toh-lá-sáp sǎh-táh-la-ná

I'd like to buy a phonecard.
ຂ້ອຍຢາກຊື້ບັດໂທລະສັບ
kòy yahk sêu bát toh-lá-sáp

I want to ...	ຂ້ອຍຕ້ອງການຈະ ...	kòy đôrng gahn jà ...
call (Singapore)	ໂທໄປ (ສິງກະໂປ)	toh bài (síng-gà-boh)
make a local call	ໂທພາຍໃນປະເທດ	toh pai nai pà tét
reverse the charges	ເກັບເງິນປາຍທາງ	gép ngéun bai táhng

How much does ... cost?	ຄ່າໂທ ... ເທົ່າໃດ?	káh tóh ... tow dai
a (three)-minute call	(ສາມ) ນາທີ	(sǎhm) náh-tée
each extra minute	ເພີ່ມນາທີລະ	pêum náh-tée là

(1000 kip) per (minute). (ນຶ່ງພັນກີບ) ຕໍ່ (ນາທີ) (neung pan géep) đòr (náh-tée)

post office

I want to send a ...	ຂ້ອຍຢາກສົ່ງ ... ອັນນຶ່ງ	kòy yahk song ... an neung
fax	ແຟັກ	fáak
letter	ຈົດໝາຍ	jót-măi
parcel	ຫໍເຄື່ອງ	hor keu·ang
postcard	ໂພສຄາດ	pot-sà-kàht
Can I have ...?	ເອົາ ... ອັນນຶ່ງ	ow ... an
	ໃຫ້ຂ້ອຍໄດ້ບໍ່?	neung hâi kòy dâi bor
an envelope	ຊອງຈົດໝາຍ	sorng jót-măi
some stamps	ສະແຕມ	sa-đaam
express mail	ສົ່ງທາງດ່ວນ	song táhng duan
registered mail	ຈົດໝາຍລົງທະບຽນ	jót-măi lohng ta-bee·an
surface mail	ທາງມະດາ	táhm-ma-dáh

Please send it (to Australia) by airmail.

ກະລຸນາສົ່ງຈົດໝາຍ   ga-lú-náh song jót-măi
(ໄປ ອົດສະຕາລີ) ທາງຍົນ   (ɓai oht-sà-đah-lee) táhng nyón

Is there any mail for me?

ມີຈົດໝາຍເຖິງຂ້ອຍບໍ່?   mée jót-măi tĕung kòy bor

bank

Where's a foreign exchange office?

ບ່ອນແລກເງິນຢູ່ໃສ?   born láak ngéun yoo săi

Can I use my credit card to withdraw money?

ຂ້ອຍໃຊ້ບັດເຄຣດິດຖອນເງິນໄດ້ບໍ່?   kòy sái bát klàir-dít tŏrn ngéun dâi bor

I'd like to change (a) ...	ຂ້ອຍຢາກປ່ຽນ ...	kòy yahk ɓee·an ...
cheque	ເຊັກໃບນຶ່ງ	sék bai neung
money	ເງິນ	ngéun
travellers cheque	ເຊັກທ່ອງທ່ຽວໃບນຶ່ງ	sék tòrng têe·o bai neung

What's the ...?	... เທ່ົາໃດ?	... tow dai
charge for that	ເຈ້ົາເອົາຄ່າບໍລິການ	jôw ow kàh bor-li-gáhn
exchange rate	ອັດຕາແລກປ່ຽນ	át-đah làak bee-an

It's ...	ມັນແມ່ນ ...	man maan ...
(1000) kip	(ໜຶ່ງພັນ) ກີບ	(neung-pán) géep
free	ໃຫ້ລ້າ	hài làh

What time does the bank open?
ທະນາຄານເປີດຈັກໂມງ?   ta-náh-káhn bֵeut ják móhng

Can I transfer money here from my bank?
ຂ້ອຍໂອນເງິນຈາກ   kòy ohn ngéun jahk
ທະນາຄານມານີ້ໄດ້ບໍ?   ta-náh-káhn máh nêe dâi bor

How long will it take to arrive?
ຈັກມື້ມັນຊິມາຮອດ?   ják mêu see máh hôrt

Has my money arrived yet?
ເງິນຂ້ອຍມາຮອດແລ້ວບໍ?   ngéun kòy máh hôrt lâa-ou bor

sightseeing

getting in

What time does it open/close?
ມັນເປີດ/ປິດເວລາຈັກໂມງ?   man bֵeut/bít wáir-láh ják móhng

Is there an admission charge?
ເກັບຄ່າຜ່ານປະຕູບໍ?   gép káh pahn bà-đoo bor

Is there a discount	ມີການລຸດ	mee gahn lùt
for ...?	ລາຄາສໍລັບ ... ບໍ?	láh-káh säm-láp ... bor
children	ເດັກນ້ອຍ	dék nóy
students	ນັກຮຽນ	nák hée an

Do you have a ...?	ເຈ້ົາມີ ... ບໍ?	jôw mée ... bor
catalogue	ປ້ຶມແບບ	bֵeum baap
guide	ປ້ຶມຄູ່ມື	bֵeum koo méu
local map	ແຜນທີ່ຕົວເມືອງ	pàan tee đua méu-ang

I'd like to see ...
ຂ້ອຍຢາກໄປເບິ່ງ ... kòy yahk bai béung ...

What's this monument?
ນີ້ແມ່ນອານຸສາວະລິຫຍັງ? nêe maan ah-nu-săh-wà-lée nyăng

What's that building?
ນັ້ນແມ່ນອາຄານຫຍັງ? nàn maan ah-káhn nyăng

Can we take photos?
ພວກເຮົາຖ່າຍຮູບໄດ້ບໍ່? púak hów tai hôop dâi bor

tours

When's the next ...?	... ເທື່ອຕໍ່ໄປແມ່ນ	... teu-a ðór bai maan
	ເວລາໃດ?	wáir-láh dai
boat trip	ການທ່ຽວທາງເຮືອ	gahn têe-o tahng héu-a
day trip	ການທ່ຽວມື້ເວັນ	gahn têe-o mêu wèn
tour	ທ່ອງທ່ຽວ	tòrng têe-o
Does the price	ລາຄາລ່ວມທັງ	láh-káh lùam tang
include (the) ...?	... ບໍ່?	... bor
accommodation	ທີ່ພັກ	tee pák
admission charge	ຄ່າຜ່ານປະຕູ	kah pahn bà-đoo
food	ອາຫານ	ah-hăhn
transport	ພະຫະນະ	pà-hà-nà

How long is the tour?
ທ່ອງທ່ຽວຫຍ້ອນຶ່ງດົນປານໃດ? tórng têe-o têe-o neung dón bahn dai

What time should we be back?
ພວກເຮົາຈະກັບມາຈັກໂມງ? púak hów jà gàp mah jàk móhng

market	ຕະຫລາດ	đa-làht
memorial	ອານຸສອນສະຖານ	ah-nu-sŏrn sa-tăhn
monument	ອະນຸສາວະລີ	à-nu-săh-wà-lée
museum	ພິພິດຫະພັນ	pi-pit-tà-pán
palace	ພະລາດສະວັງ	pà-laht-sa-wáng
ruins	ຊາກສະລັກຫັກພັງ	sàhk sá-lak-hàk-páng
shrine	ຫໍໄຫວ້	hŏr wâi
temple	ວັດ	wat

shopping

enquiries

Where's a ...?	... ຢູ່ໃສ?	... yoo săi
bank	ທະນາຄານ	ta-nā-kháhn
bookshop	ຮ້ານຂາຍປື້ມ	hâhn kăi bêum
camera shop	ຮ້ານຂາຍກ້ອງຖ່າຍຮູບ	hâhn kăi gôrng tai hóop
department store	ຮ້ານສັບພະສິນຄ້າ	hâhn sàp-pa-sĭn-kâh
market	ຕະຫລາດ	đa-làht
supermarket	ຫ້າງຂາຍເຄື່ອງ	hang kăi keu·ang

I'm looking for ...
ຂ້ອຍຊອກຫາ ...   kòy sôrk·hăh ...

Can I look at it?
ຂ້ອຍເບິ່ງໄດ້ບໍ່?   kòy beung dâi bor

Do you have any others?
ເຈົ້າມີອີກບໍ່?   jôw mée èek bor

Does it have a guarantee?
ມັນມີປະກັນບໍ່?   mán mée bà-găn bor

Can I have it sent overseas?
ຂ້ອຍສົ່ງໄປຕ່າງປະເທດໄດ້ບໍ່?   kòy song bai đáhng bà-tét dâi bor

Can you repair it?
ເຈົ້າແປງໃຫ້ແດ່ໄດ້ບໍ່?   jôw baang hài dàa dâi bor

The quality isn't very good.
ຄຸນນະພາບບໍ່ດີປານໃດ   kún-na-pàhp boh dée bahn dai

I'd like (a) ..., please.
ຂ້ອຍຂໍ ... ແດ່   kòy kŏr ... dàa

bag	ຖົງໜຶ່ງ	tŏng neung
refund	ເອົາເງິນຄືນ	ow ngeun kéun
to return this	ສົ່ງເຄື່ອງນີ້ຄືນ	sòng keu·ang nêe kéun

paying

How much is it?
ລາຄາເທົ່າໃດ?
láh-káh tow dai

Can you write down the price?
ເຈົ້າຂຽນລາຄາໃສ່ໄດ້ບໍ່?
jôw kĕe-an láh-káh sai dâi bor

That's too expensive.
ຂ້ອຍຄິດວ່າແພງໂພດ
kòy kít wah páang pôht

Do you have anything cheaper?
ມີອັນຖືກກວ່ານີ້ບໍ່
mée an tèuk gwah nêe bor

How about (100,000) kip?
(ໜຶ່ງແສນ) ກີບໄດ້ບໍ່?
(neung-sǎan) géep dâi bor

There's a mistake in the bill.
ບິນຂຽນບໍ່ຖືກ
bín kĕe-an bor tèuk

Do you accept ...?	ເຈົ້າເອົາ ... ບໍ່?	jôw ow ... bor
credit cards	ບັດເຄຼດິດ	bát kláir-dít
travellers cheques	ເຊັກທ່ອງທ່ຽວ	sék torng têe-o

I'd like ..., please.	ເອົາ ... ໃຫ້ຂ້ອຍແດ່	ow ... hâi kòy dàa
a receipt	ໃບຮັບເງິນ	bai hap ngéun
my change	ເງິນທອນຂອງຂ້ອຍ	ngéun torn kŏrng kòy

clothes & shoes

Can I try it on?
ຂ້ອຍລອງໄດ້ບໍ່?
kòy lórng dâi bor

My size is (42).
ຂະໜາດຂອງຂ້ອຍແມ່ນ
(ສີ່ສິບສອງ)
kà-naht kŏrng kòy maan
(see-síp-sŏrng)

It doesn't fit.
ມັນບໍ່ພໍດີ
mán bor por dée

small	ນ້ອຍ	nòy
medium	ກາງ	gahng
large	ໃຫຍ່	yai

books & music

Can I have a ...?
ເອົາ ... ໃຫ້ຂ້ອຍໄດ້ບໍ່? ow ... hâi kòy dâi bor

   newspaper   ໜັງສືພິມ   năng-sěu pím

   pen   ປາກາ   bah-gáh

Is there an English-language bookshop?
ມີຮ້ານຂາຍປຶ້ມພາສາອັງກິດບໍ່?   mee hâhn kǎi bêum pah-sǎh àng-gít bor

I'm looking for books/music by (a local author/artist).
ຂ້ອຍຊອກຫາປຶ້ມ/ເພັງ   kòy sôrk hǎh bêum/péng
ຂອງ (ນັກປະພັນພື້ນເມືອງ)   kǒrng (nak bà-pán pêun méu·ang)

Can I listen to this?
ຂ້ອຍຟັງເພັງນີ້ໄດ້ບໍ່?   kòy fang péng nêe dâi bor

photography

I need a/an ... film	ຂ້ອຍຕ້ອງການ ... ຟິມ	kòy đôrng gahn ... fím
for this camera.	ສໍາລັບກ້ອງຖ່າຍຮູບ	sǎm-làp gôrng tai hôop
APS	ຟິມ ແອ ພີ ເອສ	fím àa-pee-ét
B&W	ຟິມຂາວດໍາ	fím kǒw dám
colour	ຟິມສີ	fím sěe
(200) speed	ຄວາມໄວ (ສອງຮ້ອຍ)	kwáhm wái (sǎwng·hôy)
Can you ...?	ເຈົ້າ ... ໄດ້ບໍ່?	jôw ... dâi bor
burn a CD from	ເບິນ ຊີ ດີຈາກ	béun sée dee jahk
my memory card	ແມມໂມລິຄາດ	mém-moh-li kaht
	ຂອງຂ້ອຍ	kǒrng kòy
develop this film	ລ້າງຟິມນີ້	lâhng fím nêe
load my film	ໃສ່ຟິມ	sai fím
When will it be ready?	ເວລາໃດຈະແລ້ວ?	wáir-láh dai jà lâa·ou

toiletries

conditioner	ຢານວດຜົມ	yah nuat pŏm
condoms	ຖົງຢາງອະນາໄມ	tŏng yáhng à-náh-mái
deodorant	ຢາກັນກິ່ນຕົວ	yah gán gin đoo-a
insect repellent	ຢາກັນແມງໄມ້	yáh gán máang mâi
moisturiser	ຄີມທາໜ້າ	keem táh nâh
razor blades	ໃບມິດແຖ	bai mêet tăa
sanitary napkins	ຜ້າອະນາໄມ	pâh à-náh-mái
shampoo	ຢາຊະຜົມ	yáh sà pŏm
shaving cream	ຢາແຖໜວດ	yáh tăa nuat
soap	ສະບູ	sà-boo
sunscreen	ຄີມກັນແດດ	kim gán dàat
tampons	ຜ້າອະນາໄມ	pâh a-náh-mái
toilet paper	ເຈັ້ຍທ້ອງນ້ຳ	jêe-a hòrng nàm
toothbrush	ແປງຖູແຂ້ວ	ƀaang tŏo kâa·ou
toothpaste	ຢາຖູແຂ້ວ	yáh tŏo kâa·ou

meeting people

greetings, goodbyes & introductions

Hello/Hi.	ສະບາຍດີ	sa-bai dee
Goodbye/Good night.	ລາກ່ອນ	lah gorn
See you later.	ພົບກັນໃໝ່	pòp gan mai
Mr	ທ່ານ	táhn
Mrs/Miss	ນາງ/ນາງສາວ	náhng/náhng sŏw
How are you?	ເຈົ້າສະບາຍດີບໍ່?	jŏw sa-bai dee bor
Fine. And you?	ສະບາຍດີ	sa-bai dee
	ເຈົ້າເດ?	jŏw dáir
What's your name?	ເຈົ້າຊື່ຫຍັງ?	jŏw seu nyãng
My name is ...	ຂ້ອຍຊື່ ...	kòy seu ...
Pleased to meet you.	ຍິນດີທີ່ໄດ້ຮູ້ຈັກ	nyín dée tee dâi hôo-jàk

This is my ...	ນີ້ແມ່ນ ... ຂອງຂ້ອຍ	nêe maan ... kŏrng kóy
boyfriend	ແຟນ	fáan
brother (older)	ອ້າຍ	âi
brother (younger)	ນ້ອງຊາຍ	nórng sái
daughter	ລູກສາວ	lôok sŏw
father	ພໍ່	pór
friend	ເພື່ອນ	peu·an
girlfriend	ແຟນ	fáan
husband	ຜົວ	pŏo·a
mother	ແມ່	maa
partner (intimate)	ແຟນ	fáan
sister (older)	ເອື້ອຍ	êu·ay
sister (younger)	ນ້ອງສາວ	nòrng sŏw
son	ລູກຊາຍ	lôok sái
wife	ເມຍ	mée·a

Here's my ...	ນີ້ແມ່ນ ... ຂອງຂ້ອຍ	nêe maan ... kŏrng kòy
What's your ...?	... ຂອງເຈົ້າແມ່ນຫຍັງ?	... kŏrng jôw maan nyăng
address	ທີ່ຢູ່	tee yoo
email address	ອີແມວ	ée-máa·ou
phone number	ເບີໂທລະສັບ	beu tóh-la-sáp
mobile number	ເບີໂທລະສັບມືຖື	beu tóh-la-sáp méu těu

occupations

What's your occupation?

ອາຊີບເຈົ້າເຮັດຫຍັງ?   ah-sêep jôw hét nyăng

I'm a/an ...	ຂ້ອຍເປັນ ...	kòy bén ...
manual worker	ກາມະກອນ	gàm-ma-gorn
nurse	ນາງພະຍາບານ	nahng pà-yah-báhn
office worker	ພະນັກງານ	pà-nak ngáhn
	ຫ້ອງການ	hòrng gahn
student	ນັກສຶກສາ	nak séuk-săh
teacher	ຄູ	kóo
volunteer	ອາສາສະມັກ	ah-săh sà-mak
writer	ນັກຂຽນ	nak kĕe-an

background

Where are you from?	ເຈົ້າມາແຕ່ໃສ?	jôw mah đaa săi
I'm from ...	ຂ້ອຍເປັນຄົນ ...	kòy bén kón ...
Australia	ອົສຕາລີ	òr-sá-đah-lée
Canada	ການາດາ	gah-nah-dah
England	ອັງກິດ	àng-gít
New Zealand	ນິວຊີແລນ	néw-sée-láan
the USA	ອາເມລິກາ	ah-máir-li-gáh
Are you married?	ເຈົ້າແຕ່ງງານແລ້ວຫລືບໍ່?	jôw đáang ngáhn lâa-ou leu bor
I'm ...	ຂ້ອຍ ...	kòy ...
married	ແຕ່ງງານແລ້ວ	đáang ngáhn lâa-ou
single	ເປັນໂສດ	bén sóht

age

How old ...?	... ອາຍຸຈັກປີ?	... ah-nyù ják bee
are you	ເຈົ້າ	jôw
is your daughter	ລູກສາວເຈົ້າ	lóok sŏw jôw
is your son	ລູກຊາຍເຈົ້າ	lóok sái jôw

I'm ... years old.
ຂ້ອຍອາຍຸ ... ປີ   kòy ah-nyu ... bee

He/She is ... years old.
ລາວອາຍຸ ... ປີ   lów ah-nyu ... bee

classifiers				
animals, clothes	ໂຕ	đoh	**people**	ຄົນ	kón
glasses (of water etc)	ຈອກ	jòrk	**plates (of food)**	ຈານ	jahn
letters, newspapers	ສະບັບ	sá-báp	**small objects**	ໂຕ	đoh
pairs of items	ຄູ່	koo	**vehicles**	ຄັນ	kán

feelings

Are you ...?	ເຈົ້າຮູ້ສຶກ ... ບໍ່?	jôw hôo-seuk ... bor
I'm ...	ຂອຍຮູ້ສຶກ ...	kòy hôo-seuk ...
angry	ໃຈຮ້າຍ	jai hâi
cold	ໜາວ	nŏw
excited	ຕື່ນເຕັ້ນ	đéun đên
happy	ດີໃຈ	dée jai
hot	ຮ້ອນ	hôrn
hungry	ຫິວເຂົ້າ	hĕw kôw
lonely	ເຫງົາ	ngŏw
sad	ໂສກເສົ້າ	sohk sôw
sleepy	ເຫງົານອນ	ngŏw nórn
surprised	ປະຫລາດໃຈ	bà-láht jai
thirsty	ຫິວນ້ຳ	hĕw nâm
tired	ເໝື່ອຍ	meu-ay
upset	ອາລົມເສຍ	ah-lóm sĕe-a

entertainment

water sports

Is it safe to swim here?
ລອຍນ້ຳຢູ່ຫັ້ນປອດໄພບໍ່?   loy-nâhm yoo hân bort-pài bor

How much for a/an ...?	... ອັນໜຶ່ງ ລາຄາເທົ່າໃດ?	... án neung lah-kah tow dai
chair	ຕັ່ງນັ່ງ	đang nàng
umbrella	ຄັນຮົ່ມ	kán-hom

Can I hire (a) ...?	ຂ້ອຍເຊົ່າ ... ອັນໜຶ່ງໄດ້ບໍ່?	kòy sow ... an neung dâi bor
canoe	ເຮືອພາຍ	heu-a pai
guide	ຜູ້ນຳທ່ຽວ	pôo nam tee-o
life jacket	ເສື້ອຊູຊີບ	sêu-a soo síp

going out

Where are the ...?	... ຢູ່ໃສ?	... yoo săi
bars	ບາ	bah
cafés	ຮ້ານກາເຟ	hâhn gah-fáir
clubs	ສະໂມສອນ	sà-móh-sŏrn
restaurants	ຮ້ານອາຫານ	hâhn ah-hăhn

I feel like going to a/the ...	ຂ້ອຍຢາກໄປ ...	kòy yàhk bai ...
concert	ງານດົນຕີ	ngáhn don-đee
karaoke bar	ບາຄາລາໂອເກະ	bah kah-lah-or-gáir
movies	ເບິ່ງຮູບເງົາ	béung hôop ngáo
nightclub	ບາກາງຄືນ	bah gahng keun
party	ງານລ້ຽງສັນ	ngáhn sâhng-săn
performance	ເບິ່ງການສະແດງ	beung gahn-sa-daang
theatre	ໂຮງລະຄອນ	hóhng la-kórn

personal pronouns		
I	ຂ້ອຍ	kòy
you sg	ເຈົ້າ	jôw
he/she	ລາວ	lów
it	ມັນ	mán
we	ເຮົາ	hów
you pl	ພວກເຈົ້າ	pûak jôw
they	ພວກເຂົາ	pûak kŏw
possessive pronouns		
my	ຂອງຂ້ອຍ	kŏrng kòy
your sg	ຂອງເຈົ້າ	kŏrng jôw
his/her	ຂອງລາວ	kŏrng lów
our	ຂອງເຮົາ	kŏrng hów
your pl	ຂອງພວກເຈົ້າ	kŏrng pûak jôw
their	ຂອງພວກເຂົາ	kŏrng pûak kŏw

interests

Do you like ...?	ເຈົ້າມັກ ... ບໍ່?	jôw mak ... bor
I (don't) like ...	ຂ້ອຍ (ບໍ່) ມັກ ...	kóy (bor) mak ...
art	ສິລະປະ	sí-la-bà
cooking	ແຕ່ງກິນ	đaang gin
film	ໜັງ	năng
hiking	ປີນເຂົາ	ƀeen kŏw
photography	ຖ່າຍຮູບ	tai hôop
reading	ອ່ານປຶ້ມ	ahn ƀeum
sport	ກິລາ	gi-láh
travelling	ທ່ອງທ່ຽວ	tórng têe·o
watching TV	ເບິ່ງໂທລະທັດ	béung tóh-la-tát
Do you like to ...?	ເຈົ້າມັກ ... ບໍ່?	jôw mak ... bor
dance	ຟ້ອນ	fôrn
go to concerts	ໄປເບິ່ງຄອນເສີດ	ƀai beung kórn-seut
listen to music	ໄປເບິ່ງດົນຕີ	ƀai beung don-đee

food & drink

finding a place to eat

Can you	ເຈົ້າຈະ	jôw jà
recommend a ...?	ແນະນຳ ... ໄດ້ບໍ່?	nàa·nám ... dâi bor
bar	ບາ	bah
café	ຮ້ານກາເຟ	hâhn gah-fáir
restaurant	ຮ້ານອາຫານ	hâhn ah-hăhn
I'd like ..., please.	... ຂ້ອຍຢາກໄດ້	... kòy yahk dâi
a table for (four)	ໂຕະສຳລັບ (ສີ່) ຄົນ	đôh săm-làp (see) kón
the nonsmoking section	ບ່ອນປອດຢາສູບ	born ƀort yah sòop
the smoking section	ບ່ອນສູບຢາໄດ້	born sòop yah dâi

ordering food

breakfast	ອາຫານເຊົ້າ	ah-hăhn sôw
lunch	ອາຫານທ່ຽງ	ah-hăhn tee-ang
dinner	ອາຫານແລງ	ah-hăhn láang
snack	ອາຫານຫວ່າງ	ah-hăhn wâhng

Please bring the bill/menu.
ຂໍ ເຊັກ/ລາຍການອາຫານແດ່   kŏr sék/lái gahn ah-hăhn dàa

What would you recommend?
ມີຫຍັງພິເສດບໍ?   mée nyăng pi-sét bor

I'd like to try that.
ຂ້ອຍຢາກລອງກິນເບິ່ງ   kòy yahk lórng gin béung

I (don't) like it hot and spicy.
ຂ້ອຍ(ບໍ່)ມັກເຜັດ   kòy (bor) mak pét

bowl	ຖ້ວຍ	tôo-ay
chopsticks	ໄມ້ໝູ່	mâi too
cloth	ຜ້າ	pàh
cup	ຈອກ	jork
fork	ສ້ອມ	sórm
glass	ຈອກ	jork
knife	ມີດ	mêet
plate	ຈານ	jahn
spoon	ບ່ວງ	buang
teaspoon	ບ່ວງຊາ	buang sáh

drinks

... water	ນ້ຳ ...	nàm ...
boiled	ຕົ້ມ	đôm
drinking	ດື່ມບໍລິສຸດ	deum bor-li-sut
mineral	ແຮ່ທາດ	háa tâht
milk	ນ້ຳນົມຈືດ	nàm nóm jeut
orange juice	ນ້ຳໝາກກ້ຽງ	nàm màhk gêe-ang

coffee/tea ...	ກາເຟ/ຊາ ...	gah-fáir/sáh ...
with milk and sugar	ນົມຮ້ອນ	nóm hórn
without milk	ບໍ່ໃສ່ນົມ	bor sai nóm
without sugar	ບໍ່ໃສ່ນ້ຳຕານ	bor sai nâm-đahn

in the bar

I'll have (a gin).	ຂ້ອຍຊໍ(ເຫລົ້າຈິນ)	kòy kŏr (lôw jêen)
I'll buy you a drink.	ຂ້ອຍຈະຊື້ເຄື່ອງ	kòy jà sêu keu·ang
	ດື່ມໃຫ້ເຈົ້າ	deum hâi jôw
What would you like?	ເຈົ້າຈະເອົາຫຍັງ?	jôw jà ow nyăng
It's my round.	ທີ່ຂ້ອຍ	tee kòy
Cheers!	ເຊີນດື່ມ	séun deum
Same again, please.	ຊໍຄືເກົ່າແດ່	kŏr keu gow dàa

rice whisky	ເຫລົ້າຂາວ	lôw kŏw
rum	ເຫລົ້າຫລ້ຳ	lôw lâm
vodka	ເຫລົ້າໂວກາ	lôw woh-gáh

a shot of (whisky)	(ເຫລົ້າວິສກີ້) ຈອກໜຶ່ງ	(lôw wi-sà-gêe) jork neung
a bottle of (beer)	(ເບຍ) ແກ້ວໜຶ່ງ	(bee-a) gâa-ou neung
a glass of (beer)	(ເບຍ) ຈອກໜຶ່ງ	(bee-a) jork neung

a bottle/glass	ວາຍ ...	wai ...
of ... wine	ແກ້ວ/ຈອກໜຶ່ງ	gâa-ou/jork neung
red	ແດງ	daang
sparkling	ປຸກ	búk
white	ຂາວ	kŏw

self-catering

What's the local specialty?
ມີຫຍັງພິເສດບໍ່? mée nyăng pi-sèt bor

What's that?
ນັ້ນແມ່ນຫຍັງ? nàn maan nyăng

How much is (a kilo of) ...?
... (ກິໂລ) ເທົ່າໃດ? ... (gi-lóh) tow dai

I'd like ...	ຂ້ອຍຕ້ອງການ ...	kòy đôrng gahn ...
(100) grams	(ໜຶ່ງຮ້ອຍ) ກລາມ	(neung hôy) glahm
(two) kilos	(ສອງ) ກີໂລ	(sŏrng hôy) gi-loh
(three) pieces	(ສາມ) ອັນ	(sǎhm) an
(six) slices	(ຫົກ) ປ່ຽງ	(hók) ‛bee·ang

Enough.	ພໍ	pór
A bit more.	ອີກ	eek
Less.	ໜ້ອຍກວ່າ	nóy gwah

special diets & allergies

Is there a vegetarian restaurant near here?
ມີຮ້ານອາຫານເຈໃກ້ແຖວນີ້ບໍ?   mee hăhn ah-hăhn jáir gâi tăa·ou nêe bor

I don't want any meat.
ຂ້ອຍບໍ່ເອົາຊີ້ນສັດ   kòy bor ow sêen sát

Please don't use any ...	ກະລຸນາບໍ່ໃສ່ ...	ga-lú-náh bor sai ...
anchovies	ປາແດກ	‛bah dàak
chilli	ໝາກເຜັດ	màhk pét
fish sauce	ນ້ຳປາ	nâm ‛bah
MSG	ແປ້ງນົວ	‛bâang núa

I'm allergic to ...	ຂ້ອຍແພ້ ...	kòy pâa ...
caffeine	ຄາເຟອີນ	káh-fáir-in
dairy produce	ອາຫານມີນມເນີຍ	ah-hăhn nóm néui
eggs	ໄຂ່	kài
gluten	ແປ້ງເຂົ້າໜຽວ	‛bâang kòw nĕe·o
nuts	ຖົ່ວ	tua
seafood	ອາຫານທະເລ	ah-hăhn tà-láir

For other allergies see **health**, page 146.

menu decoder

bah sôm wähn	ປາສົ້ມຫວານ	sweet & sour fish
bà-torng-góh	ປະທ່ອງໂກະ	Chinese doughnuts
bêeng gûng	ປີ້ງກຸ້ງ	grilled prawns
dàm màhk-hung	ຕຳໝາກຫຸ່ງ	spicy green papaya salad
dôm yám bah	ຕົ້ມຍຳປາ	fish soup with mushrooms
fêu hàang	ເຝີແຫ້ງ	rice noodles with vegetables & meat, without broth
fêu kûa sai pak làa sêen	ເຝີຂົ້ວໃສ່ຜັກແລະຊີ້ນ	fried rice noodles with vegetables & meat
fêu sai pak làa sêen	ເຝີໃສ່ຜັກແລະຊີ້ນ	soup with rice-noodles, vegetables & meat
gaang jèut đao-hôo	ແກງຈືດເຕົ້າຮູ້	soup with vegetables, pork & bean curd
gai pát kêeng	ໄກ່ຜັດຂີງ	chicken with ginger
kòw bèe-ak gai	ເຂົ້າປຽກໄກ່	rice soup with chicken
kòw bèe-ak mõo	ເຂົ້າປຽກໝູ	rice soup with pork
kòw bèe-ak bah	ເຂົ້າປຽກປາ	rice soup with fish
kòw bôon sai nâm bah wahn	ເຂົ້າປຸ້ນໃສ່ນ້ຳປາ ຫວານ	white-flour noodles served with sweet & spicy sauce
kòw đôm	ເຂົ້າຕົ້ມ	sweetened sticky rice steamed in banana leaves
kòw kèe-ap gûng	ເຂົ້າຂຽບກຸ້ງ	shrimp chips
kòw lãhm	ເຂົ້າຫລາມ	sticky rice in coconut milk cooked in bamboo
kòw làht gaang	ເຂົ້າລາດແກງ	curry with rice
kòw mõo daang	ເຂົ້າໝູແດງ	red pork with rice
kòw nàh bét	ເຂົ້າໜ້າເປັດ	roast duck with rice
kòw nèung	ເຂົ້າໜຶ້ງ	steamed white rice
kòw nêe-o	ເຂົ້າໜຽວ	sticky rice
kòw nêe-o daang	ເຂົ້າໜຽວແດງ	sticky rice in coconut cream

kòw née-o-máhk mùang	ເຂົ້າໜຽວໝາກມ່ວງ	sticky rice in coconut cream & ripe mango
kòw-nôm	ເຂົ້າໜົມ	rice-flour cakes
kòw-nôm mòr gaang	ເຂົ້າໜົມໝໍ້ແກງ	egg custard
kòw pát boo	ເຂົ້າຜັດປູ	fried rice with crab
kòw pát gai	ເຂົ້າຜັດໄກ່	fried rice with chicken
kòw pát gûng	ເຂົ້າຜັດກຸ້ງ	fried rice with shrimp
kòw pát mõo	ເຂົ້າຜັດໝູ	fried rice with pork
làhp	ລາບ	meat salad with garlic, onions, chilli, sticky rice, lime juice & mint leaves
làhp gai	ລາບໄກ່	chicken làhp
làhp mõo	ລາບໝູ	pork làhp
làhp bah	ລາບປາ	fish làhp
làhp sêen	ລາບຊີ້ນ	beef làhp
mee hàang sai pak là sêen	ໝີ່ແຫ້ງໃສ່ຜັກແລະຊີ້ນ	yellow wheat noodles with vegetables & meat
mee nâm	ໝີ່ນ້ຳ	yellow wheat noodles in broth, with vegetables & meat
mõo sôm wãhn	ໝູສົ້ມຫວານ	stir-fried sweet & sour pork
nâm wãhn máhk gûay	ນ້ຳຫວານໝາກກ້ວຍ	banana in coconut milk
nãng kwai hãang	ໜັງຄວາຍແຫ້ງ	dried skin of water buffalo
ngúa pát nâm-mãn hõy	ງົວຜັດນ້ຳມັນຫອຍ	beef in oyster sauce
pát pák	ຜັດຜັກ	stir-fried mixed vegetables
pát sá-êw	ເຜິ້ຂົ້ວໃສ່ສະອິ້ວ	fried rice noodles with soy sauce
sãng-ka-nyãa	ສັງຂະຫຍາ	custard
tua din jeun	ຖົ່ວດິນຈືນ	fried peanuts
yám sèn wûn	ຍຳເສັ້ນຫວຸ້ນ	salad of cellophane noodles
yór díp	ຍໍດິບ	fresh spring rolls
yór jeun	ຍໍຈືນ	fried spring rolls

emergencies

basics

Help!	ຊ່ອຍແດ່	sóo·ay dàa
Stop!	ຢຸດ	yút
Go away!	ໜີໄປ	nèe bai
Thief!	ຄົນຂີ້ລັກ	kón kêe lak
Fire!	ໄຟໄໝ້	fái mài

Call ...	ຊ່ອຍເອີ້ນ ... ໃຫ້ແດ່	sóo·ay êun ... hài dàa
a doctor	ທ່ານໝໍ	tahn mŏr
an ambulance	ລົດໂຮງໝໍ	lot hóhng mŏr
the police	ຕຳຫລວດ	đam-luat

It's an emergency!
ສຸກເສີນ   súk sêun

There's been an accident!
ມີອຸບັດຕິເຫດ   mée ù-bát-đí-hét

Could I use the phone, please?
ໃຊ້ໂທລະສັບໄດ້ບໍ່?   sâi tóh-la-sáp dâi bor

Could you help me, please?
ເຈົ້າຊ່ອຍຂ້ອຍໄດ້ບໍ່?   jôw sóo·ay kòy dâi bor

I'm lost.
ຂ້ອຍຫລົງທາງ   kòy lŏng táhng

Where are the toilets?
ຫ້ອງນ້ຳຢູ່ໃສ?   hòrng nâm yoo săi

police

Where's the police station?
ສະຖານີຕຳຫລວດຢູ່ໃສ?   sa-tăh-née đam-lùat yoo săi

I want to report an offence.
ຂ້ອຍຕ້ອງການແຈ້ງຄວາມ   kòy đôrng gahn jàang kúam

I've been ...	ຂ້ອຍຖືກ ...	kòy tèuk ...
assaulted	ທຳຮ້າຍ	tam hâi
raped	ຂົ່ມຂືນ	kòm kěun
robbed	ປຸ້ນ	ɓôon

My ... was/were stolen.	... ຂອງຂ້ອຍຖືກລັກ	... körng kóy teuk làk

I've lost my ...	ຂ້ອຍເຮັດ ... ເສຍແລ້ວ	kòy hét ... sěe·a lâa·ou
backpack	ຖົງເປ້	tŏng ɓâir
bags	ຖົງເຄື່ອງ	tŏng keu·ang
credit card	ບັດເຄລດິດ	bát kláir·dít
handbag	ກະເປົາຫີ້ວ	gà·bow héw
jewellery	ເຄື່ອງປະດັບ	keu·ang ɓá·dáp
money	ເງິນ	ngéun
passport	ໜັງສືຜ່ານແດນ	năng·sěu pahn daan
travellers cheques	ເຊັກເດິນທາງ	sék deun táhng
wallet	ກະເປົາເງິນ	gà·bow ngéun

I want to contact my embassy/consulate.

ຂ້ອຍຢາກຕິດຕໍ່ສະຖານທູດ/
ກົງສຸນຂອງຂ້ອຍ

kòy yáhk đít đor sa·tăhn·tôot/
gòng·sŏon körng kòy

I have insurance.

ຂ້ອຍມີປະກັນໄພ

kóy mée ɓà·gan pái

health

medical needs

Where's the nearest ...?	... ໄກ້ທີ່ສຸດຢູ່ໃສ?	... gâi tee sút yóo săi
dentist	ໝໍປົວແຂ້ວ	mŏr ɓua kâa·ou
doctor	ທ່ານໝໍ	tahn mŏr
hospital	ໂຮງໝໍ	hóhng mŏr
(night) pharmacist	ຮ້ານຂາຍຢາ (ກາງຄືນ)	hâhn kăi yáh (gahng·keun)

I need a doctor (who speaks English).

ຂ້ອຍຕ້ອງການທ່ານໝໍ   kòy đôrng-gahn tahn mŏr

(ຮູ້ພາສາອັງກິດ)   (hôo páh-săh àng-gít)

Could I see a female doctor?

ຂ້ອຍຂໍພົບທ່ານໝໍຜູ້ຍິງໄດ້ບໍ່?   kòy kŏr pop tahn mŏr pôo nyíng đài bor

I've run out of my medication.

ຢາຂ້ອຍໝົດ   yáh kòy mót

symptoms, conditions & allergies

I'm sick.	ຂ້ອຍບໍ່ສະບາຍ	kòy bor sá-bai
It hurts here.	ເຈັບຢູ່ນີ້	jép yoo nêe
ankle	ຂໍ້ຕີນ	kôr đèen
arm	ແຂນ	kăen
back	ຫລັງ	lăng
chest	ເອິກ	éuk
ear	ຫູ	hŏo
eye	ຕາ	đah
face	ໜ້າ	nâh
finger	ນິ້ວມື	nêw méu
foot	ຕີນ	đèen
hand	ມື	méu
head	ຫົວ	hŭa
heart	ຫົວໃຈ	hŭa-jai
leg	ຂາ	kăh
mouth	ປາກ	bàhk
neck	ກ້ານຄໍ	gâhn kór
nose	ດັງ	dang
skin	ຜິວໜັງ	pĕw năng
stomach	ທ້ອງ	tòrng
teeth	ແຂ້ວ	káe-ou
throat	ຮູຄໍ	hoo kór

I need something for (a/an) ...	ຂ້ອຍຕ້ອງການຮັບໃຊ ອັນໜຶ່ງເພື່ອ ...	kòy đôrng-gahn an dai an neung pèu·a ...
asthma	ໂລກຫືດ	lôhk heut
bronchitis	ຫລອດລົມອັກເສບ	lòrt lóm ák-sèp
constipation	ຢ້ຽງທ້ອງ	nyeung tôrng
cough	ໄອ	ài
heart condition	ໂລກຫົວໃຈ	lôhk hũa-jài
infection	ການອັກເສບ	gahn àk-sép
influenza	ໄຂ້ຫວັດໃຫຍ່	kái wát nyai

I have (a) ...	ຂ້ອຍ ...	kòy ...
cold	ເປັນຫວັດ	ben wat
fever	ເປັນໄຂ້	ben kài
diarrhoea	ລົງທ້ອງ	lóng tôrng
stomachache	ປວດທ້ອງ	bùat tôrng
headache	ປວດຫົວ	bùat hũa
sore throat	ເຈັບຄໍ	jép kór
toothache	ເຈັບແຂ້ວ	jép káa·ou

antimalarial medication	ຢາກັນໄຂ້ປ່າ	yah gan kài bah
antiseptic	ຢາລ້າງເຊື້ອໂລກ	yah láhng sêu·a lôhk
aspirin	ແອສເປລິນ	àat-sá-ˈbair-lín
bandage	ຜ້າຫໍ່ບາດ	pàh hor bàht
contraceptives	ສິ່ງຄຸມກຳເນີດ	sing kùm gam-néut
diarrhoea medicine	ຢາແກ້ລົງທ້ອງ	yáh gàa lóng tôrng
insect repellent	ຢາກັນແມງໄມ້	yáh gán máang-mâi
laxatives	ຢາລະບາຍ	yah là-bai
painkillers	ຢາແກ້ປວດ	yah gàa bùat
sleeping tablets	ຢານອນຫລັບ	yah nórn láp

I'm allergic to ...	ຂ້ອຍແພ້ ...	kóy pâa ...
antibiotics	ຢາຕ້ານເຊື້ອ	yah đâhn sêu·a
anti-inflammatories	ຢາແກ້ບວມ	yah gàa buam
bees	ແມງເຜິ້ງ	maang pêung
codeine	ໂຄດີອິນ	koh-di-in
penicillin	ເປນິຊິລິນ	ˈbair-née-sée-lín

See **special diets & allergies**, page 140, for food-related allergies.

The symbols ⓝ, ⓐ and ⓥ (indicating noun, adjective and verb) have been added for clarity where an English term could be either. For food terms see the **menu decoder**, page 141.

A

accident ອຸບັດຕິເຫດ ú-bát-đí-hèt

accommodation ບ່ອນພັກ born pàk

adaptor ໝໍ້ປັບໄຟ mòr bàp fái

address ⓝ ທີ່ຢູ່ tee yoo

after ຫລັງຈາກ lãng jàhk

air conditioning ແອເຢັນ aa yén

airplane ເຮືອບິນ héu·a bin

airport ເດີນບິນ deun bin

alcohol ເຫລົ້າ lòw

all ທັງໝົດ táng mót

allergy ພູມແພ້ póom·pàa

ambulance ລົດໂຮງໝໍ lot hóhng mŏr

and ແລະ laa

ankle ຂໍ້ຕີນ kòr đeen

arm ແຂນ kăan

B

baby ເດັກນ້ອຍ dék nóy

backpack ຖົງເປ້ tohng bâir

bad ຊົ່ວ sua

bag ຖົງເຄື່ອງ tohng·keu·ang

baggage claim ບ່ອນເອົາກະເປົາ
bòrn ow gà·bow

Band-Aid ຜ້າຕິດບາດ pàh đit bàht

bank ທະນາຄານ ta·náh·káhn

bar ບາ bah

bathroom ຫ້ອງນ້ຳ hòrng nàm

battery ໝໍ້ໄຟ mòr fái

beautiful ງາມ ngáhm

bed ຕຽງ dee·ang

beer ເບຍ bee·a

before ກ່ອນ gorn

behind ທາງຫລັງ tähng lăng

bicycle ລົດຖີບ lot tèep

big ໃຫຍ່ nyai

bill ໃບບິນ bai been

black ສີດຳ sèe dam

blanket ຜ້າຫົ່ມ pàh hom

blood ເລືອດ lêu·at

blue ສີຟ້າ sée fáh

book (make a reservation) ⓥ ຈອງ jorng

both ທັງສອງ táng sŏrng

bottle ແກ້ວ gâa·ou

bottle opener ເຄື່ອງໄຂຝາແກ້ວ
keu·ang·kăi·făh·gâa·ou

boy ເດັກຊາຍ dék·sái

brakes (car) ຫ້າມ hàhm

breakfast ອາຫານເຊົ້າ ah·hăhn·sòw

broken ເພແລ້ວ páir·lâa·ou

brown ສີນ້ຳຕານ sèe·nàm·đahn

bus ລົດເມ lot·méh

business ທຸລະກິດ tu·la·git

bus stop ບ່ອນຈອດລົດ born jort lot

buy ຊື້ séu

C

café ຮ້ານກາເຟ hăhn·gah·fáir

camera ກ້ອງຖ່າຍຮູບ gôrng·tai·hôop

camp site ບ່ອນຕັ້ງເຕັ້ມ bórn·đăng·kém

cancel ຍົກເລີກ nyók·lèuk

can opener ເຄື່ອງໄຂກະປ໋ອງ
keu·ang·kăi gà·bŏrng

car ລົດ lot

cash ⓐ ເງິນສົດ ngéun-sót
cash (a cheque) ⓥ ປ່ຽນເຊັກ bee-an-sék
cell phone ໂທລະສັບມືຖື tóh-la-sáp-meu-teu
centre ສູນກາງ sōon-gahng
change (money) ⓝ ເງິນນ້ອຍ ngéun-nòy
change (money) ⓥ ແລກປ່ຽນ lâak-bee-an
cheap ຖືກ tèuk
check (bill) ໃບບິນ bai-been
check-in ⓝ ແຈ້ງເຂົ້າ jáeng-kòw
cheque (bank) ເຊັກ (ທະນາຄານ) sék (ta-náh-káhn)
child ເດັກນ້ອຍ dék-nòy
cigarette ຢາສູບ yáh-sòop
clean ⓐ ສະອາດ sá-àht
close ⓥ ປິດ bìt
coffee ກາເຟ gah-fáir
coins ຫລຽນ lěe-an
cold ⓐ ໜາວ nǒw
cold (illness) ⓝ ເປັນຫວັດ bèn-wát
collect call ໂທລະສັບເກັບເງິນປາຍທາງ
  toh-là-sap gép ngéun bai táhng
come ມາ máh
compass ເຂັມທິດ kěm-tìt
computer ຄອມພິວເຕີ kórm-piw-đěu
condoms ຖົງຢາງອະນາໄມ
  tǒng yáhng á-náh-mái
contact lenses ແກ້ວຕາຫຼມ gâa-ou đah tée-am
cook ⓥ ແຕ່ງກິນ đaang gin
cost ⓝ ລາຄາ láh-káh
credit card ບັດເຄຣດິດ bát klàir-dìt
currency exchange ບ່ອນແລກເງິນ
  born lâak ngéun
customs (immigration) ຫ້ອງການພາສີອາກອນ
  hông gahn páh-sěe-ah-gorn

D

dangerous ອັນຕະລາຍ an-đa-lái
date (time) ⓝ ວັນທີ wán tee
day ມື້ mêu
delay ⓥ ເລື່ອນ lèu-an
dentist ໝໍປົວແຂ້ວ mǒr bua gâa-ou

departure ອອກເດີນທາງ òrk déun táhng
diaper ຜ້າອານາໄມ pàh ah-nah-mai
diarrhoea ພະຍາດຖອກທ້ອງ
  pà-nyáht tòrk tòrng
dictionary ປຶ້ມວັດຈະນານຸກົມ
  bêum wat-jà-nah-nu-gohm
dinner ອາຫານແລງ ah-hǎhn láang
direct ໂດຍກົງ doy gong
dirty ເປື້ອນ béu-an
disabled person ຄົນພິການ kón pi-gahn
discount ⓝ ລຸດລາຄາ lút láh-káh
doctor ທ່ານໝໍ tahn mǒr
double bed ຕຽງຄູ່ dee-ang koo
double room ຫ້ອງຄູ່ hòrng koo
drink ⓝ ເຄື່ອງດື່ມ keu-ang deum
drive ⓥ ຂັບລົດ káp lót
drivers licence ໃບອະນຸຍາດຂັບຂີ່
  bai à-nù-nyáht káp-kee
drugs (illicit) ຢາເສບຕິດ yáh sep dìt

E

ear ຫູ hoo
east ທິດຕາເວັນອອກ tit đah-wén òrk
eat ກິນ gin
economy class ຊັ້ນປະຢັດ sán bà-yat
electricity ໄຟຟ້າ fái fâh
elevator ລິບ lip
email ອີເມລ ee-máa-ou
embassy ສະຖານທູດ sá-tǎhn tôot
emergency ດ່ວນ duan
empty ເປົ່າ bow
English ພາສາອັງກິດ páh-sǎh ang-gít
entrance ທາງເຂົ້າ tahng-kào
evening ຕອນຄ່ำ đorn kám
exchange (money) ⓥ ແລກປ່ຽນ lâak-bee-an
exit ⓝ ທາງອອກ táhng-òrk
expensive ແພງ páang
express mail ຈົດໝາຍດ່ວນ jòt-mǎi duan
eye ຕາ đah

F

far ไก gai
fast ไว wái
father พี่ por
faulty ปอม bòrm
fever ไຂ້ kài
film (camera) ຟີມ fim
finger ນີ້ວມື nêw méu
first ທີ່ນຶ່ງ tee-neung
first-aid kit ເຄື່ອງມື ພະຍາບານຂັ້ນຕົ້ນ kèu-a meu pà-nyah-bahn kân đôn
first-class (ticket) ຊັ້ນພິເສດ sân pi-sét
fish ປາ bah
fly (a plane) ບິນ bin
food ອາຫານ ah-hähn
foot ຕີນ đeen
fork ສ້ອມ sòrm
free (of charge) ໃຫ້ລ້າ hài láh
friend ເພື່ອນ peu-an
fruit ໝາກໄມ້ màhk mái
full ເຕັມ đem
funny ຕະຫລົກ đá-lók

G

gift ຂອງຂວັນ kòrng kwän
girl ເດັກຍິງ dék nying
glass (drinking) ຈອກ jòrk
glasses ແວ່ນຕາ waan đah
go ໄປ bai
good ດີ dee
green ສີຂຽວ sée-kée-o
guide ພະນັກງານນຳທ່ຽວ pà-nak-ngáhn-nám-tee-o

H

half ເຄິ່ງນຶ່ງ keung-neung
hand ມື meu
handbag ກະເປົາຖື gá-bow hěw

happy ດີໃຈ dee jai
have ມີ mée
head ຫົວ hüa
headache ເຈັບຫົວ jép hüa
heart ຫົວໃຈ hüa-jai
heart condition ໂລກຫົວໃຈ lôhk-hüa-jai
heat ຄວາມຮ້ອນ kúam hôrn
heavy ໜັກ nák
help ຊ່ວຍ suay
here ຢູ່ນີ້ yoo nêe
high ສູງ söong
highway ທາງຫລວງ táhng lüang
hike ເດີນປ່າ deun-bà
homosexual ມັກເພດດຽວກັນ màk pèt dee-o gàn
hospital ໂຮງໝໍ hóhng mór
hot ຮ້ອນ hôrn
hotel ໂຮງແຮມ hóhng háam
hungry ຫົວເຂົ້າ hěw kôw
husband ຜົວ püa

I

identification (card) ບັດປະຈຳຕົວ bát-bà-jam-đua
ill ໄຂ້ kài
important ສຳຄັນ säm-kan
included ປະກອບດ້ວຍ bá-gòrp dúay
injury ບາດເຈັບ bàht jép
insurance ປະກັນໄພ bá-gan pái
Internet ອິນເຕີແນັດ in-đeu-naat
interpreter ຜູ້ແປພາສາ póo baa páh-säh

J

jewellery ເຄື່ອງປະດັບ keu-ang bá-dáhp
job ວຽກ wêe-ak

K

key ກະແຈ ká-jaa
kilogram ກິໂລ gi-lóh

kitchen ເຮືອນຄົວ héu-an kúa
knife ມີດ mêet

L

late ຊ້າ sàh
laundry (place) ຮ້ານຊັກເຄື່ອງ
  hâhn sak keu-ang
lawyer ນັກກົດໝາຍ nak gót-mái
lesbian ທອມ tórm
leg ຂາ kah
letter ຈົດໝາຍ jót-mái
light ໄຟ fái
like ⊙ ມັກ mak
lock ⋒ ໜ່ວຍກຸນແຈ nuay gùn-jaa
long ຍາວ nyów
lost ເສຍຫາຍ sèe-a-hái
lost property office ບ່ອນແຈ້ງເຄື່ອງເສຍ
  bôrn jàang keu-ang sèe-a
love ⊙ ຮັກ hak
luggage ກະເປົາ gá-bow
lunch ອາຫານທ່ຽງ ah-hähn tee-ang

M

mail ⋒ ຈົດໝາຍ jót-mài
man ຜູ້ຊາຍ pòo sái
map ແຜນທີ່ pǎan tee
market ຕະຫລາດ dà-làht
matches ກັບຂີດ gáp kèet
meat ຊີ້ນ sêen
medicine ຢາ yáh
menu ລາຍການອາຫານ lái gahn ah-hähn
message ຂໍ້ຄວາມ kǒr kuám
milk ນົມມິນ nâm nóm
minute ນາທີ náh-tee
mobile phone ໂທລະສັບມືຖື
  tóh-la-sáp méu tĕu
money ເງິນ ngéun
month ເດືອນ deu-an
morning ຕອນເຊົ້າ đorn sôw
mother ແມ່ maa

motorcycle ລົດຈັກ lot ják
motorway ທາງລົດ tahng lot
mountain ພູດອຍ póo doy
mouth ປາກ bàhk
music ດົນຕີ don-đee

N

name ຊື່ seu
near ໃກ້ gài
new ໃໝ່ mai
news ຂ່າວ kow
newspaper ໜັງສືພິມ nǎng-sĕu pím
next ຕໍ່ໄປ dor bai
night ຄ່ຳ kám
no ບໍ່ bor
noisy ສ້ຽງດັງ song sèe-ang däng
nonsmoking ບ່ອນປອດຢາສູບ
  bôrn bort yáh sòop
north ເໜືອ néu-a
nose ດັງ dang
now ດຽວນີ້ dee-o nêe
number ຕົວເລກ đua lék

O

oil (engine) ນ້ຳມັນເຄື່ອງ nàm mán kéu-ang
old (person) ແກ່ gaa
old (thing) ເກົ່າ gow
on ຢູ່ເທິງ yoo téung
one-way (ticket) (ປີ້) ຖ້ຽວດຽວ
  (bêe) têe-o dee-o
open ⓐ ເປີດ beut
other ອື່ນ eun
outside ທາງນອກ tahng nôrk

P

package ຫໍ່ hor
painful ເຈັບ jép
painkillers ຢາແກ້ປວດ yáh gàa bùat
paper ເຈັ້ຍ jêe-a

park (car) ⓥ จอด jort
passport ໜັງສືຜ່ານແດນ năng-sĕu pahn daan
pay จ่าย jai
pen ບິກ bìk
petrol ນ້ຳມັນແອັດຊັງ nâm man àat-sáng
pharmacy ຮ້ານຂາຍຢາ hăhn-kăi-yáh
phonecard ບັດໂທລະສັບ bàht toh-la-sáp
photo ຮູບຖ່າຍ hôop tai
plate ຈານ jahn
police ຕຳຫລວດ dam-lùat
postcard ບັດໄປສະນີ bàt bai-sá-née
post office ຫ້ອງການໄປສະນີ hòrng gahn bai-sá-née
pregnant ຖືພາ tĕu páh
price ລາຄາ láh-káh

Q

quiet ງຽບ ngée-ap

R

rain ⓝ ຝົນ fŏhn
razor blades ໃບມີດແຖ bai mêet tăa
receipt ໃບຮັບເງິນ bai hap ngéun
recommend ເຫັນດີ hĕn-dee
red ສີແດງ sĕe-daang
refund ⓝ ສິ່ງເງິນຄືນ song-ngéun-kéun
registered mail ຈົດໝາຍລົງທະບຽນ jót-măi long-tà-bee-an
rent ⓥ ເຊົ່າ sow
repair ແປງ baang
reservation ການສັ່ງຈອງ gahn-sang jorng
restaurant ຮ້ານອາຫານ hăhn ah hăhn
return ⓥ ກັບຄືນ gáp-kéun
return ticket ປີ້ໄປກັບ bée bai gáp
right (direction) ເບື້ອງຂວາ bêu-ang-kŭa
road ທາງ táhng
room ຫ້ອງ hòrng
rope ເຊືອກ sĕu-ak

S

safe ⓐ ປອດໄພ bòrt pái
sanitary napkins ຜ້າອະນາໄມ páh à-nah-mái
sea ທະເລ ta-láir
seat ບ່ອນນັ່ງ born nahng
send ສົ່ງ song
service station ບ່ອນບໍລິການ born bor-li-gahn
sex ເພດ pét
shaving cream ຄິມແຖໜວດ kim tăa nuat
sheet (bed) ຜ້າປູບ່ອນ pàh boo born
shirt ເສື້ອ sêu-a
shoes ເກີບ gèup
shop ⓝ ຮ້ານຄ້າ hăhn kàh
short ສັ້ນ sàn
shower ⓥ ອາບນ້ຳ ahp nâhm
single room ຫ້ອງນອນດ່ຽວດ່ຽວ hòrng nórn dee-ang dee-ŏ
size (clothes) ຂະໜາດ ká-nàht
skin ຜິວໜັງ péw năng
skirt ກະໂປ່ງ gà-bohng
sleep ⓥ ນອນ nórn
slowly ຊ້າ sâh
small ນ້ອຍ nôy
smoke ⓥ ສູບຢາ sòop yah
soap ສະບູ sá-boo
some ບາງ bahng
soon ໃນໄວໆນີ້ náu wái wái nêe
south ທິດໃຕ້ tit dâi
souvenir ຂອງທີ່ລະລຶກ kŏrng tì-là-léuk
speak ເວົ້າ wôw
spoon ບ່ວງ búang
stamp ສະແຕມ sá-dàam
stand-by ticket ປີ້ສຳລອງ bèe săm-lórng
stomach ທ້ອງ tôrng
stop ⓥ ຢຸດ yut
stop (bus) ⓝ ບອນຈອດລົດ born jort lot
street ຖະໜົນ tá-nŏn
student ນັກຮຽນ nak hée-an
sun ຕາເວັ້ນ đah wáirn
sunblock ຢາກັນແດດ yah gan dàat

151

supermarket ຮ້ານສັບພະສິນຄ້າ
háhn sáp-pá-sín-káh

surname ນາມສະກຸນ náhm sá-gun

sweet ຫວານ wǎhn

swim ⓥ ລອຍນ້ຳ lóy nâm

T

taxi ລົດແທັກຊີ້ lot taak-sée

telephone ໂທລະສັບ toh-là-sáp

television ໂທລະທັດ toh-la-tat

temperature (weather) ອຸນນະພູມ un-na-póom

tent ຕູບຜ້າ đóop pàh

that ⓐ ນັ້ນ nân

thirsty ຫິວນ້ຳ hěw nâm

this ⓐ ນີ້ nêe

ticket ປີ້ bêe

time ⓝ ເວລາ wáir-láh

tired ເໝື່ອຍ meu-ay

tissues ເຈ້ຍອະນາໄມ jêe-a á-nah-mái

today ມື້ນີ້ mêu nêe

toilet ຫ້ອງນ້ຳ hòrng nâm

tomorrow ມື້ອື່ນ mêu eun

tonight ຄືນນີ້ kéun nêe

toothache ເຈັບແຂ້ວ jép kâa-ou

toothbrush ແປງຖູແຂ້ວ baang tôo kâa-ou

toothpaste ຢາຖູແຂ້ວ yáh-tôo-kâa-ou

torch (flashlight) ໄຟສາຍ fái-sǎi

tour ⓝ&ⓥ ທ່ອງທ່ຽວ tórng tèe-o

tourist ນັກທ່ອງທ່ຽວ nak-tórng tèe-o

tourist office ຫ້ອງຂໍ້ມູນຂ່າວສານທ່ອງທ່ຽວ
hòrng kôr moon kow-sǎhn tórng tèe-o

towel ຜ້າເຊັດໂຕ pàh set đoh

town ເມືອງ méu-ang

translate ແປ baa

travel agency ບໍລິສັດຕົວແທນຈຳໜ່າຍບີ້ຍົນ
bor-li-sat đua táan jam-nai-bêe-nyón

travellers cheque ເຊັກທ່ອງທ່ຽວ
sèk-tórng tèe-o

trousers ສົ້ງຂາຍາວ sóng kǎh-nyów

twin beds ຕຽງຄູ່ đee-ang koo

tyre ຢາງລົດ yáhng lot

U

underwear ສົ້ງຊ້ອນ sóhng-sòrn

urgent ດ່ວນ duan

V

vacant ຫວ່າງ wǎhng

vacation ພັກງານ pak gahn

vegetable ⓝ&ⓐ ຜັກ pák

vegetarian ⓝ&ⓐ ຄົນກິນເຈ kón-gin jàir

visa ວິຊາ wi-sáh

W

waiter ເດັກເສິບ dék sèup

walk ⓝ&ⓥ ຍ່າງ nyahng

wallet ກະເປົາເງິນ gà-bao ngéun

warm ເນຍ ອົບອຸ່ນ óp-un

wash ລ້າງ lâhng

water ນ້ຳ nâm

weekend ມື້ພັກງານ mêu pak gahn

west ທິດຕາເວັນຕົກ tit đah-wén đok

wheelchair ລົດເຂັນ lot kén

when ເວລາໃດ wáir-láh dai

where ຢູ່ໃສ yoo sǎi

white ສີຂາວ sěe-kǒw

who ໃຜ pǎi

why ເປັນຫຍັງ ben nyǎng

wife ເມຍ mée-a

window ປ່ອງຢ້ຽມ borng èe-am

wine ເຫລົ້າວາຍ lôw-wái

with ກັບ gáp

without ປາສະຈາກ bah-sá-jàhk

woman ແມ່ຍິງ maa-nying

write ຂຽນ kěe-an

Y

yellow ສີເຫລືອງ sěe léu-ang

yes ແມ່ນ maan

yesterday ມື້ວານນີ້ mêu wáhn nêe

Thai

consonants

ก gor gài	ข kŏr kài	ค kor kwai	ฆ kor rá-kang	ง ngor ngoo	จ jor jahn
ฉ chŏr chìng	ช chor cháhng	ซ sor sôh	ฌ chor cheu	ญ yor yĭng	ฎ dor chá-dah
ฏ đor ঠà-đàk	ฐ tŏr tăhn	ฑ tor mon-toh	ฒ tor pôo tôw	ณ nor nen	ด dor dèk
ต đor đòw	ถ tŏr tŭng	ท tor tá-hăhn	ธ tor tong	น nor nŏo	บ bor bai mái
ป ঠor ঠlah	ผ pŏr pêung	ฝ fŏr făh	พ por pahn	ฟ for fan	ภ por săm-pow
ม mor máh	ย yor yák	ร ror reu-a	ล lor ling	ว wor wăan	ศ sŏr săh-lah
ษ sŏr reu-sĕe	ส sŏr sĕu-a	ห hŏr hèep	ฬ lor jù-lah	อ or ahng	ฮ hor nók hôok

vowels (the letter อ is used as the consonant base)

อะ a	อา ah	อิ i	อี ee	อึ eu	อื eu
อุ u	อู oo	เอะ e	เอ air	แอะ aa	แอ aa
โอะ o	โอ oh	เอาะ o	ออ or	อัวะ ua	อัว oo·a
เอียะ ee·a	เอีย ee·a	เอือะ eu·a	เอือ eu·a	เออะ eu	เออ eu
อำ am	ไอ ai	ใอ ai	เอา ow	อาย ai	อาว ow
อิว ew	แอว aa·ao	เอว e·ou	เอย er·i	อวย oo·ay	ออย oy
อัย ai	อุย oo·i	เอิ eu	เอียว ee·o	เอือย eu·ay	โอย oy
ไอย ai					

introduction

Cradled between Cambodia, Laos, Malaysia and Myanmar, the Kingdom of Thailand is something of a Tower of Babel, with numerous dialects spoken from north to south. What has come to be known as Standard Thai is actually the dialect spoken in Bangkok and the surrounding provinces. The number of native speakers of Thai is estimated to be between 25 and 37 million. Standard Thai is the official language of administration, education and the media, and most Thais understand it even if they speak another dialect. All words and phrases in this chapter are in Standard Thai as it will be understood throughout the country.

Thai belongs to the Tai language group, meaning that it's closely related to a number of languages spoken outside the borders of present-day Thailand. Some of these are Lao (Laos), Khampti (India) and Lue (China). It has borrowed a number of words from languages such as Mon (Myanmar) and Khmer (Cambodia). Ancient languages also continue to influence Thai. Just as English relied on Latin and ancient Greek for coining new words or formalising grammar rules, Thai has adopted Sanskrit and Pali as linguistic models. More recently, English has become a major influence, particularly in words related to technology or business.

The elegant characters of the Thai script are a source of fascination for those experiencing the language for the first time. The curved symbols seem to run together but they're all divisible into distinct alphabetical units. The consonants are classified into three categories depending on the kinds of vowels they're associated with. Vowels are indicated by symbols, or combinations of symbols, that may appear before, after or even around the consonant – there's no punctuation or spaces between words. The complete Thai alphabet is shown on the page opposite. The Thai government has instituted the Royal Thai General Transcription System (or RTGS) as a standard method of writing Thai using a 26-letter Roman alphabet. You'll notice its use in official documents, road signs and on maps.

While RTGS is convenient for writing it's not comprehensive enough to account for all sounds in Thai. In this book we've devised pronunciation guides based on how the language sounds when it's spoken – just follow the coloured pronunciation guides provided next to each phrase.

The details of the grammar system are beyond the scope of this book, but the basic rules are explained in simple terms. We hope it will encourage you to explore further and help you create your own sentences.

pronunciation

vowel sounds

For the Thai pronunciation guides we've used hyphens to separate syllables from each other – the word ang-grìt (meaning 'English') is made up of two distinct syllables: ang and grìt. In some words we've divided the diphthongs (ie vowel sound combinations) further with a dot (·) to help you separate vowel sounds and avoid mispronunciation – the word kĕe·an (write) is actually pronounced as one syllable with two separate vowel sounds. Accents above vowels (like à, é and ò) relate to the tones (see below).

symbol	english equivalent	thai example	symbol	english equivalent	thai example
a	run	bàt	i	bit	bìt
aa	bad	gàa	o	hot	bòt
ah	father	gah	oh	note	đoh
ai	aisle	jài	oo	moon	kôo
air	flair	wair-lah	or	for	pôr
e	bed	pen	aa-ou	aa followed by u	láa-ou
ee	see	bee	ow	cow	bow
eu	her	beu	oy	boy	soy
ew	new	néw	u	put	sùk

tones

Thai uses a system of carefully-pitched tones to make distinctions between words, so some vowels are pronounced at a high or low pitch while others swoop or glide in a sing-song manner. There are five distinct tones in Thai: mid, low, falling, high and rising. The accent marks above the vowel remind you which one to use. Note that the mid tone has no accent.

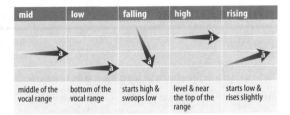

mid	low	falling	high	rising
a	à	â	á	ǎ
middle of the vocal range	bottom of the vocal range	starts high & swoops low	level & near the top of the range	starts low & rises slightly

consonant sounds

Watch out for the b̖ sound, which is halfway between a 'b' and a 'p', and the d̖ sound, which is halfway between a 'd' and a 't'.

symbol	english equivalent	thai example	symbol	english equivalent	thai example
b	**b**ig	bòr	l	**l**ike	ling
b̖	s**p**in	b̖lah	m	**m**at	máh
ch	**ch**art	chìng	n	**n**ut	nǒo
d	**d**og	dèk	ng	si**ng**	ngoo
d̖	s**t**op	d̖òw	p	**p**ush	pahn
f	**f**ull	fǎh	r	**r**at	reu·a
g	**g**et	gài	s	**s**it	sǎh-lah
h	**h**at	hèep	t	**t**ap	tów
j	**j**unk	jahn	w	**w**atch	wát
k	**k**ite	kài	y	**y**es	yàhk

phrasebuilder

be

The word ฿en เป็น (be) is used to join the subject (doer of an action) with a noun.

I'm a teacher.   ผม/ดิฉันเป็นครู   pŏm/dì-chăn ฿en kroo m/f
                                             (lit: I-m/f be teacher)

counters/classifiers

Thai nouns are the same in singular and plural. However, when counting things, you need to use an extra word which 'classifies' the noun. It always goes after the noun and the number. The box on page 172 lists some common classifiers.

four dogs   หมาสี่ตัว   măh sèe đoo-a
                                  (lit: dogs four đoo-a)

have

Possession is expressed by placing the word mee มี (have) before the object:

I have a bicycle.
ผม/ดิฉันมีรถจักรยาน   pŏm/dì-chăn mee rót-jàk-gà-yahn m/f
                          (lit: I-m/f have bicycle)

negatives

Any verb or adjective can be negated by placing the word mâi ไม่ (not) in front of it:

I don't have any cash.
ผม/ดิฉันไม่มีตางค์   pŏm/dì-chăn mâi mee đahng m/f
                        (lit: I-m/f not have cash)

pronouns

In Thai, there are different words for 'you' depending on the level of politeness. The pronouns 'I' and 'my' have different masculine and feminine forms, marked with m/f throughout this chapter. For a complete list of Thai pronouns, see the box on page 163.

THAI – phrasebuilder

158

questions

To form a yes/no question, place the word măi ไหม (no literal translation) at the end of a statement. To answer, just repeat the verb for 'yes' and add măi ไม่ (not) before the verb for 'no':

Do you want a beer?   เอาเบียร์ไหม   ow bee·a măi
                                                    (lit: want beer măi)

Yes/No.   เอา/ไม่เอา   ow/măi ow
                                                    (lit: want/not want)

requests

The word kŏr ขอ (roughly equivalent to 'please give me' or 'may I ask for') is used at the beginning of the sentence to make polite requests – often the word nòy หน่อย (a little) is added to the end of the sentence:

Can I have some rice?
ขอข้าวหน่อย   kŏr kôw nòy
                               (lit: please-give-me rice a-little)

verbs

Thai verbs don't change according to tense. You can specify the time by adding one of the following words: gam-lang กำลัง (no literal meaning) for a present action, ja จะ (will) for the future and láa-ou แล้ว (already) for the past. The first two words are used before the verb, and the third one comes at the end of a sentence.

I'm washing the clothes.   กำลังซักเสื้อผ้า   gam-lang sák sêu·a pâh
                                                        (lit: gam-lang wash clothes)

He/She will buy rice.   เขาจะซื้อข้าว   kŏw jà séu kôw
                                                        (lit: he/she will buy rice)

We've been to Bangkok.   เราไปกรุงเทพฯแล้ว   row bai grung têp láa-ou
                                                        (lit: we Bangkok go already)

phrasebuilder – ไทย

basics

language difficulties

Do you speak English?
พูดภาษาอังกฤษได้ไหม   pôot pah-săh ang-grìt dâi măi

Do you understand?
คุณเข้าใจไหม   kun kôw jai măi

I (don't) understand.
ผม/ดิฉัน (ไม่) เข้าใจ   pŏm/dì-chăn (mâi) kôw jai m/f

What does (à-nah-kót) mean?
(อนาคต) แปลว่าอะไร   (à-nah-kót) blaa wâh à-rai

How do you ...?	... อย่างไร	... yàhng rai
pronounce this	ออกเสียง	òrk sĕe·ang
write (Saraburi)	เขียน(สระบุรี)	kĕe·an (sà-rà-bù-ree)

Could you please ...?	... ได้ไหม	... dâi măi
repeat that	พูดอีกที	pôot èek tee
speak more slowly	พูดช้าๆ	pôot cháa cháa
write it down	เขียนลงให้	kĕe·an long hâi

essentials

Yes.	ใช่	châi
No.	ไม่	mâi
Please.	ขอ	kŏr
Thank you (very much).	ขอบคุณ(มากๆ)	kòrp kun (mâhk mâhk)
You're welcome.	ยินดี	yin dee
Excuse me.	ขอโทษ	kŏr tôht
Sorry.	ขอโทษ	kŏr tôht

numbers

0	ศูนย์	sŏon		17	สิบเจ็ด	sìp-jèt
1	หนึ่ง	nèung		18	สิบแปด	sìp-bàat
2	สอง	sŏrng		19	สิบเก้า	sìp-gôw
3	สาม	săhm		20	ยี่สิบ	yêe-sip
4	สี่	sèe		21	ยี่สิบเอ็ด	yêe-sìp-èt
5	ห้า	hâh		22	ยี่สิบสอง	yêe-sìp-sŏrng
6	หก	hòk		30	สามสิบ	săhm-sìp
7	เจ็ด	jèt		40	สี่สิบ	sèe-sìp
8	แปด	bàat		50	ห้าสิบ	hâh-sìp
9	เก้า	gôw		60	หกสิบ	hòk-sìp
10	สิบ	sìp		70	เจ็ดสิบ	jèt-sìp
11	สิบเอ็ด	sìp-èt		80	แปดสิบ	bàat-sìp
12	สิบสอง	sìp-sŏrng		90	เก้าสิบ	gôw-sìp
13	สิบสาม	sìp-săhm		100	หนึ่งร้อย	nèung róy
14	สิบสี่	sìp-sèe		1000	หนึ่งพัน	nèung pan
15	สิบห้า	sìp-hâh		10,000	หนึ่งหมื่น	nèung mèun
16	สิบหก	sìp-hòk		1,000,000	หนึ่งล้าน	nèung láhn

numerals									
0	1	2	3	4	5	6	7	8	9
๐	๑	๒	๓	๔	๕	๖	๗	๘	๙

time & dates

While the Western twelve-hour clock divides the day between two time periods (am and pm), the Thai system uses four periods. From midnight to 6am times begin with the word đee ตี (strike), from 6am until midday they end with the word chów เช้า (morning), from midday to 6pm they begin with the word bai บ่าย (afternoon) and from 6pm until midnight they end with the word tûm ทุ่ม (thump).

What time is it?	กี่โมงแล้ว	gèe mohng láa-ou
It's 3am.	ตีสาม	đee săhm
It's 6am.	หกโมงเช้า	hòk mohng chów
It's 2pm.	บ่ายสองโมง	bài sŏrng mohng
It's 9pm.	สามทุ่ม	săhm tûm

To give times after the hour, just add the number of minutes following the hour. To give times before the hour, add the number of minutes beforehand:

It's 4.30pm.

บ่ายสี่โมงครึ่ง   bài sèe mohng krêung

(lit: afternoon four hours half)

It's 4.15pm.

บ่ายสี่โมงสิบห้านาที   bài sèe mohng sìp-hâh nah-tee

(lit: afternoon four hours fifteen minutes)

It's 3.45pm.

อีกสิบห้านาทีบ่ายสี่โมง   èek sìp-hâh nah-tee bài sèe mohng

(lit: another fifteen minutes afternoon four hours)

Monday	วันจันทร์	wan jan
Tuesday	วันอังคาร	wan ang-kahn
Wednesday	วันพุธ	wan pút
Thursday	วันพฤหัสบดี	wan pá-réu-hàt
Friday	วันศุกร์	wan sùk
Saturday	วันเสาร์	wan sŏw
Sunday	วันอาทิตย์	wan ah-tít

January	เดือนมกราคม	deu·an má-gà-rah-kom
February	เดือนกุมภาพันธ์	deu·an gum-pah-pan
March	เดือนมีนาคม	deu·an mee-nah-kom
April	เดือนเมษายน	deu·an mair-săh-yon
May	เดือนพฤษภาคม	deu·an préut-sà-pah-kom
June	เดือนมิถุนายน	deu·an mí-tù-nah-yon
July	เดือนกรกฎาคม	deu·an gà-rák-gà-dah-kom
August	เดือนสิงหาคม	deu·an sĭng-hăh-kom
September	เดือนกันยายน	deu·an gan-yah-yon
October	เดือนตุลาคม	deu·an đù-lah-kom
November	เดือนพฤศจิกายน	deu·an préut-sà-ji-gah-yon
December	เดือนธันวาคม	deu·an tan-wah-kom

What date is it today?

วันนี้วันที่เท่าไร   wan née wan têe tôw-rai

It's (27 September).

วันที่(ยี่สิบเจ็ด   wan têe (yêe-sìp-jèt

เดือนกันยายน)   deu·an gan-yah-yŏn)

yesterday ...	... เมื่อวาน	... mêu·a wahn
tomorrow ...	พรุ่งนี้ ...	prûng née ...
morning	เช้า	chów
afternoon	บ่าย	bài
evening	เย็น	yen
last ...	... ที่แล้ว	... tee láa·ou
next ...	... หน้า	... nâh
week	อาทิตย์	ah-tít
month	เดือน	deu·an
year	ปี	bee
last night	เมื่อคืนนี้	mêu·a keun née
since (May)	ตั้งแต่(พฤษภาคม)	đâng đàa (préut-sà-pah-kom)
until (June)	จนถึง(มิถุนายน)	jon tĕung (mí-tù-nah-yon)

personal & possessive pronouns		
I m/f	ผม/ดิฉัน	pŏm/dì-chăn **m/f**
I m&f (neutral)	ฉัน	chăn
you sg inf	เธอ	teu
you sg pol	คุณ	kun
he/she	เขา	kŏw
it	มัน	man
we	เรา	row
you pl	คุณ	kun
they	เขา	kŏw
my m/f	ของผม/ดิฉัน	kŏrng pŏm/dì-chăn **m/f**
your sg	ของคุณ	kŏrng kun
his/her	ของเขา	kŏrng kŏw
our	ของเรา	kŏrng row
your pl	ของคุณ	kŏrng kun
their	ของเขา	kŏrng kŏw

weather

What's the weather like?

อากาศเป็นอย่างไร		ah-gàht ben yàhng rai

It's ...	มัน ...	man ...
cold	หนาว	nŏw
(very) hot	ร้อน (มาก)	rórn (mâhk)
rainy	มีฝน	mee fŏn
windy	มีลม	mee lom

spring	หน้าใบไม้ผลิ	nâh bai mái plì
summer	หน้าร้อน	nâh rórn
autumn	หน้าใบไม้ร่วง	nâh bai mái rôo·ang
winter	หน้าหนาว	nâh nŏw

cool season	หน้าหนาว	nâh nŏw
dry season	หน้าแล้ง	nâh láang
hot season	หน้าร้อน	nâh rórn
rainy season	หน้าฝน	nâh fŏn

border crossing

I'm ...	ผม/ดิฉัน ...	pŏm/dì-chăn ... m/f
in transit	เดินทางผ่าน	deun tahng pàhn
on business	มาธุระ	mah tú-rá
on holiday	มาพักผ่อน	mah pák pòrn

I'm here for ...	ผม/ดิฉัน มาพักที่นี่ ...	pŏm/dì-chăn mah pák têe née ... m/f
(10) days	(สิบ) วัน	(sìp) wan
(two) months	(สอง) เดือน	(sŏrng) deu·an
(three) weeks	(สาม) อาทิตย์	(săhm) ah-tít

I'm going to (Ayutthaya).

ผม/ดิฉันกำลังไป(อยุธยา)	pŏm/dì-chăn gam-lang bai (à-yút-tá-yah) m/f

I'm staying at the (Bik Hotel).

พักอยู่ที่(โรงแรมบิ๊ก)	pák yòo têe (rohng raam bík)

I have nothing to declare.

ไม่มีอะไรที่จะแจ้ง	mâi mee à-rai têe jà jâang

I have something to declare.
มีอะไรที่จะต้องแจ้ง   mee à-rai têe jà đôrng jâang

That's (not) mine.
นั่น (ไม่ใช่) ของผม/ดิฉัน   nân (mâi châi) kŏrng pŏm/dì-chăn **m/f**

I didn't know I had to declare it.
ไม่รู้ว่าต้องแจ้งอันนี้ด้วย   mâi róo wâh đôrng jâang an née dôo·ay

transport

tickets & luggage

Where can I buy a ticket?
ต้องซื้อตั๋วที่ไหน   đôrng séu đŏo·a têe năi

Do I need to book?
ต้องจองล่วงหน้าหรือเปล่า   đôrng jorng lôo·ang nâh rĕu Ъlòw

One ... ticket to (Chiang Mai), please.	ขอตั๋ว ...ไป (เชียงใหม่)	kŏr đŏo·a ...Ъai (chee·ang mài)
one-way	เที่ยวเดียว	têe·o dee·o
return	ไปกลับ	Ъai glàp

I'd like to ... my ticket, please.	ผม/ดิฉันอยาก จะขอ ... ตั๋ว	pŏm/dì-chăn yàhk jà kŏr ... đŏo·a **m/f**
cancel	ยกเลิก	yók lêuk
change	เปลี่ยน	Ъlèe·an
confirm	ยืนยัน	yeun yan

I'd like a ... seat, please.	ต้องการที่นั่ง ...	đôrng gahn têe nâng ...
nonsmoking	ในเขตห้ามสูบบุหรี่	nai kèt hâhm sòop bù-rèe
smoking	ในเขตสูบบุหรี่ได้	nai kèt sòop bù-rèe dâi

How much is it?
ราคาเท่าไร   rah-kah tôw-rai

Is there air conditioning?
มีแอร์ไหม   mee aa măi

Is there a toilet?
มีส้วมไหม   mee sôo·am măi

How long does the trip take?

การเดินทางใช้เว   gahn deun tahng chái wair-lah
ลานานเท่าไร   nahn tôw-rai

Is it a direct route?

เป็นทางตรงไหม   ben tahng drong măi

Where can I find a luggage locker?

จะหาตู้ฝากกระเป๋าได้ที่ไหน   jà hăh đôo fàhk grà-bŏw dâi têe năi

My luggage	กระเป๋าของ	grà-bŏw kŏrng
has been ...	ผม/ดิฉันโดน ... แล้ว	pŏm/dì-chăn dohn ... láa-ou m/f
damaged	เสียหาย	sĕe-a hăi
lost	หายไป	hăi bai
stolen	ขโมย	kà-moy

getting around

Where does flight (TG 132) arrive/depart?

เที่ยวบิน(ทีจีหนึ่งสามสอง)   têe-o bin (tee jee nèung săhm sŏrng)
เข้า/ออกที่ไหน   kôw/òrk têe năi

Where's (the) ...?	... อยู่ที่ไหน	... yòo têe năi
arrivals hall	เที่ยวบินขาเข้า	têe-o bin kăh kôw
departures hall	เที่ยวบินขาออก	têe-o bin kăh òrk
duty-free shop	ที่ขายของปลอดภาษี	têe kăi kŏrng blòrt pah-sĕe
gate (12)	ประตูที่ (สิบสอง)	bra-đoo têe (sìp-sŏrng)

Is this the ... to	อันนี้เป็น ...ไป	an née ben ... bai
(Chiang Mai)?	(เชียงใหม่) ใช่ไหม	(chee-ang mài) châi măi
boat	เรือ	reu-a
bus	รถเมล์	rót mair
plane	เครื่องบิน	krêu-ang bin
train	รถไฟ	rót fai

When's the ...	รถเมล์คัน ...	rót mair kan ...
bus?	มาเมื่อไร	mah mêu-a rai
first	แรก	râak
last	สุดท้าย	sùt tái
next	ต่อไป	đòr bai

What time does it leave?
ออกกี่โมง
òrk gèe mohng

How long will it be delayed?
จะเสียเวลานานเท่าไร
jà sĕe·a wair·lah nahn tôw·rai

What station is this?
ที่นี่สถานีไหน
têe née sà·tăh·nee năi

What's the next stop?
ที่จอดต่อไปคือที่ไหน
têe jòrt đòr pai keu têe năi

Does it stop at (Saraburi)?
รถจอดที่(สระบุรี)ไหม
rót jòrt têe (sà·rà·bù·ree) măi

Please tell me when we get to (Chiang Mai).
เมื่อถึง(เชียงใหม่)
กรุณาบอกด้วย
mêu·a tĕung (chee·ang mài)
gà·rú·nah bòrk dôo·ay

How long do we stop here?
เราจะหยุดที่นี่นานเท่าไร
row jà yùt têe née nahn tôw·rai

Is this seat available?
ครับ/ค่ะ ที่นั่งนี้ว่างไหม
kráp/kâ têe nâng née wâhng măi m/f

I'd like a taxi ...
ต้องการรถแท็กซี่ ...
đôrng gahn rót táak·sêe ...
  at (9am)
เมื่อ(สามโมงเช้า)
mêu·a (săhm mohng chów)
  now
เดี๋ยวนี้
dĕe·o née
  tomorrow
พรุ่งนี้
prûng née

Is this ... available?
... อันนี้ว่างหรือเปล่า
... an née wâhng rĕu blòw
  bicycle-rickshaw
สามล้อ
săhm lór
  motorcycle-taxi
ตุ๊กๆ
đúk đúk
  taxi
รถแท็กซี่
rót táak·sêe

How much is it to ...?
ไป ... เท่าไร
pai ... tôw·rai

Please put the meter on.
ขอเปิดมิเตอร์ด้วย
kŏr bèut mí·đeu dôo·ay

Please take me to (this address).
ขอพาไป(ที่นี่)
kŏr pah bai (têe née)

Please slow down.
ขอให้ช้าลง
kŏr hâi cháh long
Please stop here.
ขอหยุดตรงนี้
kŏr yùt đrong née
Please wait here.
ขอคอยอยู่ที่นี่
kŏr koy yòo têe née

car, motorbike & bicycle hire

I'd like to hire a bicycle.
ต้องการเช่ารถจักรยาน · đôrng gahn chôw rót jàk-gà-yahn

I'd like to hire a ...	อยากจะเช่า ...	yàhk jà chôw ...
car	รถเก๋ง	rót gěng
motorbike	รถมอเตอร์ไซค์	rót mor-đeu-sai

with ...	กับ ...	gàp ...
air conditioning	แอร์	aa
a driver	คนขับ	kon kàp

How much for	ค่าเช่า...	kâh chôw ...
... hire?	ละเท่าไร	lá tôw-rai
hourly	ชั่วโมง	chôo·a mohng
daily	วัน	wan
weekly	อาทิตย์	ah-tít

I need a mechanic.	ต้องการช่างรถ	đôrng gahn châhng rót
I've run out of petrol.	หมดน้ำมัน	mòt nám man
I have a flat tyre.	ยางแบน	yahng baan

air	ลม	lom
oil	น้ำมันเครื่อง	nám man krêu·ang
petrol	เบนซิน	ben-sin
tyre	ยางรถ	yahng rót

directions

Where's a/the ...?	... อยู่ที่ไหน	... yòo têe năi
bank	ธนาคาร	tá-nah-kahn
city centre	ใจกลางเมือง	jai glahng meu·ang
hotel	โรงแรม	rohng raam
market	ตลาด	đà-làht
police station	สถานีตำรวจ	sà-tăh-nee đam-ròo·at
post office	ที่ทำการไปรษณีย์	têe tam gahn brai-sà-nee
public toilet	สุขาสาธารณะ	sù-kăh săh-tah-rá-ná
tourist office	สำนักงานท่องเที่ยว	săm-nák ngahn tôrng têe·o

Is this the road to (Ban Bung Wai)?

ทางนี้ไป(บ้านบุ่งหวาย)ไหม   tahng née bai (bâhn bùng wăi) măi

Can you show me (on the map)?

ให้ดู(ในแผนที่)ได้ไหม   hâi doo (nai păan têe) dâi măi

What's the address?

ที่อยู่คืออะไร   têe yòo keu à-rai

How far is it?

อยู่ไกลเท่าไร   yòo glai tôw-rai

How do I get there?

ไปทางไหน   bai tahng năi

It's ...	อยู่ ...	yòo ...
across from ...	เยื้อง ...	yéu·ang ...
behind ...	ที่หลัง ...	têe lăng ...
far	ไกล	glai
here	ที่นี่	têe née
in front of ...	ตรงหน้า ...	drong nâh ...
left	ซ้าย	sái
near	ใกล้ๆ ...	glâi glâi ...
next to ...	ข้างๆ ...	kâhng kâhng ...
opposite ...	ตรงกันข้าม ...	drong gan kâhm ...
right	ขวา	kwăh
straight ahead	ตรงไป	drong bai
there	ที่นั่น	têe nán

Turn ...	เลี้ยว ...	lée·o ...
at the corner	ตรงหัวมุม	drong hŏo·a mum
at the traffic lights	ตรงไฟจราจร	drong fai jà-rah-jorn
left/right	ซ้าย/ขวา	sái/kwăh

by bus	โดยรถเมล์	doy rót mair
by taxi	โดยแท็กซี่	doy táak-sêe
by train	โดยรถไฟ	doy rót fai
on foot	เดินไป	deun bai

north	ทิศเหนือ	tít nĕu·a
south	ทิศใต้	tít đâi
east	ทิศตะวันออก	tít đà-wan òrk
west	ทิศตะวันตก	tít đà-wan đòk

ทางเข้า/ทางออก	tahng kôw/tahng òrk	**Entrance/Exit**
เปิด/ปิดแล้ว	bèut/bìt láa·ou	**Open/Closed**
มีห้องว่าง	mee hôrng wâhng	**Vacancies**
ไม่มีห้องว่าง	mâi mee hôrng wâhng	**No Vacancies**
สอบถาม	sòrp tăhm	**Information**
สถานีตำรวจ	sà-tăh-nee đam-ròo·at	**Police Station**
ห้าม	hâhm	**Prohibited**
ส้วม	sôo·am	**Toilets**
ชาย/หญิง	chai/yĭng	**Men/Women**
ร้อน/เย็น	rórn/yen	**Hot/Cold**

accommodation

finding accommodation

Where's a ...?	... อยู่ที่ไหน	... yòo têe năi
bungalow	บังกะโล	bang-gà-loh
camping ground	ค่ายพักแรม	kâi pák raam
guesthouse	บ้านพัก	bâhn pák
hotel	โรงแรม	rohng raam

Can you recommend	แนะนำที่...	náa nam têe ...
somewhere ...?	ได้ไหม	dâi măi
cheap	ราคาถูก	rah-kah tòok
good	ดีๆ	dee dee
nearby	ใกล้ๆ	glâi glâi
romantic	โรแมนติก	roh-maan-đĭk

I'd like to book a room, please.
ขอจองห้องหน่อย kŏr jorng hôrng nòy

I have a reservation.
จองห้องมาแล้ว jorng hôrng mah láa·ou

My name is ...
ชื่อ... chêu ...

Do you have a ... room?	มีห้อง ... ไหม	mee hôrng ... mǎi
single	เดี่ยว	dèe·o
double	เตียงคู่	đee·ang kôo
twin	สองเตียง	sǒrng đee·ang

How much is it per ...?	... ละเท่าไร	... lá tôw-rai
night	คืน	keun
person	คน	kon

Can I pay ...?	จ่ายเป็น... ได้ไหม	jài ben ... dâi mǎi
by credit card	บัตรเครดิต	bàt krair-dìt
with a travellers cheque	เช็คเดินทาง	chék deun tahng

For (three) nights/weeks.
เป็นเวลา(สาม) คืน/อาทิตย์   ben wair-lah (sǎhm) keun/ah-tít

From (July 2) to (July 6).
จากวันที่(สองกรกฎาคม)   jàhk wan têe (sǒrng gà-rák-gà-dah-kom)
ถึงวันที่(หกกรกฎาคม)   těung wan têe (hòk gà-rák-gà-dah-kom)

Can I see it?
ดูได้ไหม   doo dâi mǎi

Can I camp here?
พักแรมที่นี่ได้ไหม   pák raam têe née dâi mǎi

Is there a camp site nearby?
มีที่ปักเตนต์อยู่แถวนี้ไหม   mee têe bàk đen yòo tǎa·ou née mǎi

requests & queries

When's breakfast served?
อาหารเช้าจัดกี่โมง   ah-hǎhn chów jàt gèe mohng

Where's breakfast served?
อาหารเช้าจัดที่ไหน   ah-hǎhn chów jàt têe nǎi

Please wake me at (seven).
กรุณาปลุกให้เวลา   gà-rú-nah blùk hâi wair-lah
(เจ็ด) นาฬิกา   (jèt) nah-lí-gah

Could I have my key, please?
ขอกุญแจห้องหน่อย   kǒr gun-jaa hôrng nòy

Do you have a ...?	มี ... ไหม	mee ... măi
mosquito net	มุ้ง	múng
safe	ตู้เซฟ	đôo-sép

It's too ...	... เกินไป	... geun bai
expensive	แพง	paang
noisy	เสียงดัง	sĕe·ang dang
small	เล็ก	lék

The ... doesn't work.	... เสีย	... sĕe·a
air conditioner	แอร์	aa
fan	พัดลม	pát lom
toilet	ส้วม	sôo·am

This ... isn't clean.	... นี้ไม่สะอาด	... née mâi sà·àht
pillow	หมอนใบ	mŏrn bai
sheet	ผ้าปูนอน	pâh boo norn
towel	ผ้าเช็ดตัว	pâh chét đoo·a

checking out

What time is checkout?
ต้องออกห้องกี่โมง
đôrng òrk hôrng gèe mohng

Can I leave my luggage here?
ฝากกระเป๋าไว้ที่นี่ได้ไหม
fàhk grà·bŏw wái têe née dâi măi

Could I have my ..., please?	ขอ ... หน่อย	kŏr ... nòy
deposit	เงินมัดจำ	ngeun mát jam
passport	หนังสือเดินทาง	năng-sĕu deun tahng
valuables	ของมีค่า	kŏrng mee kâh

classifiers					
animals, clothes	ตัว	đoo·a	plates of food	จาน	jahn
glasses (of water etc)	แก้ว	gâa·ou	small objects	อัน	an
letters, newspapers	ฉบับ	chà·bàp	vehicles	คัน	kan

communications & banking

the internet

Where's the local Internet café?
ที่ไหนร้านอินเตอร์เนต   têe năi ráhn in-đeu-nét
ที่ใกล้เคียง   têe glâi kee·ang

How much is it per hour?
คิดชั่วโมงละเท่าไร   kít chôo·a mohng lá tôw-rai

I'd like to ...	อยากจะ ...	yàhk jà ...
check my email	ตรวจอีเมล	đròo·at ee-mairn
get Internet access	ติดต่อทาง	đit đòr tahng
	อินเตอร์เนต	in-đeu-nét
use a printer	ใช้เครื่องพิมพ์	chái krêu·ang pim
use a scanner	ใช้เครื่องสแกน	chái krêu·ang sà-gaan

mobile/cell phone

I'd like a mobile/cell phone for hire.
ต้องการเช่าโทรศัพท์มือถือ   đôrng gahn chôw toh-rá-sàp meu tĕu

I'd like a SIM card.
ต้องการบัตรซิม   đôrng gahn bàt sim

What are the rates?
อัตราการใช้เท่าไร   àt-đrah gahn chái tôw-rai

telephone

What's your phone number?
เบอร์โทรของคุณคืออะไร   beu toh kŏrng kun keu à-rai

The number is ...
เบอร์ก็คือ ...   beu gôr keu ...

Where's the nearest public phone?
ตู้โทรศัพท์ที่ใกล้เคียงอยู่ที่ไหน   đôo toh-rá-sàp têe glâi kee·ang yòo têe năi

I'd like to buy a phonecard.
อยากจะซื้อบัตรโทรศัพท์   yàhk jà séu bàt toh-rá-sàp

I want to ...	อยากจะ ...	yàhk jà ...
call (Singapore)	โทรไปประเทศ (สิงคโปร์)	toh bai brà-têt (sǐng-ká-boh)
make a local call	โทรภายใน จังหวัดเดียวกัน	toh pai nai jang-wàt dee-o gan
reverse the charges	โทรเก็บปลายทาง	toh gèp blai tahng
How much does ... cost?	... คิดเงินเท่าไร	... kít ngeun tôw-rai
a (three)-minute call	โทร (สาม) นาที	toh (sǎhm) nah-tee
each extra minute	ทุกนาทีต่อไป	túk nah-tee đòr bai
(3 baht) per (minute).	(สามบาท)	(sǎhm bàht)
	ต่อหนึ่ง (นาที)	đòr nèung (nah-tee)

post office

I want to send a ...	ผม/ดิฉันอยาก จะส่ง ...	pǒm/dì-chăn yàhk jà sòng ... m/f
fax	แฟกซ์	fàak
letter	จดหมาย	jòt-mǎi
parcel	พัสดุ	pát-sà-dù
postcard	ไปรษณียบัตร	brai-sà-nee-yá-bàt
I want to buy a/an ...	ผม/ดิฉันอยาก จะซื้อ ...	pǒm/dì-chăn yàhk jà séu ... m/f
envelope	ซองจดหมาย	sorng jòt-mǎi
stamp	แสตมป์	sà-đaam

express mail	ไปรษณีย์ด่วน	brai-sà-nee dòo·an
registered mail	ลงทะเบียน	long tá-bee·an
sea mail	ไปรษณีย์ทางทะเล	brai-sà-nee tahng tá-lair

Please send it by airmail to (Australia).

ขอส่งทางอากาศไปประเทศ (ออสเตรเลีย)	kǒr sòng tahng ah-gàht bai brà-têt (or-sà-đrair-lee·a)

Is there any mail for me?

มีจดหมายสำหรับผม/ดิฉัน ด้วยไหม	mee jòt-mǎi sǎm-ràp pǒm/dì-chăn dôo·ay mǎi m/f

bank

Where's a/an ...?	... อยู่ที่ไหน	... yòo têe nǎi
automated teller machine	ตู้เอทีเอ็ม	đôo air-tee-em
foreign exchange office	ที่แลกเงินต่างประเทศ	têe lâak ngeun đàhng brà-têt
I'd like to ...	อยากจะ...	yàhk jà ...
Where can I ...?	... ได้ที่ไหน	... dâi têe nǎi
arrange a transfer	โอนเงิน	ohn ngeun
cash a cheque	ขึ้นเช็ค	kêun chék
change money	แลกเงิน	lâak ngeun
change a travellers cheque	แลกเช็คเดินทาง	lâak chék deun tahng
get a cash advance	รูดเงินจากบัตรเครดิต	rôot ngeun jàhk bàt krair-dìt
withdraw money	ถอนเงิน	tǒrn ngeun
What's the ...?	... เท่าไร	... tôw-rai
charge for that	ค่าธรรมเนียม	kâh tam-nee-am
exchange rate	อัตราแลกเปลี่ยน	àt-đrah lâak blèe-an
It's ...		
(12) baht	(สิบสอง) บาท	(sìp sǒrng) baht
free	ไม่มีค่าธรรมเนียม	mâi mee kâh tam-nee-am

What time does the bank open?
ธนาคารเปิดกี่โมง

tá-nah-kahn bèut gèe mohng

Has my money arrived yet?
เงินของผม/ดิฉัน
มาถึงหรือยัง

ngeun kǒrng pǒm/dì-chǎn
mah těung rěu yang m/f

sightseeing

getting in

What time does it open/close?
เปิด/ปิดกี่โมง
bèut/bìt gèe mohng

What's the admission charge?
ค่าเข้าเท่าไร
kâh kôw tôw-rai

Is there a discount for …?	ลดราคาสำหรับ … ไหม	lót rah-kah săm-ràp … măi
children	เด็ก	dèk
students	นักศึกษา	nák sèuk-săh

I'd like a …	ผม/ดิฉันต้องการ …	pŏm/dì-chăn đôrng gahn m/f
catalogue	คู่มือแนะนำ	kôo meu náa nam
guide	ไกด์	gai
local map	แผนที่ท้องถิ่น	păan têe tórng tìn

I'd like to see …
ผม/ดิฉันอยากจะดู …
pŏm/dì-chăn yàhk jà doo … m/f

What's that?
นั่นคืออะไร
nân keu à-rai

Can we take photos?
ถ่ายรูปได้ไหม
tài rôop dâi măi

tours

When's the next …?	… ต่อไปออกกี่โมง	… đòr bai òrk gèe mohng
boat trip	เที่ยวเรือ	têe-o reu-a
day trip	เที่ยวรายวัน	têe-o rai wan
tour	ทัวร์	too-a

Is (the) … included?	รวม … ด้วยไหม	roo-am … dôo-ay măi
accommodation	ค่าพัก	kâh pák
admission charge	ค่าเข้า	kâh kôw
food	ค่าอาหาร	kâh ah-hăhn
transport	ค่าขนส่ง	kâh kŏn sòng

How long is the tour?

การเที่ยวใช้เวลานานเท่าไร   gahn têe-o chái wair-lah nahn tôw-rai

What time should we be back?

ควรจะกลับมากี่โมง   koo-an jà glàp mah gèe mohng

city centre	ใจกลางเมือง	jai glahng meu-ang
market	ตลาด	đà-làht
monument	อนุสาวรีย์	à-nú-sǎh-wá-ree
museum	พิพิธภัณฑ์	pí-pít-tá-pan
palace	วัง	wang
ruins	ซากโบราณสถาน	sâhk boh-rahn-ná sà-tǎhn
statue	รูปปั้น	rôop bân
shrine	แท่นพระะ	tâan prá
temple	วัด	wát

shopping

enquiries

Where's a ... ?	... อยู่ที่ไหน	... yòo têe nǎi
bank	ธนาคาร	tá-nah-kahn
bookshop	ร้านขายหนังสือ	ráhn kǎi nǎng-sěu
camera shop	ร้านขายกล้อง	ráhn kǎi glôrng
	ถ่ายรูป	tài rôop
department store	ห้างสรรพสินค้า	hâhng sàp-pá-sǐn-káh
(floating) market	ตลาด(น้ำ)	đà-làht (nám)
newsagency	ร้านขายหนังสือพิมพ์	ráhn kǎi nǎng-sěu pim
supermarket	ซูเปอร์มาร์เก็ต	soo-ъeu-mah-gèt

---

male & female

In Thai, the pronoun 'I' changes depending on the gender of the speaker – so a man will refer to himself as pǒm ผม while a woman will refer to herself as dì-chǎn ดิฉัน. The two forms are marked as m/f throughout this chapter. Thai also has a neutral form of 'I' (ie used by both men and women) – chǎn ฉัน. When being polite to others, it's customary to add the word kráp ครับ (if you're a man) or kâ ค่ะ (if you're a woman) as a kind of a 'softener' to the end of questions and statements.

Where can I buy (a padlock)?
จะซื้อ(แม่กุญแจ) ได้ที่ไหน   jà séu (mâa gun·jaa) dâi têe nǎi

I'd like to buy …
อยากจะซื้อ …   yàhk jà séu …

Can I look at it?
ขอดูหน่อย   kŏr doo nòy

Do you have any others?
มีอีกไหม   mee èek mǎi

Does it have a guarantee?
มีรับประกันด้วยไหม   mee ráp bràgan dôo·ay mǎi

Can I have it sent overseas?
จะส่งเมืองนอกให้ได้ไหม   jà sòng meu·ang nôrk hâi dâi mǎi

Can I have my … repaired here?
ที่นี่ซ่อม … ได้ไหม   têe née sôrm … dâi mǎi

It's faulty.
มันบกพร่อง   man bòk prôrng

I'd like (a) …, please.   อยากจะ… ครับ/ค่ะ   yàhk jà … kráp/kâ m/f
  bag   ถุง   tǔng
  refund   ได้เงินคืน   dâi ngeun keun
  to return this   เอามาคืน   ow mah keun

paying

How much is it?
เท่าไรครับ/คะ   tôw·rai kráp/ká m/f

Can you write down the price?
เขียนราคาให้หน่อยได้ไหม   kěe·an rah·kah hâi nòy dâi mǎi

That's too expensive.
แพงไป   paang bai

What's your lowest price?
เท่าไรราคาต่ำสุด   tôw·rai rah·kah đàm sùt

I'll give you (five baht).
จะให้(ห้าบาท)   jà hâi (hâh bàht)

There's a mistake in the bill.
บิลใบนี้ผิดนะครับ/ค่ะ   bin bai née pìt ná kráp/kâ m/f

Do you accept ...?	รับ ... ไหม	ráp ... măi
credit cards	บัตรเครดิต	bàt krair-dìt
debit cards	บัตรธนาคาร	bàt tá-nah-kahn
travellers cheques	เช็คเดินทาง	chék deun tahng
I'd like ..., please.	ขอ ... หน่อย	kŏr ... nòy
my change	เงินทอน	ngeun torn
a receipt	ใบเสร็จ	bai sèt

clothes & shoes

Can I try it on?
ลองใส่ได้ไหม — lorng sài dâi măi

My size is (42).
ฉันใช้ขนาด (เบอร์สี่สิบสอง) — chăn chái kà-nàht (beu sèe sip sŏrng)

It doesn't fit.
ไม่ถูกขนาด — mâi tòok kà-nàht

small	เล็ก	lék
medium	กลาง	glahng
large	ใหญ่	yài

books & music

I'd like a ...	ต้องการ ...	dôrng gahn ...
newspaper	หนังสือพิมพ์	năng-sĕu pim
(in English)	(ภาษาอังกฤษ)	(pah-săh ang-grìt)
pen	ปากกา	pàhk-gah

Is there an English-language bookshop?
มีร้านขายหนังสือภาษา — mee ráhn kăi năng-sĕu pah-săh
อังกฤษไหม — ang-grìt măi

I'm looking for something by (Carabao).
กำลังหาชุดเพลง — gam-lang hăh chút pleng
(วงคาราบาว) — (wong kah-rah-bow)

Can I listen to this?
ฟังได้ไหม — fang dâi măi

photography

Can you ...?	... ได้ไหม	... dâi măi
burn a CD from	อัดซีดีจาก	àt see-dee jàhk
my memory card	หน่วยเมมโมรี่	mem-moh-rêe
develop this film	ล้างฟิล์มนี้	láhng fim née
load my film	ใส่ฟิล์มให้	sài fim hâi

| When will it be ready? | จะเสร็จเมื่อไร | jà sèt mêu·a-rai |

I need a ... film	ต้องการฟิล์ม ...	dôrng gahn fim ...
for this camera.	สำหรับกล้องนี้	săm-ràp glôrng née
APS	เอพีเอ็ส	air-pee-ét
B&W	ขาวดำ	kŏw dam
colour	สี	sĕe
slide	สไลด์	sà-lai
(200) speed	มีความไว	mee kwahm wai
	(สองร้อย)	(sŏrng róy)

toiletries

conditioner	ยานวดผม	yah nôo·at pŏm
condoms	ถุงยางอนามัย	tŭng yahng à-nah-mai
deodorant	ยาดับกลิ่นตัว	yah dàp glìn đoo·a
insect repellent	ยากันแมลง	yah gan má-laang
moisturiser	น้ำยาบำรุง	nám yah bam-rung
	ความชื้น	kwahm chéun
razor blades	ใบมีดโกน	bai mêet gohn
sanitary napkins	ผ้าอนามัย	pâh à-nah-mai
shampoo	น้ำยาสระผม	nám yah sà pŏm
shaving cream	ครีมโกนหนวด	kreem gohn nòo·at
soap	สบู่	sà-bòo
sunscreen	ครีมกันแดด	kreem gan dàat
tampons	แทมพอน	taam-porn
toilet paper	กระดาษห้องน้ำ	grà-dàht hôrng nám
toothbrush	แปรงสีฟัน	ɓraang sĕe fan
toothpaste	ยาสีฟัน	yah sĕe fan

meeting people

greetings, goodbyes & introductions

Hello.	สวัสดี	sà-wàt-dee
Hi.	หวัสดี	wàt-dee
Goodbye.	ลาก่อน	lah gòrn
Good night.	ราตรีสวัสดิ์	rah-đree sà-wàt
Mr	นาย	nai
Mrs/Ms	นาง	nahng
Miss	นางสาว	nahng sŏw

How are you?
สบายดีไหม — sà-bai dee măi

Fine. And you?
สบายดีครับ/ค่ะ — sà-bai dee kráp/kâ
แล้วคุณล่ะ — láa·ou kun lâ m/f

What's your name?
คุณชื่ออะไร — kun chêu à-rai

My name is ...
ผม/ดิฉันชื่อ ... — pŏm/dì-chăn chêu ... m/f

I'm pleased to meet you.
ยินดีที่ได้รู้จัก — yin-dee têe dâi róo jàk

This is my ...	นี่คือ ... ของผม/ดิฉัน	nêe keu ... kŏrng pŏm/dì-chăn m/f
brother (older)	พี่ชาย	pêe chai
brother (younger)	น้องชาย	nórng chai
daughter	ลูกสาว	lôok sŏw
father	บิดา/พ่อ	bì-dah/pôr pol/inf
friend	เพื่อน	pêu·an
husband	ผัว	pŏo·a
mother	มารดา/แม่	mahn-dah/mâa pol/inf
partner (intimate)	แฟน	faan
sister (older)	พี่สาว	pêe sŏw
sister (younger)	น้องสาว	nórng sŏw
son	ลูกชาย	lôok chai
wife	เมีย	mee·a

Here's my ...	นี่คือ ... ของผม/ดิฉัน	nêe keu ... kŏrng pŏm/dì-chăn **m/f**
What's your ...?	... ของคุณคืออะไร	... kŏrng kun keu à-ra
address	ที่อยู่	têe yòo
email address	ที่อยู่อีเมล	têe yòo ee-men
mobile number	เบอร์มือถือ	beu meu tĕu
phone number	เบอร์	beu

occupations

What's your occupation?	คุณมีอาชีพอะไร	kun mee ah-chêep à-rai
I'm a/an ...	ฉันเป็น ...	chăn ben ...
nurse	บุรุษพยาบาล/ นางพยาบาล	bù-rùt pá-yah-bahn/ nahng pá-yah-bahn **m/f**
office worker	พนักงานสำนักงาน	pá-nák ngahn săm-nák ngahn
student	นักศึกษา	nák sèuk-săh
teacher	ครู	kroo
tradesperson	ช่าง	châhng
writer	นักเขียน	nák kĕe-an

background

Where are you from?	คุณมาจากไหน	kun mah jàhk năi
I'm from ...	ผม/ดิฉันมาจาก ประเทศ ...	pŏm/dì-chăn mah jàhk brà-têt ... **m/f**
Australia	ออสเตรเลีย	or-sà-đrair-lee-a
Canada	แคนาดา	kaa-nah-dah
England	อังกฤษ	ang-grìt
Ireland	ไอร์แลนด์	ai-laan
New Zealand	นิวซีแลนด์	new see-laan
the USA	สหรัฐอเมริกา	sà-hà-rát à-mair-rí-gah
Are you married?	คุณแต่งงานหรือยัง	kun đaang ngahn rĕu yang
I'm ...	ผม/ดิฉัน ...	pŏm/dì-chăn ... **m/f**
married	แต่งงานแล้ว	đaang ngahn láa-ou
single	เป็นโสดอยู่	ben sòht yòo

age

How old ...?	... อายุเท่าไร	... ah-yú tôw-rai
are you	คุณ	kun
is your daughter	ลูกสาวของคุณ	lôok sŏw kŏrng kun
is your son	ลูกชายของคุณ	lôok chai kŏrng kun

| I'm ... years old. | ฉันอายุ ... ปี | chăn ah-yú ... bee |
| He/She is ... years old. | เขาอายุ ... ปี | kŏw ah-yú ... bee |

feelings

I'm (not) ...	ผม/ดิฉัน(ไม่) ...	pŏm/dì-chăn (mâi) ... m/f
Are you ...?	คุณ ... ไหม	kun ... măi
cold	หนาว	nŏw
happy	ดีใจ	dee jai
hot	ร้อน	rórn
hungry	หิว	hĕw
sad	เศร้า	sôw
thirsty	หิวน้ำ	hĕw nám

entertainment

beach

Where's the ... beach?	ชายหาด ... อยู่ที่ไหน	chai hàht ... yòo têe năi
best	ที่ดีที่สุด	têe dee têe sùt
nearest	ที่ใกล้ที่สุด	têe glâi têe sùt
public	สาธารณะ	săh-tah-rá-ná

How much for a chair/an umbrella?
เก้าอี้/ร่มเท่าไร
gôw-êe/rôm tôw-rai

Is it safe to swim/dive here?
ที่นี่ว่าย/กระโดด
têe née wâi/grà-dòht
น้ำปลอดภัยไหม
nám blòrt pai măi

What time is high/low tide?
น้ำขึ้น/ลงกี่โมง
nám kêun/long gèe mohng

water sports

Can I book a lesson?
จองเวลาเรียนได้ไหม · jorng wair-lah ree-an dâi măi

Can I hire (a) ...?	เช่า... ได้ไหม	chôw ... dâi măi
canoe	เรือคนู	reu-a ká-noo
diving equipment	อุปกรณ์ดำน้ำ	ùp-bà-gorn dam nám
guide	ไกด์	gai
life jacket	เสื้อชูชีพ	sêu-a choo chêep
motorboat	เรือติดเครื่อง	reu-a đìt krêu-ang
sailboard	กระดานโต้ลม	grà-dahn đôh lom
sailing boat	เรือใบ	reu-a bai
snorkelling	อุปกรณ์ดำน้ำใช้	ùp-bà-gorn dam
gear	ท่อหายใจ	nám chái tôr hăi jai
surfboard	กระดานโต้คลื่น	grà-dahn đôh klêun

Are there any ...?	มี... ไหม	mee ... măi
reefs	หินโสโครก	hĭn sŏh-krôhk
rips	กระแสใต้น้ำ	grà-săa đâi nám
water hazards	อันตรายในน้ำ	an-đà-rai nai nám

going out

Where can I find ...?	จะหา... ได้ที่ไหน	jà hăh ... dâi têe năi
clubs	ไนท์คลับ	nai kláp
gay venues	สถานบันเทิง สำหรับคนเกย์	sà-tăhn ban-teung săm-ràp kon gair
pubs	ผับ	pàp

I feel like going to a/the ...	ผม/ดิฉันรู้สึก อยากจะไป ...	pŏm/dì-chăn róo-sèuk yàhk jà bai ... m/f
concert	ดูการแสดง	doo gahn sà-daang
folk opera	ลิเก	lí-gair
full-moon party	งานปาร์ตี้พระจันทร์เต็มดวง	ngahn bah-đêe prá jan đem doo-ang
karaoke bar	คาราโอเกะ	kah-rah-oh-gé
movies	ดูหนัง	doo năng
performance	ดูงานแสดง	doo ngahn sà-daang

interests

Do you like ...?	ชอบ ... ไหม	chôrp ... mǎi
I (don't) like ...	ผม/ดิฉัน(ไม่) ชอบ ...	pŏm/dì-chăn (mâi) chôrp ... m/f
art	ศิลปะ	sĭn-lá-bà
cooking	ทำอาหาร	tam ah-hǎhn
drawing	เขียนภาพ	kĕe-an pâhp
movies	ดูหนัง	doo năng
nightclubs	ไนท์คลับ	nai kláp
photography	ถ่ายภาพ	tài pâhp
reading	อ่านหนังสือ	àhn năng-sĕu
sport	กีฬา	gee-lah
surfing the Internet	เล่นอินเตอร์เนต	lên in-đeu-nét
swimming	ว่ายน้ำ	wâi nám
travelling	การท่องเที่ยว	tôrng têe-o
watching TV	ดูโทรทัศน์	doo toh-rá-tát
Do you ...?	คุณ ... ไหม	kun ... mǎi
dance	เต้นรำ	đên ram
go to concerts	ไปดูการแสดง	bai doo gahn sà-daang
listen to music	ฟังดนตรี	fang don-đree

food & drink

finding a place to eat

Can you recommend a ...?	แนะนำ ... ได้ไหม	náa-nam ... dâi mǎi
bar	บาร์	bah
café	ร้านกาแฟ	ráhn gah-faa
restaurant	ร้านอาหาร	ráhn ah-hǎhn
I'd like ..., please.	ขอ ... หน่อย	kŏr ... nòy
a table for (five)	โต๊ะสำหรับ(ห้า) คน	đó sǎm-ràp (hâh) kon
the nonsmoking section	ที่เขตห้ามสูบบุหรี่	têe kèt hâhm sòop bù-rèe
the smoking section	ที่เขตสูบบุหรี่ได้	têe kèt sòop bù-rèe dâi

ordering food

breakfast	อาหารเช้า	ah-hăhn chów
lunch	อาหารกลางวัน	ah-hăhn glahng wan
dinner	อาหารเย็น	ah-hăhn yen
snack	อาหารว่าง	ah-hăhn wâhng

bowl	ชาม	chahm
chopsticks	ตะเกียบ	đà-gèe·ap
cloth	ผ้า	pàh
cup	ถ้วย	tôo·ay
fork	ส้อม	sôrm
glass	แก้ว	gâa·ou
knife	มีด	mêet
plate	จาน	jahn
spoon	ช้อน	chórn
teaspoon	ช้อนชา	chórn chah

I'd like the …, please. ขอ … หน่อย — kŏr … nòy

bill	บิลล์	bin
drink list	รายการเครื่องดื่ม	rai gahn krêu·ang dèum
menu	รายการอาหาร	rai gahn ah-hăhn

What would you recommend?
คุณแนะนำอะไรบ้าง — kun náa-nam à-rai bâhng

I'll have that.
เอาอันนั้นนะ — ow an nán ná

drinks

(cup of) coffee …	กาแฟ(ถ้วยหนึ่ง) …	gah-faa (tôo·ay nèung) …
(cup of) tea …	ชา(ถ้วยหนึ่ง) …	chah (tôo·ay nèung) …
with milk	ใส่นม	sài nom
without sugar	ไม่ใส่น้ำตาล	mâi sài nám-đahn

boiled water	น้ำต้ม	nám đôm
orange juice	น้ำส้มคั้น	nám sôm kán
soft drink	น้ำอัดลม	nám àt lom
sparkling mineral water	น้ำแร่อัดลม	nám râa àt lom
still mineral water	น้ำแร่ธรรมดา	nám râa tam-má-dah

in the bar

I'll have ...	เอา ...	ow ...
I'll buy you a drink.	ฉันจะซื้อของดื่มให้คุณ	chăn jà séu kŏrng dèum hâi kun
What would you like?	จะรับอะไร	jà ráp à-rai
Cheers!	ไชโย	chai-yoh

herbal liquor	เหล้ายาดอง	lôw yah dorng
jungle liquor	เหล้าเถื่อน	lôw tèu·an
Mekong whisky	วิสกีแม่โขง	wít-sà-gee mâa kŏhng

a jug of (beer)	(เบียร์) เหยือกหนึ่ง	(bee·a) yèu·ak nèung
a glass of (beer)	(เบียร์) แก้วหนึ่ง	(bee·a) gâa·ou nèung
a shot of (whisky)	(วิสกี) ช็อตหนึ่ง	(wít-sà-gee) chórt nèung

a (bottle) of ... wine	ไวน์ ... (ขวดหนึ่ง)	wai ... (kòo·at nèung)
red	แดง	daang
sparkling	เหล้าองุ่นสปาร์คลิ่ง	lôw à-ngùn sà-bah-klîng
white	ขาว	kŏw

self-catering

What's the local speciality?
อาหารรสเด็ดๆของแถว
นี้คืออะไร
ah-hăhn rót dèt dèt kŏrng
tăa·ou née keu à-rai

What's that?
นั่นคืออะไร
nân keu à-rai

How much is (a kilo of) ...?
... (กิโลหนึ่ง) เท่าไร
... (gì-loh nèung) tôw-rai

I'd like ...	ต้องการ ...	đôrng gahn ...
(200) grams	(สองร้อย) กรัม	(sŏrng róy) gram
(two) kilos	(สอง) กิโล	(sŏrng) gì-loh
(three) pieces	(สาม) ชิ้น	(săhm) chín
(six) slices	(หก) ชิ้น	(hòk) chín

Enough.	พอแล้ว	por láa·ou
A bit more.	อีกหน่อย	èek nòy
Less.	น้อยลง	nóy long

special diets & allergies

Is there a vegetarian restaurant near here?

| มีร้านอาหารเจ | mee ráhn ah·hǎhn jair |
| อยู่แถวๆนี้ไหม | yòo tǎa·ou tǎa·ou née mǎi |

Do you have vegetarian food?

| มีอาหารเจไหม | mee ah·hǎhn jair mǎi |

Could you prepare	ทำอาหารไม่	tam ah·hǎhn mâi
a meal without ...?	ใส่ ... ได้ไหม	sài ... dâi mǎi
butter	เนย	neu·i
eggs	ไข่	kài
fish	ปลา	blah
meat	เนื้อแดง	néu·a daang
meat stock	ซุปก้อนเนื้อ	súp gôrn néu·a
MSG	ชูรส	choo·rót
pork	เนื้อหมู	néu·a mǒo
poultry	เนื้อไก่	néu·a gài

I'm allergic to ...	ผม/ดิฉันแพ้ ...	pǒm/dì·chǎn páa ... **m/f**
chilli	พริก	prík
dairy produce	อาหารจำพวกนม	ah·hǎhn jam·pôo·ak nom
eggs	ไข่	kài
fish sauce	น้ำปลา	nám blah
gelatine	วุ้น	wún
gluten	แป้ง	bâang
honey	น้ำผึ้ง	nám pêung
MSG	ชูรส	choo·rót
nuts	ถั่ว	tòo·a
seafood	อาหารทะเล	ah·hǎhn tá·lair
shellfish	หอย	hǒy

For other allergies see **health**, page 194.

THAI – food & drink

menu decoder

bah-tôrng-gŏh	ปาท่องโก๋	fried wheat pastry
bà-mèe hâang	บะหมี่แห้ง	noodles with meat, seafood or vegetables
bèt đǔn	เป็ดตุ๋น	steamed duck soup with soy sauce & spices
blah dàat dee-o	ปลาแดดเดียว	fried fish served with a spicy mango salad
blah mèuk bîng	ปลาหมึกปิ้ง	dried squid roasted over hot coals
blah nêung	ปลานึ่ง	freshwater fish steamed with vegetables
blah pŏw	ปลาเผา	fish in foil roasted over hot coals
blah tôrt	ปลาทอด	fried fish
bor-bée-a sòt	ปอเปี๊ยะสด	fresh spring rolls
bor-bée-a tôrt	ปอเปี๊ยะทอด	fried spring rolls
đà-gôh	ตะโก้	steamed sweet made from tapioca flour, coconut milk & seaweed
đôm yam gûng	ต้มยำกุ้ง	hot shrimp salad with lime, chilli & herbs
đôw hôo	เต้าหู้	tofu (soybean curd)
gaang kěe-o wǎhn	แกงเขียวหวาน	green curry
gaang pèt	แกงเผ็ด	red curry
gaang lee-ang	แกงเลียง	spicy soup of cauliflower, greens & chicken, shrimp or pork
gaang lěu-ang	แกงเหลือง	spicy fish curry with green beans
gaang râht kôw	แกงราดข้าว	curry with rice
gài đǔn	ไก่ตุ๋น	chicken soup with soy sauce
gài tôrt	ไก่ทอด	fried chicken
gée-o	เกี๊ยว	won ton (pork or fish in dough)
glôo-ay bòo-at chee	กล้วยบวชชี	banana chunks in coconut milk
glôo-ay tôrt	กล้วยทอด	fried battered banana

gŏo·ay đĕe·o nám	ก๋วยเตี๋ยวน้ำ	rice noodles with meat & pickled cabbage
hŏy tôrt	หอยทอด	oysters fried with beaten eggs, mung bean sprouts & spring onions
jóhk mŏo	โจ๊กหมู	thick rice soup with pork meatballs
kài yát sâi	ไข่ยัดใส้	omelette with pork, tomatoes & chillies
kà-nŏm krók	ขนมครก	mixture of coconut milk & rice flour
kôw đôm	ข้าวต้ม	boiled rice soup
kôw đôm gà-tí	ข้าวต้มกะทิ	sticky rice & coconut in a banana leaf
kôw lăhm	ข้าวหลาม	steamed sticky rice & coconut
kôw mŏo daang	ข้าวหมูแดง	red pork with rice
kôw nĕe·o má-môo·ang	ข้าวเหนียวมะม่วง	sweet made of mangoes
kôw gaang	ข้าวแกง	curry over rice
nám blah	น้ำปลา	fish sauce made of fermented anchovies
nám prík đah daang	น้ำพริกตาแดง	very dry & hot chilli dip
néu·a đŭn	เนื้อตุ๋น	beef soup with soy sauce & spices
prík bòn	พริกปน	dried red chilli, flaked or ground
roh-đee	โรตี	fried, round flat wheat bread
roh-đee gaang	โรตีแกง	flat bread dipped in a curry sauce
roh-đee glôo·ay	โรตีกล้วย	flat bread stuffed with banana chunks
sà-đé	สะเต๊ะ	barbecued meat with a spicy peanut sauce
sah-lah-bow	ซาลาเปา	steamed buns filled with stewed pork or sweet bean paste
săng-kà-yăh	สังขยา	custard
see-éw dam	ซีอิ๊วดำ	'black soy' – heavy, dark soy sauce
see-éw kŏw	ซีอิ๊วขาว	'white soy' – light soy sauce
yam	ย่ำ	hot salad with lime, chilli & herbs

emergencies

basics

Help!	ช่วยด้วย	chôo·ay dôo·ay
Stop!	หยุด	yùt
Go away!	ไปให้พ้น	ɓai hâi pón
Thief!	ขโมย	kà·moy
Fire!	ไฟไหม้	fai mâi

Call an ambulance!
ตามรถพยาบาล
đahm rót pá·yah·bahn

Call a doctor!
เรียกหมอหน่อย
rêe·ak mŏr nòy

Call the police!
เรียกตำรวจหน่อย
rêe·ak đam·ròo·at nòy

It's an emergency!
เป็นเหตุฉุกเฉิน
ɓen hèt chùk·chĕun

There's been an accident.
มีอุบัติเหตุ
mee ù·bàt·đi·hèt

Could you help me, please?
ช่วยได้ไหม
chôo·ay dâi măi

Can I use your phone?
ใช้โทรศัพท์ของคุณได้ไหม
chái toh·rá·sàp kŏrng kun dâi măi

I'm lost.
ผม/ดิฉันหลงทาง
pŏm/dì·chăn lŏng tahng m/f

Where are the toilets?
ห้องน้ำอยู่ที่ไหน
hôrng nám yòo têe năi

police

Where's the police station?
สถานีตำรวจอยู่ที่ไหน
sà·tăh·nee đam·ròo·at yòo têe năi

I want to report an offence.
ผม/ดิฉันอยากจะแจ้งความ
pŏm/dì·chăn yàhk jà jâang kwahm m/f

I've been ...	ผม/ดิฉันโดน ...	pŏm/dì-chăn dohn ... m/f
assaulted	ทำร้ายร่างกาย	tam rái râhng gai
raped	ข่มขืน	kòm kĕun
robbed	ปล้น	ป̂lôn

I've lost my ...	ผม/ดิฉันทำ ...	pŏm/dì-chăn tam ...
	หายแล้ว	hăi láa-ou m/f
My ... was/were	... ของ ผม/ดิฉัน	... kŏrng pŏm/dì-chăn
stolen.	ถูกขโมย	tòok kà-moy m/f
backpack	เป้	ป̂âir
bags	กระเป๋า	grà-ป̌ŏw
credit card	บัตรเครดิต	bàt krair-dìt
handbag	กระเป๋าหิ้ว	grà-ป̌ŏw hêw
jewellery	เพชรพลอย	pét ploy
money	เงิน	ngeun
passport	หนังสือเดินทาง	năng-sĕu deun tahng
travellers cheques	เช็คเดินทาง	chék deun tahng
wallet	กระเป๋าเงิน	grà-ป̌ŏw ngeun

I want to contact my embassy.
ผม/ดิฉันอยากจะติดต่อสถานทูต   pŏm/dì-chăn yàhk jà ติ̀t ต̀òr sà-tăhn tôot m/f

I want to contact my consulate.
ผม/ดิฉันอยากจะติดต่อกงศุล   pŏm/dì-chăn yàhk jà ติ̀t ต̀òr gong-sŭn m/f

I have insurance.
ผม/ดิฉันมีประกันอยู่   pŏm/dì-chăn mee ป̀rà-gan yòo m/f

health

medical needs

Where's the	... ที่ใกล้เคียง	... têe glâi kee-ang
nearest ...?	อยู่ที่ไหน	yòo têe năi
dentist	หมอฟัน	mŏr fan
doctor	หมอ	mŏr
hospital	โรงพยาบาล	rohng pá-yah-bahn
(night)	ร้านขายยา	ráhn kăi yah
pharmacist	(กลางคืน)	(glahng keun)

I need a doctor (who speaks English).
ผม/ดิฉันต้องการหมอ   pŏm/dì-chăn dôrng gahn mŏr
(ที่พูดภาษาอังกฤษได้)   (têe pôot pah-săh ang-grìt dâi) m/f

Could I see a female doctor?
พบกับคุณหมอผู้หญิงได้ไหม   póp gàp kun mŏr pôo yĭng dâi măi

I've run out of my medication.
ยาของผม/ดิฉันหมดแล้ว   yah kŏrng pŏm/dì-chăn mòt láa·ou m/f

symptoms, conditions & allergies

I'm sick.	ผม/ดิฉันป่วย	pŏm/dì-chăn bòo·ay m/f
It hurts here.	เจ็บตรงนี้	jèp drong née
ankle	ข้อเท้า	kôr tów
arm	แขน	kăan
back	หลัง	lăng
chest	หน้าอก	nâh òk
ear	หู	hŏo
eye	ตา	đah
finger	นิ้ว	néw
foot	เท้า	tów
hand	มือ	meu
head	หัว	hŏo·a
heart	หัวใจ	hŏo·a jai
leg	ขา	kăh
mouth	ปาก	bàhk
neck	คอ	kor
nose	จมูก	jà-mòok
skin	ผิวหนัง	pĕw năng
stomach	ท้อง	tórng
teeth	ฟัน	fan
throat	คอหอย	kor hŏy

I have (a/an) ...	ผม/ดิฉัน ...	pŏm/dì-chăn ... m/f
asthma	เป็นโรคหืด	ben rôhk hèut
bronchitis	เป็นโรคหลอดลมอักเสบ	ben rôhk lòrt lom àk-sèp
constipation	ท้องผูก	tórng pòok
cough	เป็นไอ	ben ai
diarrhoea	เป็นท้องร่วง	ben tórng rôo·ang
fever	เป็นไข้	ben kâi
headache	ปวดหัว	bòo·at hŏo·a
heart condition	เป็นโรคหัวใจ	ben rôhk hŏo·a ja
heat stroke	แพ้แดด	páa dàat
nausea	คลื่นใส้	klêun sâi
pain	ปวด	bòo·at
sore throat	เจ็บคอ	jèp kor
toothache	ปวดฟัน	bòo·at fan

antifungal cream	ยาฆ่าเชื้อรา	yah kâh chéu·a rah
antimalarial medication	ยาป้องกันมาเลเรีย	yah bôrng gan mah-lair-ree·a
antiseptic	ยาฆ่าเชื้อ	yah kâh chéu·a
bandage	ผ้าพันแผล	pâh pan plăa
Band-Aid	ปลาสเตอร์	blah-sà-đeu
contraceptives	ยาคุมกำเนิด	yah kum gam-nèut
diarrhoea medicine	ยาระงับอาการท้องร่วง	yah rá-ngáp ah-gahn tórng rôo·ang
insect repellent	ยากันแมลง	yah gan má-laang
laxatives	ยาระบาย	yah rá-bai
painkillers	ยาแก้ปวด	yah gâa bòo·at
rehydration salts	เกลือแร่	gleu·a râa
sleeping tablets	ยานอนหลับ	yah norn làp

I'm allergic to ...	ผม/ดิฉันแพ้ ...	pŏm/dì-chăn páa ... m/f
antibiotics	ยาปฏิชีวนะ	yah bà-đì-chee-wá-ná
anti-inflammatories	ยาแก้อักเสบ	yah gâa àk-sèp
aspirin	ยาแอสไพริน	yah àat-sà-pai-rin
bees	ตัวผึ้ง	đoo·a pêung
penicillin	ยาเพนนิซิลลิน	yah pen-ní-sin-lin
sulphur-based drugs	ยาที่ประกอบด้วยซัลเฟอร	yah têe brà-gòrp dôo·ay san-feu

See **special diets & allergies**, page 188, for food-related allergies.

The symbols ⓝ, ⓐ and ⓥ (indicating noun, adjective and verb) have been added for clarity where an English term could be either. For food terms see the **menu decoder**, page 189.

A

accident อุบัติเหตุ ù-bàt-đi-hèt
accommodation ที่พัก têe pák
adaptor หม้อแปลง mór ʾblaang
address ⓝ ที่อยู่ têe yòo
after หลัง lăng
air-conditioned ปรับอากาศ ʾbràp ah-gàht
airplane เครื่องบิน krêu-ang bin
airport สนามบิน sà-năhm bin
alcohol เหล้า lôw
all ทั้งหมด táng mòt
allergy การแพ้ gahn páa
ambulance รถพยาบาล rót pá-yah-bahn
and และ láa
ankle ข้อเท้า kôr tów
arm แขน kăan
automated teller machine (ATM) ตู้เอทีเอ็ม
  đôo air tee em

B

back (body) หลัง lăng
backpack เป้ ʾbâir
baby ทารก tah-rók
bad เลว le-ou
bag กระเป๋า grà-ʾbŏw
baggage claim ที่รับกระเป๋า têe ráp grà-ʾbŏw
bank ⓝ ธนาคาร tá-nah-kahn
bank account บัญชี ธนาคาร
  ban-chee tá-nah-kahn
bar ⓝ บาร์ bah
bathroom ห้องน้ำ hôrng nám
battery ถ่านไฟฉาย tàhn fai chǎi
beach ชายหาด chai hàht

beautiful สวย sŏo-ay
bed เตียง đee-ang
beer เบียร์ bee-a
before ก่อน gòrn
behind ข้างหลัง kâhng lăng
bicycle รถจักรยาน rót jàk-gà-yahn
big ใหญ่ yài
bill บิลล์ bin
black สีดำ sěe dam
blanket ผ้าห่ม pâh hòm
blood เลือด lêu-at
blood group กลุ่มเลือด glum lêu-at
blue สีฟ้า sěe fáh
book (make a reservation) ⓥ จอง jorng
both ทั้งสอง táng sŏrng
bottle ขวด kòo-at
bottle opener เครื่องเปิดขวด
  krêu-ang ʾbèut kòo-at
boy (child/teen) เด็กชาย/หนุ่ม dèk chai/nùm
breakfast อาหารเช้า ah-hăhn chów
broken หักแล้ว hàk láa-ou
bus รถเมล์ rót mair
business ธุรกิจ tú-rá-gìt
bus stop ป้ายรถเมล์ ʾbâi rót mair
but แต่ว่า đàa wâh
buy ซื้อ séu

C

café ร้านกาแฟ ráhn gah-faa
camera กล้องถ่ายรูป glôrng tài rôop
camp site ที่ปักเต็นท์ têe bàk đén
cancel ยกเลิก yók lêuk
can opener เครื่องเปิดกระป๋อง
  krêu-ang ʾbèut grà-ʾbŏrng

car รถยนต์ rót yon
cash ⑩ เงินสด ngeun sòt
cash (a cheque) ⓥ แลก lâak
cell phone โทรศัพท์มือถือ toh-rá-sàp meu teu
centre ศูนย์กลาง sŏon glahng
change (money) ⓥ แลกเปลี่ยน lâak blèe-an
cheap ถูก tòok
check (bill) บิลล์ bin
check-in ⑩ เช็คอิน chék in
cheque (bank) ⑩ เช็ค chék
chest (body) หน้าอก nâh òk
child เด็ก dèk
cigarette บุหรี่ bù-rèe
clean ⓐ สะอาด sà-àht
closed ปิดแล้ว bìt láa-ou
coffee กาแฟ gah-faa
coins เหรียญ rĕe-an
cold ⓐ เย็น yen
cold (illness) ⑩ หวัด wàt
collect call โทรเก็บปลายทาง
  toh gèp blai tahng
come มา mah
compass เข็มทิศ kĕm tít
computer คอมพิวเตอร์ korm-pew-đeu
condoms ถุงยางอนามัย tŭng yahng à-
  nai-mai
contact lenses เลนส์สัมผัส len săm-pàt
cook ⓥ ทำอาหาร tam ah-hăhn
cost ⑩ มีราคา mee rah-kah
credit card บัตรเครดิต bàt crair-dìt
currency exchange การแลกเงิน
  gahn lâak ngeun
customs (immigration) ศุลกากร
  sŭn-lá-gah-gorn

D

dangerous อันตราย an-đà-rai
date (time) ⑩ วันที่ wan têe
day วัน wan
delay ⑩ การเสียเวลา gahn sĕe-a wair-lah
dentist หมอฟัน mŏr fan
departure ขาออก kăh òrk

diaper ผ้าอ้อม pâh òrm
diarrhoea ท้องเสีย tórng sĕe-a
dictionary พจนานุกรม pót-jà-nah-nú-grom
dinner อาหารมื้อเย็น ah-hăhn méu yen
direct ทางตรง tahng đrong
dirty สกปรก sòk-gà-bròk
disabled (person) พิการ pí-gahn
discount ราคาส่วนลด rah-kah sòo-an lót
doctor หมอ mŏr
double bed เตียงคู่ dee-ang kôo
double room ห้องคู่ hôrng kôo
down ลง long
drink ⑩ เครื่องดื่ม krêu-ang dèum
drive ⓥ ขับ kàp
drivers licence ใบขับขี่ bai kàp kèe
drugs (illicit) ยาเสพติด yah sèp đit
dummy (pacifier) หัวนมเทียม
  hŏo-a nom tee-am

E

ear หู hŏo
east ทิศตะวันออก tít đà-wan òrk
eat ทาน tahn
economy class ชั้นประหยัด chán brà-yàt
electricity ไฟฟ้า fai fáh
elevator ลิฟต์ líp
email อีเมล ee-men
embassy สถานทูต sà-tăhn tôot
emergency เหตุฉุกเฉิน hèt chùk-chĕun
empty ⓐ ว่าง wâhng
English อังกฤษ ang-grìt
enough พอ por
entrance ทางเข้า tahng kòw
evening ตอนเย็น đorn yen
exchange (money) ⓥ แลกเปลี่ยน lâak blèe-an
exchange rate อัตราการแลกเปลี่ยน
  àt-đrah gahn lâak blèe-an
exit ⑩ ทางออก tahng òrk
expensive แพง paang
express mail ไปรษณีย์ด่วน
  brai-sà-nee dòo-an
eye ตา đah

F

face (body) ใบหน้า bai nâh
far ไกล glai
fast เร็ว re·ou
father พ่อ pôr
faulty บกพร่อง bok prôrng
fever ไข้ kâi
film (camera) ฟิล์ม fim
finger นิ้ว néw
first ที่หนึ่ง têe nèung
first-aid kit ชุดปฐมพยาบาล
    chút bà·tŏm pá·yah·bahn
first-class (ticket) ⓐ ชั้นหนึ่ง chán nèung
fish ปลา blah
flashlight (torch) ไฟฉาย fai chǎi
fly (a plane) ⓥ บิน bin
food อาหาร ah·hăhn
foot เท้า tów
fork ส้อม sôrm
free (of charge) ฟรี free
friend เพื่อน pêu·an
fruit ผลไม้ pŏn·lá·mái
full เต็ม đem
funny ตลก đà·lòk

G

gift ของขวัญ kŏrng kwăn
girl (child/teen) เด็กหญิง/สาว dèk yĭng/sŏw
glass (drinking) แก้ว gâa·ou
glasses แว่นตา wâan đah
go ไป bai
good ดี dee
green สีเขียว sĕe kĕe·o
guide ⓝ ไกด์ gai

H

half ⓐ ครึ่ง krêung
hand มือ meu
handbag กระเป๋าพาย grà·bŏw pai
happy ดีใจ dee jai

have มี mee
head หัว hŏo·a
headache ปวดหัว bòo·at hŏo·a
heart หัวใจ hŏo·a jai
heart condition โรคหัวใจ rôhk hŏo·a jai
heat ⓝ ความร้อน kwahm rórn
heavy หนัก nàk
help ⓝ ความช่วยเหลือ kwahm chôo·ay lĕu·a
help ⓥ ช่วย chôo·ay
here ที่นี่ têe née
high สูง sŏong
highway ทางหลวง tahng lŏo·ang
hike ⓥ เดินป่า deun bàh
homosexual คนรักร่วมเพศ kon rák rôo·am pêt
hospital โรงพยาบาล rohng pá·yaa·bahn
hot ร้อน rórn
hotel โรงแรม rohng raam
hungry หิว hěw
husband ผัว pŏo·a

I

identification (card) หลักฐานส่วนตัว
    làk tăhn sòo·an đoo·a
ill ป่วย bòo·ay
important สำคัญ săm·kan
included รวมด้วย roo·am dôo·ay
injury ที่บาดเจ็บ têe bàht jèp
insurance การประกัน gahn brà·gan
Internet อินเตอร์เนต in·đeu·nét
interpreter ล่าม lâhm

J

jewellery เครื่องเพชรพลอย krêu·ang pét ploy
job งาน ngahn

K

key ลูกกุญแจ lôok gun·jaa
kilogram กิโลกรัม gi·loh·gram
kitchen ครัว kroo·a
knife มีด mêet

F

L

late ช้า cháh
laundry (place) ที่ซักผ้า têe sák pâh
lawyer ทะนายความ tá-nai kwahm
left-luggage office ห้องรับฝากกระเป๋า
    hôrng ráp fàhk grà-bŏw
leg ขา kăh
lesbian เล็สเบียน lét-bee-an
less น้อยกว่า nóy gwàh
letter จดหมาย jòt-măi
lift (elevator) ลิฟต์ líp
light ⓝ ไฟ fai
like ⓥ ชอบ chôrp
lock ⓝ กุญแจ gun-jaa
long ยาว yow
lost หาย hăi
lost property office ที่แจ้งของหาย
    têe jâang kŏrng hăi
love ⓥ รัก rák
luggage กระเป๋า grà-bŏw
lunch อาหารกลางวัน ah-hăhn glahng wan

M

mail จดหมาย jòt-măi
man ผู้ชาย pôo chai
map แผนที่ păan têe
market ตลาด dà-làht
matches ไม้ขีดไฟ mái kèet fai
meat เนื้อ néu-a
medication ยา yah
menu รายการอาหาร rai gahn ah-hăhn
message ข้อความฝาก kôr kwahm fàhk
milk น้ำนม nám nom
minute นาที nah-tee
mobile phone โทรศัพท์มือถือ
    toh-rá-sàp meu tĕu
money เงิน ngeun
month เดือน deu-an
morning ตอนเช้า dorn chów
mother แม่ mâa
motorcycle รถมอเตอร์ไซค์ rót mor-đeu-sai

motorway ทางด่วน tahng dòo-an
mountain ภูเขา poo kŏw
mouth ปาก bàhk
music ดนตรี don-đree

N

name ชื่อ chêu
nappy ผ้าอ้อม pâh ôrm
nausea คลื่นไส้ klêun sâi
near ใกล้ glâi
neck คอ kor
new ใหม่ mài
news ข่าว kòw
newspaper หนังสือพิมพ์ năng-sĕu pim
next หน้า nâh
night คืน keun
no ไม่ mâi
noisy เสียงดัง sĕe-ang dang
nonsmoking ไม่สูบบุหรี่ mâi sòop bù-rèe
north ทิศเหนือ tít nĕu-a
nose จมูก jà-mòok
now เดี๋ยวนี้ dĕe-o née
number หมายเลข măi lêk

O

oil (engine) น้ำมันเครื่อง nám man krêu-ang
old (person) แก่ gàa
old (thing) เก่า gòw
on บน bon
one-way (ticket) เที่ยวเดียว têe-o dee-o
open ⓐ&ⓥ เปิด bèut
other อื่น èun
outside ข้างนอก kâhng nôrk

P

package ห่อ hòr
pain ความปวด kwahm bòo-at
painkillers ยาแก้ปวด yah gâa bòo-at
paper กระดาษ grà-dàht
park (car) ⓥ จอด jòrt

passport หนังสือเดินทาง năng-sěu deun tahng
pay จ่าย jài
pen ปากกา pàhk-gah
petrol เบนซิน ben-sin
pharmacy ร้านขายยา ráhn kǎi yah
phonecard บัตรโทรศัพท์ bàt toh-rá-sàp
photo ภาพถ่าย pâhp tài
plate จาน jahn
police ตำรวจ ɗam-ròo-at
postcard ไปรษณียบัตร ɓrai-sà-nee-yá-bàt
post office ที่ทำการไปรษณีย์
    tée tam gahn ɓrai-sà-nee
pregnant ตั้งครรภ์ ɗâng kan
price ราคา rah-kah

Q

quiet เงียบ ngêe-ap

R

rain ⓝ ฝน fǒn
razor มีดโกน mêet gohn
receipt ใบเสร็จ bai sèt
red สีแดง sěe daang
refund ⓝ เงินคืน ngeun keun
registered mail ไปรษณีย์ลงทะเบียน
    ɓrai-sà-nee long tá-bee-an
rent ⓥ เช่า chôw
repair ซ่อม sôrm
reservation การจอง gahn jorng
restaurant ร้านอาหาร ráhn ah-hǎhn
return ⓥ กลับ glàp
return ticket ตั๋วไปกลับ ɗǒo-a bai glàp
right (correct) ถูกต้อง tòok ɗôrng
right (direction) ขวา kwǎh
road ถนน tà-nǒn
room ห้อง hôrng
rope เชือก chêu-ak

S

safe ⓐ ปลอดภัย ɓlòrt pai
sanitary napkins ผ้าอนามัย pâh à-nah-mai

sea ทะเล tá-lair
seat ที่นั่ง têe nâng
send ส่ง sòng
service station ปั๊มน้ำมัน ɓám nám-man
sex การร่วมเพศ gahn rôo-am pêt
shaving cream ครีมโกนหนวด
    kreem gohn nòo-at
sheet (bed) ผ้าปูนอน pâh ɓoo norn
shirt เสื้อเชิ๊ต sêu-a chéut
shoes รองเท้า rorng tów
shop ⓝ ร้าน ráhn
short สั้น sân
shower ⓝ ฝักบัว fàk boo-a
single room ห้องเดี่ยว hôrng dèe-o
size (general) ขนาด kà-nàht
skin ผิวหนัง pěw năng
skirt กระโปรง grà-ɓrohng
sleep ⓥ นอน norn
slowly อย่างช้า ๆ yàhng cháh cháh
small เล็ก lék
smoke ⓥ ควัน kwan
soap สบู่ sà-bòo
soon เร็ว ๆ นี้ re-ou re-ou née
south ทิศใต้ tít ɗâi
souvenir shop ร้านขายของที่ระลึก
    ráhn kǎi kǒrng tée rá-léuk
speak พูด pôot
spoon ช้อน chórn
stamp ⓝ แสตมป์ sà-ɗáam
stand-by ticket ตั๋วแสตนด์บาย
    ɗǒo-a sà-ɗáan-bai
station (train) สถานี sà-tǎh-nee
stomach ท้อง tórng
stomachache เจ็บท้อง jèp tórng
stop ⓝ หยุด yùt
stop (bus) ป้าย ɓâi
street ถนน tà-nǒn
student นักศึกษา nák sèuk-sǎh
sun พระอาทิตย์ prá ah-tít
sunblock ครีมกันแดด kreem gan dàat
supermarket ซูเปอร์มาร์เก็ต soo-beu-mah-gèt
surname นามสกุล nahm sà-gun
sweet ⓐ หวาน wǎhn
swim ⓥ ว่ายน้ำ wâi nám

T

taxi รถแท็กซี่ rót táak-sêe
teeth ฟัน fan
telephone ⓥ โทร toh
television โทรทัศน์ toh-rá-tát
temperature (weather) อุณหภูมิ un-hà-poom
tent เต็นท์ đén
that ⓐ นั่น nán
thirsty หิวน้ำ hĕw nám
this ⓐ นี้ née
throat คอหอย kor hŏy
ticket ตั๋ว đŏo-a
time ⓝ เวลา wair-lah
tired เหนื่อย nèu-ay
tissues กระดาษทิชชู่ grà-dàht tít-chôo
today วันนี้ wan née
toilet ส้วม sôo-am
tomorrow พรุ่งนี้ prûng née
tonight คืนนี้ keun née
tooth ฟัน fan
toothache ปวดฟัน bòo-at fan
toothbrush แปรงสีฟัน braang sĕe fan
toothpaste ยาสีฟัน yah sĕe fan
torch (flashlight) ไฟฉาย fai chăi
tour ⓝ ทัวร์ too-a
tourist นักท่องเที่ยว nák tôrng têe-o
tourist office สำนักงานท่องเที่ยว
  săm-nák ngahn tôrng têe-o
towel ผ้าเช็ดตัว pâh chét đoo-a
town เมือง meu-ang
train รถไฟ rót fai
translate แปล blaa
travel agency บริษัทท่องเที่ยว
  bor-rí-sàt tôrng têe-o
travellers cheque เช็คเดินทาง chék deun tahng
trousers กางเกง gahng-geng
twin beds สองเตียง sŏrng đee-ang
tyre ยางรถ yahng rót

U

underwear กางเกงใน gahng-geng nai

up ขึ้น kêun
urgent ด่วน dòo-an

V

vacant ว่าง wâhng
vacation เที่ยวพักผ่อน têe-o pák pòrn
vegetable ผัก pàk
vegetarian ⓝ คนกินเจ kon gin jair
vegetarian ⓐ เจ jair
visa วีซ่า wee-sâh

W

waiter คนเดินโต๊ะ kon deun đó
walk ⓥ เดิน deun
wallet กระเป๋าเงิน grà-bŏw ngeun
warm ⓐ อุ่น ùn
wash ล้าง láhng
watch ⓝ นาฬิกา nah-lí-gah
watch ⓥ ดู doo
water น้ำ nám
weekend วันเสาร์อาทิตย์ wan sŏw ah-tít
west ทิศตะวันตก tít đà-wan đòk
wheelchair รถเข็นคนพิการ
  rót kĕn kon pí-gahn
when เมื่อไร mêu-a rai
where ที่ไหน têe năi
white สีขาว sĕe kŏw
who ใคร krai
why ทำไม tam mai
wife เมีย mee-a
window หน้าต่าง nâh đàhng
wine เหล้าไวน์ lôw wai
with กับ gàp
without ไม่มี mâi mee
woman ผู้หญิง pôo yĭng
write เขียน kĕe-an

Y

yellow สีเหลือง sĕe lĕu-ang
yes ใช่ châi
yesterday เมื่อวาน mêu-a wahn

Vietnamese

alphabet

A a aa	*Ă ă* uh	*Â â* uh	*B b* be	*C c* se
D d ze	*Đ đ* đe	*E e* a	*Ê ê* e	*G g* zhe
H h haat	*I i* ee	*K k* ğaa	*L l* e·luh	*M m* e·muh
N n e·nuh	*O o* o	*Ô ô* aw	*Ơ ơ* er	*P p* be
Q q koo	*R r* e·ruh	*S s* e·suh	*T t* de	*U u* u
U ư uhr	*V v* ve	*X x* ek·suh	*Y y* ee·gret	

introduction

Vietnamese is the official language of Vietnam, spoken by about 85 million people worldwide. Its distant ancestor was born in the area of the Red River, now in northern Vietnam. It was strongly influenced by Indic and Malayo-Polynesian languages, but this all changed when the Chinese took control of the coastal nation in the 2nd century BC.

Nearly 30 dynasties of Chinese rulers held sway in Vietnam for over a millennium. This period saw literary Chinese used as the language of literature, academia, science, politics and the Vietnamese aristocracy. However, Vietnamese was spoken in everyday life, and it was written in *chữ nôm* (jũhr nawm). This script was comprised of Chinese characters adapted to express Vietnamese sounds, and it was in common usage until the early 20th century. Almost 70% of Vietnamese words are derived from Chinese sources as well – this vocabulary is termed *Hán Việt* (haán vee·uht) (Sino-Vietnamese). Following a century of fighting for independence, the Vietnamese gained control of their own land in 939 AD. Common Vietnamese, written in *chữ nôm,* gained prestige as the nation rebuilt itself, and Vietnamese literature flourished.

The first European missionaries appeared in Vietnam in the 16th century. The French gradually emerged as the region's dominant European power, adding Vietnam to Indochina in 1859. French vocabulary began to be used in Vietnamese, and in 1910 the Latin-based *quốc ngữ* (gwáwk ngũhr) alphabet was declared the language's official written form. This 29-letter phonetic alphabet had been invented in the 17th century by a French Jesuit missionary, and even today virtually all writing is in *quốc ngữ.* The Vietnamese alphabet is shown on the page opposite.

There are three main varieties of Vietnamese – northern (Hanoi dialect), southern (Saigon dialect) and central (Hué dialect), and we've generally used the northern variety. The language we've provided in this chapter should be understood throughout the country. When we've given both northern and southern pronunciation, the two options are marked as Ⓝ and Ⓢ and separated with a slash.

Once you've got a hang of the tones and the few challenging vowel sounds, you should be on your way. The coloured phonetic guides that accompany each phrase in this chapter will make this task easier. You'll find that Vietnamese grammar is quite simple and once you master the basic rules given on the following pages, you'll be able to explore further and learn to build your own sentences.

pronunciation

vowel sounds

Accents above vowels (like à, é and ô) relate to the tones (see next page). The table at the top of the next page shows various combinations of Vietnamese vowel sounds.

symbol	english equivalent	vietnamese example	transliteration
a	at	*me*	ma
aa	father	*ba*	baa
ai	aisle	*ai*	ai
ay	play	*bay*	bay
aw	law	*số*	saw
e	bet	*ghê*	ge
ee	feet	*đi*	dee
er	her	*phở*	fer
i	fit	*thích*	tík
o	lot	*lo*	lo
oh	doh!	*phau*	foh
oo	through	*đủ*	doỏ
oy	boy	*tôi*	doy
ow	cow	*sao*	sow
u	book	*lúc*	lúp
uh	but	*gặp*	guhp
uhr	fur (without the 'r')	*từ*	dùhr

symbol	vietnamese example	transliteration	symbol	vietnamese example	transliteration
ay·oo	*meo*	may·oo	oo·ee	*mùi*	moo·èe
aw·ee	*mỗi*	maw·ée	oo·uh	*muốn*	moo·úhn
ee·e	*miếng*	mee·éng	uhr·ee	*mười*	muhr·èe
ee·oo	*phiều*	fee·òo	uhr·er	*được*	đuhr·erk
ee·uh	*mía*	mee·úh	uhr·oo	*mưu*	muhr·oo
o·ee	*mọi*	mo·ẹe	uhr·uh	*mưa*	muhr·uh

tones

Vietnamese uses a system of six carefully-pitched tones to make distinctions between words – some vowels are pronounced at a high or low pitch while others swoop or glide in a sing-song manner. The accent marks above the vowel remind you which one to use. Note that the mid tone has no accent.

mid level	low falling	low rising	high broken	high rising	low broken
ā	à	ả	ẫ	á	ạ
middle of the vocal range	begins low & falls lower	begins low, dips noticeably & then rises to a higher pitch	begins above mid level, dips slightly & then rises sharply	begins high & rises sharply	begins low, falls to a lower level & then stops

symbol	english equivalent	vietnamese example	transliteration
b	**bed**	*ba*	baa
ch	**chill**	*trà*	chà
d	**stop**	*tin*	din
đ	**dog**	*để*	đày
f	**fit**	*pha*	faa
g	**gap**	*ga, ghen tị*	gaa, gen dẹe
ğ	**skill**	*cá, kem*	ğá, ğam
h	**hat**	*hát*	hát
j	**jam**	*chó*	jó
k	**kit**	*khách*	kaák
l	**let**	*lý*	lée
m	**mat**	*trung, me*	chum, ma
n	**not**	*nóng*	nóm
ng	**sing**	*ngon, anh*	ngon, ang
ny	**canyon**	*nhà*	nyà
p	**top**	*súp, tóc*	súp, dóp
r	**red**	*rất*	rúht
s	**sad**	*sữa, xin*	sũhr·a, sin
t	**top**	*thích*	tík
v	**vase**	*vịt*	vịt
w	**water**	*quá*	ğwá
z	**zoo**	*giấy, do*	záy, zo

phrasebuilder

be

The verb *là* laà (be) is used to join the subject (doer of an action) with a noun, but it's not necessary with adjectives.

I'm a student.	*Tôi là sinh viên.*	doy laà sing vee·uhn
		(lit: I be student)
I'm thirsty.	*Tôi khát nước.*	doy kaát nuhr·érk
		(lit: I thirsty)

counters/classifiers

Vietnamese nouns are the same in singular and plural. When counting things however, Vietnamese uses 'classifiers' (extra words which categorise things with similar properties) between the numbers and the nouns. The box on page 222 lists some common classifiers.

three mango trees
  ba cây xoaì   baa ğay swaì
                                  (lit: three plant mango)

have

To say you possess something in Vietnamese, use the word *có* ğó (have):

I have a visa.
  Tôi có visa.   doy ğó vee·saa
                                  (lit: I have visa)

negatives

For negative statements, add the word *không* kawm (no) before the verb.

I don't have a visa.
  Tôi không có visa.   doy kawm ğó vee·saa
                                  (lit: I no have visa)

pronouns

Vietnamese pronouns vary depending on gender, age, social position and level of intimacy. For a list of the most common pronouns that will be suitable for most situations you're likely to encounter, see the box on page 230.

questions

The easiest way to form a yes/no question in Vietnamese is to add the word *không* kawm (no) to the end of a sentence. Answer 'yes' by repeating the key verb and 'no' by saying *không* kawm plus the verb.

Is there a room available?	*Có phòng không?*	ğó fòm kawm (lit: have room no)
Yes.	*Có.*	ğó (lit: have)
No.	*Không có.*	kawm ğó (lit: no have)

requests

To make a polite request, place the word *xin* sin (roughly equivalent to 'please' or 'could you') before the verb.

Please speak more slowly.
Xin bạn nói chậm hơn.   sin baạn nóy juhm hern
(lit: please you speak slow more)

verbs

Vietnamese verbs never change their forms, but you can add some modifiers before the verb to indicate tense. Use *đang* đaang (presently) for the present, *đã* đaã (past) for the past, and *sẽ* sã (will) for the future.

She's in Nha Trang.	*Cô ấy đang ở Hà Nội.*	ğaw áy đaang ẻr haà nọy (lit: she presently at Hanoi)
He went to Danang.	*Anh ấy đã đi Đà Nẵng.*	aang áy đaã đee đaà nũhng (lit: he past go Danang)
I'm going to Hanoi.	*Tôi sẽ đi Nha Trang.*	doy sã đee nyaa chaang (lit: I will go Nha Trang)

basics

language difficulties

Do you speak English?
Bạn có nói tiếng Anh không?   bạan ğó nóy dee·úhng aang kawm

Do you understand?
Bạn hiểu không?   bạan heé·oo kawm

I understand.
Hiểu.   heé·oo

I don't understand.
Không hiểu.   kawm heé·oo

What does (toy) mean?
(Thôi) có nghĩa gì?   (toy) ğó ngyeẽ·uh zèe

How do you ...?	*... như thế nào?*	... nyuhr té nòw
pronounce this	*Phát âm từ này*	faát aảm dùhr này
write (Hanoi)	*Viết từ (Hà Nội)*	vee·úht dùhr (haà nọy)

Could you please ...?	*Bạn có thể ...*	bạan ğó té ...
	được không?	đuhr·ẹrk kawm
repeat that	*lập lại*	lụhp lại
speak more slowly	*nói chậm hơn*	nóy jụhm hern
write it down	*viết ra*	vee·úht raa

essentials

Yes.	*Vâng.*	vuhng
No.	*Không.*	kawm
Please.	*Xin.*	sin
Thank you	*Cảm ơn*	ğaảm ern
(very much).	*(rất nhiều).*	(zúht nyee·oò)
You're welcome.	*Không có gì.*	kawm ğó zeè
Excuse me.	*Xin lỗi.*	sin lõy
Sorry.	*Xin lỗi.*	sin lõy

numbers

0	*không*	kawm	15	*mười lăm*	muhr·eè luhm
1	*một*	mạwt	16	*mười sáu*	muhr·eè sóh
2	*hai*	hai	17	*mười bảy*	muhr·eè bảy
3	*ba*	baa	18	*mười tám*	muhr·eè daám
4	*bốn*	báwn	19	*mười chín*	muhr·eè jín
5	*năm*	nuhm	20	*hai mươi*	hai muhr·ee
6	*sáu*	sóh	21	*hai mươi mốt*	hai muhr·ee máwt
7	*bảy*	bảy	22	*hai mươi hai*	hai muhr·ee hai
8	*tám*	daám	30	*ba mươi*	ba hai muhr·ee
9	*chín*	jín	40	*bốn mươi*	báwn muhr·ee
10	*mười*	muhr·eè	50	*năm mươi*	nuhm muhr·ee
11	*mười một*	muhr·eè mạwt	60	*sáu mươi*	sów muhr·ee
12	*mười hai*	muhr·eè hai	70	*bảy mươi*	bảy muhr·ee
13	*mười ba*	muhr·eè ba	80	*tám mươi*	daám muhr·ee
14	*mười bốn*	muhr·eè báwn	90	*chín mươi*	jín muhr·ee

100	*một trăm*	mạwt chuhm
1000	*nghìn/ngàn* ⓝ/ⓢ	ngyìn/ngaàn ⓝ/ⓢ
1,000,000	*triệu*	chee·oọ
10,000,000	*tý*	deé

time & dates

What time is it?	*Mấy giờ rồi?*	máy zèr zòy
It's (one) o'clock.	*Một giờ rồi.*	(mạwt) zèr zòy
It's (ten) o'clock.	*(Mười) giờ rồi.*	(muhr·eè) zèr zòy
Quarter past (ten).	*(Mười) giờ mười lăm phút.*	(muhr·eè) zèr muhr·eè luhm fút
Half past (ten).	*(Mười) giờ rưỡi.*	(muhr·eè) zèr zũhr·ee
Quarter to (ten).	*(Mười) giờ kém mười lăm.*	(muhr·eè) zèr ǧám muhr·eè luhm
At what time ...?	*Lúc mấy giờ ...?*	lúp máy zèr ...
At (ten).	*Lúc (mười) giờ.*	lúp (muhr·eè) zèr

| What date is it today? | Hôm nay là ngày mấy? | hawm nay laà ngày máy |
| It's (18 October). | Hôm nay là (mười tám, tháng mười). | hawm nay laà (muhr·eè daám taáng muhr·eè) |

Monday	thứ hai	túhr hai
Tuesday	thứ ba	túhr baa
Wednesday	thứ tư	túhr duhr
Thursday	thứ năm	túhr nuhm
Friday	thứ sáu	túhr sóh
Saturday	thứ bảy	túhr bảy
Sunday	chủ nhật	joỏ nyụht

January	tháng một	taáng mạwt
February	tháng hai	taáng hai
March	tháng ba	taáng baa
April	tháng tư	taáng duhr
May	tháng năm	taáng nuhm
June	tháng sáu	taáng sóh
July	tháng bảy	taáng bảy
August	tháng tám	taáng daám
September	tháng chín	taáng jín
October	tháng mười	taáng muhr·eè
November	tháng mười một	taáng muhr·eè mạwt
December	tháng mười hai	taáng muhr·eè hai

since (May)	từ (tháng năm)	dùhr (taáng nuhm)
until (June)	cho đến (tháng sáu)	jo dén (taáng sóh)
last night	buổi tối hôm qua	boỏ·ee dóy hawm ğwaa

last ...	... trước	... chuhr·érk
next ...	... sau	... soh
week	tuần	dwùhn
month	tháng	taáng
year	năm	nuhm

yesterday ...	... hôm qua	... hawm ğwaa
tomorrow ...	... ngày mai	... ngày mai
morning	sáng	saáng
afternoon	chiều	jee·oò
evening	tối	dóy

weather

What's the weather like?
Thời tiết thế nào?　　　　　　　　ter·eè dee·úht té nòw

It's ...	*Trời ...*	cher·eè ...
cold	*lạnh*	laạng
(very) hot	*(rất) nóng*	(zúht) nóm
raining	*mưa*	muhr·uh
warm	*ấm*	úhm
windy	*gió to*	zó do

dry season	*mùa khô*	moo·ùh kaw
monsoon season	*mùa mưa bão*	moo·ùh muhr·uh bõw
wet season	*mùa mưa*	moo·ùh muhr·uh

spring	*mùa xuân*	moo·ùh swuhn
summer	*mùa hè*	moo·ùh hà
autumn	*mùa thu*	moo·ùh too
winter	*mùa đông*	moo·ùh đawm

border crossing

I'm ...	*Tôi ...*	doy ...
in transit	*đang quá cảnh*	đaang ğwaá ğaảng
on business	*đang đi công tác*	đaang dee ğawm daák
on holiday	*đang đi nghỉ*	đaang dee ngyeẻ

I'm here for ...	*Tôi ở đây ...*	doy ẻr đay ...
(10) days	*(mười) ngày*	(muhr·eè) ngày
(two) months	*(hai) tháng*	(hai) túhng
(three) weeks	*(ba) tuần*	(ba) dwùhn

I'm going to (Hanoi).
Tôi sẽ đi (Hà Nội).　　　　　　doy sã đee (haà nọy)

I'm staying at the (Hotel Lotus).
Tôi đang ở (Khách Sạn Hoa Sen).　　doy đaang ẻr (kaák saạn hwaa san)

I have nothing to declare.
Tôi không có gì để khai báo.　　　doy kawm ğó zeè để kai bów

I have something to declare.
   Tôi cần khai báo.   doy ğùhn kai bów

That's (not) mine.
   Cái đó (không phải) của tôi.   ğaí đó (kawm fai) ğoỏ·uh doy

I didn't know I had to declare it.
   Tôi đã không biết tôi   doy đã kawm bee·úht doy
   phải khai báo cái đó.   fai kai bów ğaí đó

transport

tickets & luggage

Where can I buy a ticket?
   Tôi có thể mua vé ở đâu?   doy ğó tẻ moo·uh vá ér đoh

Do I need to book?
   Tôi có cần giữ chỗ   doy ğó ğùhn zữhr jãw
   trước không?   chuhr·érk kawm

One ... ticket to	*Một vé ...*	mạwt vá ...
(Saigon), please.	*đi (Sài Gòn).*	đee (sài gòn)
one-way	*một chiều*	mạwt jee·oò
return	*khú hồi*	kúhr hòy

I'd like to ... my	*Tôi muốn ...*	doy moo·úhn ...
ticket, please.	*vé này.*	vá này
cancel	*húy bỏ*	hweẻ bỏ
change	*thay đổi*	tay đỏy
collect	*lấy*	lay
confirm	*xác nhận*	saák nyuhn

I'd like a ... seat, please.	*Tôi muốn chỗ ...*	doy moo·úhn jãw ...
nonsmoking	*không hút thuốc*	kawm hút too·úhk
smoking	*hút thuốc*	hút too·úhk

How much is it?
   Bao nhiêu tiền?   bow nyee·oo dee·ùhn

Is there air conditioning?
   Có điều hòa không?   ğó đee·oò hwaà kawm

Is there a toilet?
Có vệ sinh không? — ğó vẹ sing kawm

How long does the trip take?
*Cuộc hành trình này
mất bao lâu?* — ğoo·uhk haàng chìng này
múht bow loh

Is it a direct route?
*Đây có phải là lộ trình
trực tiếp không?* — đay ğó fai laà lạw chìng
chụhrk dee·úhp kawm

Where can I find a luggage locker?
Tủ khóa đừng hành lý ở đâu? — doỏ kwaá đùhrng haàng leé ẻr đoh

My luggage	*Hành lý của*	haàng leé ğoỏ·uh
has been ...	*tôi đã bị ...*	doy đaã beẹ ...
damaged	*laàm huhr*	làm hư
lost	*mất*	múht
stolen	*lấy cắp*	láy ğúhp

getting around

Where does flight (VN631) depart?
*Cửa nào chuyến bay
(VN631) cất cánh?* — ğủhr·uh nòw jwee·úhn bay
(ve en sóh ba mạwt) ğúht ğaáng

Where does flight (VN631) arrive?
*Cửa nào chuyến bay
(VN631) đến?* — ğủhr·uh nòw jwee·úhn bay
(ve en sóh ba mạwt) đen

Where's (the) ...?	... *ở đâu?*	... ẻr đoh
arrivals hall	*Ga đến*	gaa đén
departures hall	*Ga đi*	gaa đee
duty-free shop	*Cửa hàng
miễn thuế*	ğủhr·uh haàng
meẽ·uhn twé
gate (6)	*Cửa (sáu)*	ğủhr·uh (sóh)

Is this the ...	... *này đi tới*	... này đee der·eé
to (Hué)?	*(Huế) phải không?*	(hwé) fai kawm
boat	*Thuyền*	twee·ùhn
bus	*Xe buýt*	sa bweét
plane	*Máy bay*	máy bay
train	*Xe lửa*	sa lủhr·uh

When's the	*Mấy giờ thì chuyến*	máy zèr tèe chweé·uhn
... bus?	*xe buýt ... chạy?*	sa bweét ... der·chạy
first	*đầu tiên*	đòh dee·uhn
last	*cuối cùng*	ğoo·eé ğùm
next	*kế tiếp*	ğé dee·úhp

What time does it get to (Dalat)?
Mấy giờ tới (Đà Lạt)?   máy zèr der·eé (đaà lạạt)

How long will it be delayed?
Nó sẽ bị đình hoãn bao lâu?   nó sã beḍ đìng hwaãn bow loh

What station is this?
Trạm này là trạm nào?   chụhm này laà chụhm nòw

What's the next stop?
Trạm kế tới là trạm nào?   chụhm ğé der·eé laà chụhm nòw

Which carriage is for (Hanoi)?
Toa xe nào là (Hà Nội)?   dwaa sa nòw laà (haà nọy)

Does it stop at (Vinh)?
Xe này có ngừng ở (Vinh) không?   sa này ğó ngùhrng èr (ving) kawm

Please tell me when we get to (Nha Trang).
Xin cho tôi biết khi   sin jo doy bee·úht kee
chúng ta (Nha Trang).   júm daa đén (nyaa chaang)

How long do we stop here?
Chúng ta ngừng ở đây bao lâu?   júm daa ngùhrng èr đay bow loh

Is this seat available?
Chỗ này có ai ngồi không?   jãw này ğó ai ngòy kawm

That's my seat.
Chỗ này là chỗ của tôi.   jãw này laà jãw ğoó·uh doy

Is this ...	*... này có đang*	... này ğó đaang
available?	*trống không?*	cháwm kawm
cyclo	*Xích lô*	sík law
motorcycle-taxi	*Xe ôm*	sa awm

I'd like a taxi ...	*Tôi muốn một*	doy moo·úhn mạwt
	chiếc taxi ...	jee·úhk dúhk·see ...
at (9am)	*lúc (chín giờ sáng)*	lúp (jín zèr saáng)
now	*ngay*	ngay
tomorrow	*ngày mai*	ngày mai

transport – *tiếng Việt*

Is this taxi free?
Taxi này có đang trống không?   dúhk·see này ğó đaang cháwm kawm

How much is it to ...?
Đi đến ... mất bao nhiêu tiền?   dee đén ... múht bow nyee·oo dee·ùhn

Please put the meter on.
Xin bật đồng hồ lên.   sin bụht đàwm hàw len

Please take me to (this address).
Làm ơn đưa tôi tới   laàm ern đuhr·uh doy der·eé
(địa chỉ này).   (đee·ụh jeé này)

Please ...   *Làm ơn ...*   laàm ern ...
   slow down   *chậm lại*   jụhm lại
   stop here   *dừng lại ở đây*   zùhrng lại ẻr đay
   wait here   *đợi ở đây*   đer·eẹ ẻr day

car, motorbike & bicycle hire

I'd like to hire a ...   *Tôi muốn xe ...*   doy moo·úhn sa ...
   bicycle   *đạp*   đaạp
   car   *hơi*   her·ee
   motorbike   *môtô*   maw·taw

with ...   *có ...*   ğó ...
   air conditioning   *máy lạnh*   máy laạng
   a driver   *người lái xe*   nguhr·eè laí sa

How much for ... hire?   *Bao nhiêu một ...?*   bow nyee·oo mạwt ...
   hourly   *tiếng*   dee·úhng
   daily   *ngày*   ngày
   weekly   *tuần*   dwùhn

air   *không khí*   lawm keé
oil   *dầu*   zòh
petrol   *xăng*   suhng
tyre   *bánh xe*   baáng sa

I need a mechanic.
Tôi cần thợ sửa xe.   doy ğùhn tẹr sủhr·uh sa

I've run out of petrol.
Tôi bị hết dầu xăng.   doy beẹ hét zòh suhng

I have a flat tyre.
Bánh xe tôi bị xì.   baáng sa doy beẹ seè

directions

Where's the ...?	*... ở đâu?*	*... ềr đoh*
bank	*Ngân hàng*	nguhn haàng
city centre	*Trung tâm*	chum duhm
	thành phố	taàng fáw
hotel	*Khách sạn*	kaák sạan
market	*Chợ*	jẹr
police station	*Đồn cảnh sát*	đàwn ğaảng saát
post office	*Bưu điện*	buhr·oo đee·ụhn
public toilet	*Nhà vệ sinh công cộng*	nyaà vẹ sing ğawm ğawm
tourist office	*Phòng thông*	fòm tawm
	tin du lịch	din zoo lịk

Is this the road to (Dien Bien Phu)?
Đường này đi   đuhr·èrng này đee
(Điện Biên Phụ) không?   (đee·uhn bee·uhn foọ) kawm

Can you show me (on the map)?
Xin chỉ giùm (trên bản đồ này)?   sin jeẻ zùm (chen baản đầw này)

What's the address?
Đĩa chị là gì?   đeẽ·uh jẹe laà zeè

How far is it?
Bao xa?   bow saa

How do I get there?
Tôi có thể đến tới bằng   doy ğó tẻ đén der·eé bùhng
đường nào?   đuhr·èrng nòw

by bus	*bằng xe buýt*	bùhng sa bweét
by taxi	*bằng xe taxi*	bùhng sa dúhk·see
by train	*bằng xe lửa*	bùhng sa lủhr·uh
on foot	*đi bộ*	đee bạw

Turn ...	Rẽ/Quẹo ... ⑬/⑤	zã/ğway·oọ ... ⑬/⑤
at the corner	ở góc đường	ér gấwp đuhr·èrng
at the traffic lights	tại đèn giao thông	daị đàn zow tawm
left/right	trái/phải	chaí/fai

It's ...	Nó ...	nó ...
behind ...	đằng sau ...	đùhng soh ...
close	gần đây	gùhn đay
far	xa	saa
here	ở đây	ér đay
in front of ...	đằng trước ...	đùhng chuhr·érk ...
left	trái	chaí
near ...	gần ...	gùhn ...
next to ...	bên cạnh ...	ben ğaạng ...
on the corner	ở góc	ér gấwp
	phố/đường ⑬/⑤	fáw/đuhr·èrng ⑬/⑤
opposite ...	đối diện ...	đóy zee·ụhn ...
right	phải	fai
straight ahead	thẳng tới trước	tủhng der·eé chuhr·érk
there	ở đó	ér đó

north	hướng bắc	huhr·érng búhk
south	hướng nam	huhr·érng naam
east	hướng đông	huhr·érng đawm
west	hướng tây	huhr·érng day

signs

Lối Vào/Lối Ra	lóy vòw/lóy raa	**Entrance/Exit**
Mở/Đóng	mér/dáwm	**Open/Closed**
Còn Phòng	ğòn fòm	**Vacancies**
Hết Phòng	hét fòm	**No Vacancies**
Tin Tức	din dúhrk	**Information**
Đồn Cảnh Sát	đàwn ğaản saát	**Police Station**
Cấm Chụp ảnh	gúhm chụp aảng	**No Photography or**
Quay Phim	gway feem	**Video Taping**
Vệ Sinh	vạy sịng	**Toilets**
Nam/Nữ	naam/nũhr	**Men/Women**
Nóng/Lạnh	nóm/laạng	**Hot/Cold**

accommodation

finding accommodation

Where's a ...?	*... ở đâu?*	*... èr đoh*
bed and breakfast	*Nhà nghỉ*	*nyà ngyeẻ*
camping ground	*Nơi cắm trại*	*ner·ee gùhm chaị*
guesthouse	*Nhà nghỉ*	*nyà ngyeẻ*
hotel	*Khách sạn*	*kaák saạn*
Can you recommend	*Bạn có thể giới*	*baạn ğó tẻ zer·eẻ*
somewhere ...?	*thiệu cho tôi chỗ ...?*	*tee·oọ jo doy jõ ...*
cheap	*rẻ*	*zả*
good	*tốt*	*dáwt*
nearby	*gần đây*	*gùhn đay*
romantic	*lãng mạn*	*laãng maạn*

I'd like to book a room, please.
Làm ơn cho tôi đặt phòng. laàm ern jo doy đụht fòm

I have a reservation.
Tôi đã đặt trước. doy đaã đụht chuhr·érk

My name is ...
Tên tôi là ... den doy laà ...

Do you have a ... room?	*Bạn có phòng ...?*	*baạn ğó fòm ...*
double	*đôi*	*đoy*
single	*đơn*	*đern*
twin	*hai giường*	*hai zuhr·èng*
How much is it per ...?	*Giá bao nhiêu cho ...?*	*zaá bow nyee·oo jo ...*
night	*một đêm*	*maạwt đem*
person	*một người*	*maạwt nguhr·èe*

For (three) nights/weeks.
　Cho (ba) đêm/tuần.　　　jo (baa) đam/dwùhn

From (July 2) to (July 6).
　Từ (mùng hai tháng bảy)　dùhr (mùm hai taáng bảy)
　đến (mùng sáu tháng bảy).　đén (mùm sóh taáng bảy)

Can I see it?
　Tôi có thể xem phòng được không?　doy ğó tẻ sam fòm đuhr·ẹrk kawm

Can I camp here?
　Tôi có thể cắm trại ở đây?　doy ğó tẻ ğứhm chại ẻr đay

Is there a camp site nearby?
　Có nơi cắm trại gần đây không?　ğó ner·ee ğứhm chại gùhn đay kawm

Can I pay ...?　　*Tôi có thể trả bằng ...?*　doy ğó tẻ chaả bùhng ...
　by credit card　　*thẻ tín dụng*　　tả dín zụm
　with a travellers　*séc du lịch*　　sák zoo lịk
　　cheque

requests & queries

When's breakfast served?
　Bữa sáng được phục vụ khi nào?　bũhr·a saáng đụhr·erk fụp voọ kee nòw

Where's breakfast served?
　Bữa sáng được phục vụ ở đâu?　bũhr·a saáng đụhr·erk fụp voọ ẻr đoh

Please wake me at (seven).
　Làm ơn đánh thức tôi　laàm ern đaáng túhrk doy
　vào lúc (bảy giờ).　vòw lúp (bảy zèr)

Could I have my key, please?
　Làm ơn cho tôi chìa　laàm ern cho doy chee·à
　khoá của tôi?　kwaá ğoỏ·uh doy

Do you have a ...?　*Bạn có ... không?*　bạan ğó ... kawm
　mosquito net　*một cái màn*　mạwt ğải maàn
　safe　　*két sắt*　　ğát súht

The room is too ...　*Phòng của tôi quá ...*　fòm ğoỏ·uh doy ğwaá ...
　expensive　*đắt*　　đúht
　noisy　　*ồn*　　àwn
　small　　*nhỏ*　　nyảw

The ... doesn't work.	Cái ... bị hỏng.	ğái ... beẹ hỏng
air conditioner	máy điều hoà	máy đee·oò hwaà
fan	quạt	ğwaạt
toilet	la-bô	laa-baw

This ... isn't clean.	Cái ... này không sạch.	ğái ... này kawm saạk
pillow	gối	góy
sheet	tấm ra	dúhm zaa
towel	khăn tắm	kuhn dúhm

checking out

What time is checkout?
Trả phòng vào lúc mấy giờ?   chả fòm vòw lúp máy zèr

Can I leave my luggage here?
Tôi có thể để lại hành lý   doy ğó tẻ đẻ lại haàng leé
ở đây không?   ẻr đay kawm

Could I have my ...., please?	Tôi có thể xin lại ... không?	doy ğó tẻ sin lại ... kawm
deposit	tiền đặt cọc	dee·èn đụht ğọp
passport	hộ chiếu	haạ chee·oó
valuables	những đồ có giá trị	nyũhrng đàw ğó zá cheẹ

communications & banking

the internet

Where's the local Internet café?
Internet càfê gần nhất ở đâu?   in·ter·net ğà·fe gùhn nyúht ẻr đoh

How much is it per hour?
Bao nhiêu tiền cho một tiếng?   bow nyee·oo dee·ùhn jo mạwt dee·úhng

I'd like to ...	Tôi muốn ...	doy moo·úhn ...
check my email	kiểm tra email	keé·uhm chaa ee·mayl
get Internet access	vào mạng	vòw maạng
use a printer	dùng máy in	zùm máy in
use a scanner	dùng máy scan	zùm máy skaan

mobile/cell phone

I'd like a mobile/cell phone for hire.
*Tôi muốn thuê một điện
thoại di động.*
doy moo·úhn twe mạwt đee·ụhn
twại zee đạwm

I'd like a SIM card for your network.
*Tôi muốn mua một SIM
điện thoại.*
doy moo·úhn moo·uh mạwt sim
đee·ụhn twại

What are the rates?
Giá bao nhiêu?
zaá bow nyee·oo

telephone

What's your phone number?
*Xin cho biết số máy
điện thoại của bạn?*
sin jo bee·úht sáw máy
đee·ụhn twại ğoỏ·uh bạạn

The number is ...
Số điện thoại là ...
sáw đee·ụhn twại làà ...

Where's the nearest public phone?
*Điện thoại công cộng
gần nhất ở đâu?*
đee·ụhn twại ğọm ğọm
gùhn nyúht ẻr đoh

I'd like to buy a phonecard.
*Tôi muốn mua một
thẻ gọi điện thoại.*
doy moo·úhn moo·uh mạwt
tả gọy đee·ụhn twại

I want to ...	*Tôi muốn ...*	doy moo·úhn ...
call (Singapore)	*gọi (Singapore)*	gọy (sin·gaa·paw)
make a local call	*gọi một cuộc
nội hạt*	gọy mạwt ğoo·ụhk
nọy hạạt
**reverse the
charges**	*người nghe
trả tiền*	nguhr·eè ngya
chả đee·ùhn

classifiers					
animals	con	ğon	**people**	*người*	nguhr·eè
couples, pairs	đôi	đoy	**plants**	cây	ğay
inanimate objects	caí	ğaí	**vehicles**	xe	sa

VIETNAMESE – communications & banking

How much does ... cost?	Giá ... bao nhiêu?	zaá ... bow nyee·oo
a (three)-minute call	một cuộc điện thoại (ba) phút	mạwt ğoo·uhk đee·uhn twại (baa) fút
each extra minute	mỗi một phút tiếp sau	mỗy mạwt fút dee·úhp soh

(500) dong per (30) seconds.
(Năm trăm) đồng cho (ba mươi) giây.   (nuhm chuhm) đàwm jo (baa muhr·ee) zay

post office

I want to send a ...	Tôi muốn gửi một ...	doy moo·úhn gúhr·ee mạwt ...
fax	bản fax	baản faak
letter	lá thư	laá tuhr
parcel	bưu phẩm	buhr·oo fủhm
postcard	bưu ảnh	buhr·oo aảng

I want to buy a/an ...	Tôi muốn mua một ...	doy moo·úhn moo·uh mạwt ...
envelope	phong bì	fom bee̊
stamp	cái tem	ğaí dam

Please send it to (Australia) by ...	Xin hãy gửi nó bằng ... đến (Úc).	sin hãy gúhr·ee nó bùhng ... đén (úp)
airmail	đường hàng không	đuhr·èrng haàng kawm
express mail	chuyển phát nhanh	jweẻ·uhn faát nyaang
registered mail	thư bảo đảm	tuhr bỏw đaảm
sea mail	đường biển	đuhr·èrng beẻ·uhn
surface mail	đường bộ	đuhr·èrng bạw

Is there any mail for me?
Có thư nào của tôi không?   ğó tuhr nòw ğoỏ·uh doy kawm

bank

I'd like to ...	Tôi muốn ...	doy moo·úhn ...
Where can I ...?	Tôi có thể ... ở đâu?	doy ğó tẻ ... ẻr đoh
cash a cheque	đổi séc ra tiền mặt	đỏy sák zaa dee·ùhn mụht
change money	đổi tiền	đỏy dee·ùhn
change a travellers cheque	đổi séc du lịch	đỏy sák zuu lịk
get a cash advance	rút tiền tạm ứng	zút dee·ùhn đaạm úhrng
withdraw money	rút tiền	zút dee·ùhn

What's the ...?	... là bao nhiêu?	... laà bow nyee·oo
charge for that	Phí cho cái đó	feé jo ğaí đó
exchange rate	Tỉ giá hối đoái	deẻ zaá hóy đwaí

It's ...		
(10,000) dong	(Mười nghìn) đồng.	muhr·eè ngyìn đàwm
free	Miễn phí.	meẻ·uhn feé

What time does the bank open?
Mấy giờ ngân hàng mở cửa? — máy zèr nguhn haàng mẻr ğủhr·uh

Has my money arrived yet?
Tiền của tôi đã đến chưa? — dee·ùhn ğoỏ·uh doy đaã đén juhr·uh

sightseeing

getting in

What time does it open/close?
Mấy giờ nó mở/đóng cửa? — máy zèr nó mẻr/đáwm ğủhr·uh

What's the admission charge?
Vé vào cửa hết bao nhiêu? — vá vòw ğủhr·uh hét bow nyee·oo

Is there a discount for ...?	... có được giảm giá không?	... ğó duhr·ẹrk zaảm zaá kawm
children	Trẻ em	chả am
students	Sinh viên	sing vee·uhn

I'd like a ...	Tôi muốn có một ...	doy moo·úhn ğó mạwt ...
catalogue	quyển ca-ta-lô	ğwee·úhn ğaa·daa·law
guide	người hướng dẫn	nguhr·eè huhr·érng zũhn
local map	bản đồ địa phương	baản đàw đee·ụh fuhr·erg

I'd like to visit ...		
Tôi muốn thăm ...		doy moo·úhn tuhm ...

What's that?
Đó là cái gì? — đó laà ğaí zeè

Can I take a photo?
Tôi có thể chụp ảnh
được không? — doy ğó tẻ jụp aảng
đuhr·erk kawm

tours

When's	Khi nào là chuyến	kee nòw laà jwee·úhn
the next ...?	... tới?	... der·eé
boat trip	du thuyền	zoo twee·ùhn
day trip	du lịch nội nhật	zoo lịk nọy nyụht
tour	thăm quan	tuhm ğwaan

Is (the) ...	Nó có bao gồm	nó ğó bow gàwm
included?	... không?	... kawm
accommodation	chỗ ở	jãw ẻr
admission charge	giá vé	zaá vá
food	đồ ăn	dàw uhn
transport	phương tiện đi lại	fuhr·erng dee·ụhn đee lại

How long is the tour?
Chuyến đi thăm quan
này là dài bao lâu? — jwee·úhn đee tuhm ğwaan
này laà zài bow loh

What time should we be back?
Mấy giờ chúng tôi được về? — máy zèr júm doy đuhr·ẹrk vè

market	chợ	jer
monument	di tích lịch sử	zee dík lịk súhr
museum	viện bảo tàng	vee·uhn bỏw daàng
old city	khu phố cổ	koo fáw gẳw
pagoda	chùa	joo·ùh
palace	cung điện	ğum dee·uhn
ruins	sự đổ nát	sụhr đảw naát
statues	bức tượng	búhrk duhr·erng
temple	một đền Phật Giáo	mạwt đèn fụht zów

shopping

enquiries

Where's a ...?	... ở đâu?	... ér đoh
bank	Ngân hàng	nguhn haàng
book shop	Tiệm sách	dee·uhm saák
camera shop	Tiệm bán máy	dee·uhm baán máy
	chụp hình	júp hìng
department store	Trung tâm	chum duhm
	mua bán	moo·uh baán
market	Chợ	jer
newsagency	Thông tấn xã	tawm dúhn saã
supermarket	Siêu thị	see·oo tẹ

I'd like to buy ...
Tôi muốn mua ...
doy moo·óhn moo·uh ...

Where can I buy (a padlock)?
Tôi có thể mua (khoá) ở đâu?
doy ğó tảy moo·uh (kwaá) ér đoh

Can I look at it?
Tôi có thể xem nó không?
doy ğó tảy sam nó kawm

Do you have any others?
Bạn có cái khác không?
bạn ğó ğaí kaák kawm

Does it have a guarantee?
Nó có được bảo hành không?
nó ğó đuhr·ẹrk bỏw haàng kawm

Can I have it sent overseas?
  Có thể gửi nó ra nước   ğó tảy gủhr·ee nó zaa nuhr·érk
  ngoài không?   ngwai kawm

Can I have my ... repaired?
  Ở đây có sửa ... không?   ẹr đay ğó sủhr·uh ... kawm

It's faulty.
  Nó bị hỏng rồi.   nó beẹ hỏm zòy

I'd like (a) ...	*Làm ơn cho tôi ...*	laàm ern jo doy ...
bag	*cái túi*	ğaí doo·eé
refund	*tiền hoàn lại*	dee·ùhn hwaàn lại
to return this	*trả lại cái này*	chaả lại ğaí này

paying

How much is it?
  Nó bao nhiêu tiền?   nó bow nyee·oo dee·ùhn

Can you write down the price?
  Bạn có thể viết giá được không? baạn ğó tảy vee·úht zaá đuhr·ẹrk kawm

That's too expensive.
  Cái đó quá đắt.   ğaí đó ğwaá đúht

Can you lower the price?
  Có thể giảm giá được không? ğó tảy zaảm zaá đuhr·ẹrk kawm

I'll give you (10,000) dong.
  Tôi chỉ trả (mười nghìn)   doy jeé chaả (muhr·eè ngìn)
  đồng thôi.   đàwm toy

There's a mistake in the bill.
  Có sự nhầm lẫn trên hoá đơn. ğó sụhr nyùhm lũhn chen hwaá đern

Do you accept ...?	*Bạn có dùng ... không?*	baạn ğó zùm ... kawm
credit cards	*thẻ tín dụng*	tả dín zụm
debit cards	*thẻ trừ tiền*	tả chùhr dee·ùhn
travellers cheques	*séc du lịch*	sák zoo lịk

I'd like ..., please.	*Làm ơn cho tôi ...*	laàm ern jo doy ...
a receipt	*hoá đơn*	hwaá đern
my change	*tiền thừa*	dee·ùhn tùhr·uh

clothes & shoes

Can I try it on?
Tôi có thể mặc thử được không?　　doy ğó tảy mụhk tủhr đuhr·ẹrk kawm

My size is (40).
Cỡ của tôi là (bốn mươi).　　ğẽr ğoo·uh doy laà (báwn muhr·ee)

It doesn't fit.
Nó không vừa.　　nó kawm vuhr·ùh

small	*bé*	bá
medium	*trung bình*	chum bìng
large	*to*	do

books & music

I'd like a …　　*Tôi muốn có một …*　　doy moo·úhn ğó mạwt …
　newspaper　　*tờ báo*　　dèr bów
　　(in English)　　*(bằng Tiếng Anh)*　　(bùhng dee·úhng aang)
　pen　　*bút bi*　　bút bee

Is there an English-language bookshop?
Có hiệu sách Tiếng Anh　　ğó hee·ọo saák dee·úhng aang
ở đây không?　　ẻr day kawm

I'm looking for something by (Hong Nhung).
Tôi đang tìm một cái gì đó　　doy daang dìm mạwt ğaí zeè đó
của ca sỹ (Hồng Nhung).　　ğoỏ·uh ğaa seẽ (hàwm nyum)

Can I listen to this?
Tôi có thể nghe thử cái này?　　doy ğó tảy ngya tủhr ğaí này

What's his/her best recording?
Đĩa nào của anh/cô　　deẽ·uh nòw ğoỏ·uh aang/ğaw
ấy là hay nhất?　　áy laà hay nyúht

photography

I need a ... film for this camera.	Tôi cần loại phim ... cho máy ảnh này.	doy ğühn lwaj feem ... jo máy aảng này
APS	APS	aa·pe·es
B&W	B&W	chúhng đén
colour	màu	mòh
slide	đèn chiếu	đàn jee·oó
(200) speed	(hai trăm) tốc độ	(hai chuhm) dáwp đạw

Can you ...?	Bạn có thể ... không?	bạan ğó tảy ... kawm
develop this film	rửa cuộn	zửh·uh ğoo·uhn
	phim này	feem này
load my film	bỏ phim trong máy	bỏ feem chom máy
transfer photos	chuyển ảnh từ	jweẻ·uhn aảng dùhr
from my camera	máy ảnh của	máy aảng goỏ·uh
to CD	tôi sang đĩa CD	doy saang đeẻ·uh se·đe

When will it be ready?	Khi nào nó sẽ xong?	kee nòw nó sã som

toiletries

conditioner	thuốc xả tóc	too·úhk saả dóp
condoms	bao cao su	bow ğow soo
deodorant	chất khử mùi	júht kửhr moo·eè
insect repellent	thuốc trừ sâu	too·úhk chùhr soh
	bọ túc	bọ dúhrk
moisturiser	kem dưỡng da	ğan zửhr·erng zaa
	cho mướt	jo muhr·ért
razor blades	lưỡi dao cạo	lũhr·ee zow ğọw
sanitary napkins	băng vệ sinh	buhng vẹ sing
shampoo	dầu gội đầu	zòh goy đòh
shaving cream	kem cạo rau	ğam ğọw zoh
soap	xà phòng	saà fòm
sunscreen	kem chống nắng	ğam jáwm núhng
toilet paper	giấy vệ sinh	záy vẹ sing
toothbrush	bàn chải đánh răng	bàan jaỉ đáang zuhng
toothpaste	kem đánh răng	ğam đáang zuhng

personal & possessive pronouns		
I	*tôi*	doy
you sg	*bạn*	baạn
he	*ông ấy*	awm áy
she	*bà ấy*	baà áy
it	*cái đó*	ğaí dó
we excl/incl	*chúng tôi/ta*	júm doy/daa
you pl	*các bạn*	kaák baạn
they	*họ*	họ
my	*của tôi*	ğoỏ·uh doy
your sg	*của bạn*	ğoỏ·uh baạn
his	*của ông ấy*	ğoỏ·uh awm áy
her	*của bà ấy*	ğoỏ·uh baà áy
our excl/incl	*của chúng tôi/ta*	ğoỏ·uh júm doy/daa
your pl	*của các bạn*	ğoỏ·uh kaák baạn
their	*của họ*	ğoỏ·uh họ

meeting people

greetings, goodbyes & introductions

Hello.	*Xin chào.*	sin jòw
Hi.	*Chào.*	jòw
Goodbye.	*Tạm biệt.*	daạm bee·ụht
Good night.	*Chúc ngủ ngon.*	júp ngoỏ ngon
Mr/Sir	*Anh/Ông*	aang/awm
Mrs/Madam	*Chị/Bà*	jeẹ/baà
Miss/Ms	*Cô*	ğaw

How are you?	Bạn khoẻ không?	bạan kwả kawm
Fine. And you?	Khoẻ. Còn bạn thì sao?	kwả ğòn bạan teè sow
What's your name?	Tên bạn là gì?	den bạan làà zeè
My name is …	Tên tôi là …	den doy làà …
I'm pleased to meet you.	Tôi rất vui được gặp bạn.	doy zúht voo·ee đuhr·ẹrk ğụhp bạan

This is my …	Đây là … của tôi.	đay làà … ğoỏ·uh doy
brother (older)	anh	aang
brother (younger)	em	am
boyfriend	bạn trai	bạan chai
daughter	con gái	ğon gái
father	bố	báw
friend	bạn	bạan
girlfriend	bạn gái	bạan gái
husband	chồng	jòm
mother	mẹ	mạ
partner (intimate)	tình nhân	đìng nyuhn
sister (older)	chị	jeẹ
sister (younger)	em	am
son	con trai	ğon chai
wife	vợ	vẹr

| What's your (address)? | (Địa chỉ) của bạn là gì? | (dee·ụh jeẻ) ğoỏ·uh bạan làà zeè |

Here's my …	Đây là … của tôi.	đay làà … ğoỏ·uh doy
(email) address	địa chỉ (email)	đee·ụh jeẻ (ee·mayl)
fax number	số fax	sáw faak
(mobile) number	số điện thoại (di động)	sáw đee·ụhn twại (zee đạwm)

occupations

| What's your occupation? | Bạn làm nghề gì? | bạan lààm ngyè zeè |

I'm a/an …	Tôi là …	doy làà …
chef	đầu bếp	đòh bép
doctor	bác sĩ	baák seẽ
farmer	nông dân	nawm zuhn
teacher	giáo viên	zów vee·uhn

background

Where are you from?	Bạn từ đâu đến?	baạn dùhr doh dén
I'm from ...	Tôi từ ...	doy dùhr ...
Australia	Úc	úp
Canada	Ca-na-đa	ğaa·naa·đaa
England	Anh	aang
Ireland	Ái-len	aí·laan
New Zealand	Tân Tây Lan	duhn day laan
the USA	Mỹ	meẽ
Are you married?	Bạn lập gia đình chưa?	baạn lụhp zaa đìng juhr·uh
I'm ...	Tôi ...	doy ...
married	đã lập gia đình	daã lụhp zaa đìng
single	độc thân	đạwp tuhn

age

How old ...?	... bao nhiêu tuổi?	... bow nyee·oo dóy
are you	Bạn	baạn
is your daughter	Con gái của bạn	ğon gaí ğoỏ·uh baạn
is your son	Con trai của bạn	ğon chai ğoỏ·uh baạn
I'm ... years old.	Tôi ... tuổi.	doy ... dóy
He/She is ... years old.	Anh/Cô ấy ... tuổi.	ang/ğaw áy ... dóy

feelings

I'm (not) ...	Tôi (không) thấy ...	doy (kawm) táy ...
Are you ...?	Bạn có thấy ... không?	baạn ğó táy ... kawm
cold	lạnh	laạng
happy	vui	voo·ee
hot	nóng	nóm
hungry	đói	đóy
sad	buồn	boo·ùhn
thirsty	khát nước	kaát nuhr·érk
tired	mệt mỏi	mẹt mỏy

entertainment

beach

Where's the ... beach?	*Bãi biển ... ở đâu?*	baĩ beé·uhn ... ér doh
best	*đẹp nhất*	đạp nyúht
nearest	*gần nhất*	ğùhn nyúht
public	*công cộng*	ğawm ğạwm
How much for	*Một cái ... bao*	mạwt ğaí ... bow
a/an ...?	*nhiêu tiền?*	nyee·oo dee·ùhn
chair	*ghế*	gé
umbrella	*ô*	aw

Is it safe to dive/swim here?
Có an toàn để lặn/bơi   ğó aan dwaàn đẻ lụhn/ber·ee
ở đây không?   ẹr đay kawm

What time is high/low tide?
Mấy giờ thuỷ triều lên/xuống?   máy zèr tweé chee·oò len/soo·úhng

water sports

Can I book a lesson?
Tôi có thể đặt buổi học không?   doy ğó tẻ đụht boỏ·ee họp kawm

Can I hire (a) ...?	*Tôi có thể thuê ... không?*	doy ğó tẻ twe ... kawm
boat	*thuyền*	twee·ùhn
canoe	*ca-nô*	ğa·naw
diving equipment	*đồ lặn nước*	đàw lụhn nuhr·érk
guide	*người hướng dẫn*	nguhr·eè huhr·érng zũhn
kayak	*xuổng cai-ac*	soo·ùhng ğai·aak
life jacket	*áo phao*	ów fow
motorboat	*xuồng máy*	soo·ùhng máy
sailboard	*ván buồm*	vaán boo·ùhm
sailing boat	*thuyền buồm*	twee·ùhn boo·ùhm
snorkelling	*thiết bị lặn*	tee·úht bẹe lụhn
gear	*bằng ống thở*	bùhng áwm tẻr
surfboard	*ván lướt sóng*	vaán luhr·ért sóm

Are there any ...?	Có ... ở đây không?	ğó ... èr đay kawm
reefs	san hô	saan haw
rips	dòng nước xiết chảy	zòm nuhr·érk see·úht jày
water hazards	những hiểm	nyũhrng heẻ·uhm
	hoạ do nước	hwaạ zo nuhr·érk

going out

Where can I find ...?	Tôi có thể tìm	doy ğó tẻ dìm
	các ... ở đâu?	kaák ... èr đoh
clubs	vũ trường	voõ chuhr·èrng
gay venues	quán mà giới	ğwaán màa zer·eé
	đồng tính hay đến	đàwm díng hay đén
pubs	quán rượu	ğwaán zee·oọ
I feel like going to a/the ...	Tôi muốn đi ...	doy moo·úhn đee ...
concert	nghe hoà nhạc	ngye hwàa nyaạk
karaoke bar	hát karaoke	haát ğaa·raa·o·ğe
movies	xem phim	sam feem
party	dự tiệc	zụhr dee·ụhk
performance	xem trình diễn	sam chìng zeẽ·uhn
water-puppet theatre	xem múa rối	sam moo·úh zóy

interests

Do you like ...?	Bạn có thích ... không?	baạn ğó tík ... kawm
I (don't) like ...	Tôi (không) thích ...	doy (kawm) tík ...
cockfighting	chọi gà	joy gàa
cooking	nấu ăn	nóh uhn
movies	xem phim	sam feem
music	nghe nhạc	ngya nyaạk
photography	chụp ảnh	jup ảng
reading	đọc sách	đọp saák
sport	chơi thể thao	jer·ee tẻ tow
surfing the Internet	lướt mạng	luhr·ért maạng
travelling	đi du lịch	đee zoo lịk
watching TV	xem vô tuyến	sam vaw dwee·úhn

Do you like to ...?	Bạn có ... không?	baạn ğó ... kawm
dance	biết khiêu vũ	bee·úht kee·oo voõ
go to concerts	hay đi nghe nhạc	hay đee ngya nyaạk
listen to music	nghe nhạc	ngya nyaạk

food & drink

finding a place to eat

Can you	Bạn có thể giới	baạn ğó tẻ zer·eé
recommend a ...?	thiệu một ... không?	tee·oọ mạwt ... kawm
bar	quán bar	ğwaán baa
café	quán càfê	ğwaán ğaà·fe
restaurant	nhà hàng	nyaà haàng

I'd like ..., please.	Xin cho tôi ...	sin jo doy ...
a table for (five)	một bàn cho	mạwt baàn jo
	(năm) người	(nuhm) nguhr·eè
the nonsmoking	bàn trong khu	baàn chom koo
section	không hút thuốc	kawm hút too·úhk
the smoking section	bàn có hút thuốc	baàn ğó hút too·úhk

ordering food

breakfast	ăn sáng	uhn saáng
lunch	ăn trưa	uhn chuhr·uh
dinner	ăn tối	uhn dóy
snack	ăn nhẹ	uhn nyạ

I'd like (the) ..., please.	Tôi muốn ...	doy moo·úhn ...
bill	hoá đơn	hwaá đern
drink list	thực đơn đồ uống	tụhrk đern đàw oo·úhng
menu	thực đơn	tụhrk đern
that dish	món kia	món ğee·uh

What would you recommend?

Bạn có giới thiệu những món gì?   baạn ğó zer·eé tee·oọ nyũhrng món zeè

bowl	*bát/chén* ⑧/⑤	baát/jén ⑧/⑤
chopsticks	*đũa*	đoõ·uh
cloth	*khăn trải bàn*	kuhn chaỉ baàn
cup	*cái tách*	ğaí daák
fork	*cái nĩa*	ğaí neẽ·uh
glass	*cốc/ly* ⑧/⑤	ğáwp/lee ⑧/⑤
knife	*con dao*	ğon zow
plate	*đĩa*	deẽ·uh
spoon	*thìa*	tee·ùh
teaspoon	*muỗng nhỏ*	moõ·uhng nyỏ

drinks

(cup of) coffee ...	*(một cốc) càfê ...*	(mạwt ğáwp) ğaà·fe ...
(cup of) tea ...	*(một cốc) trà ...*	(mạwt ğáwp) chaà ...
with milk	*có sữa*	ğó sũhr·uh
without sugar	*không có đường*	kawm ğó đuhr·èrng
orange juice	*nước cam*	nuhr·érk ğaam
soft drink	*nước ngọt*	nuhr·érk ngọt
... water	*nước ...*	nuhr·érk ...
boiled	*sôi*	soy
hot	*nóng*	nóm
sparkling mineral	*sô-đa*	saw·đaa
still mineral	*suối*	soo·eé

in the bar

I'll have ...
  Cho tôi ...   jo doy ...

I'll buy you a drink.
  Cho tôi mua một ly   jo doy moo·uh mạwt lee
  rượu cho bạn.   zee·oọ jo baạn

What would you like?
  Bạn thích uống gì?   baạn tík oo·úhng zeè

Cheers!
  Chúc sức khoẻ!   júp súhrk kwả

gin	*gin*	jin
rum	*rom*	zom
vodka	*vốtka*	váwt·ğaa

a bottle of (wine)	*một chai (rượu vang)*	mạwt jai (zee·oọ vaang)
a glass of (beer)	*một cốc (bia)*	mạwt ğáwp (bi·uh)
a shot of (whisky)	*một ngụm rượu (uytky)*	mạwt ngụm zee·oọ (wit·ğee)

... wine	*rượu vang ...*	zee·oọ vaang ...
red	*đỏ*	đỏ
sparkling	*có ga*	ğó gaa
white	*trắng*	chaáng

self-catering

What's the local speciality?
  Có những đặc sản gì ở đây?   ğó nyũhrng đụhk saản zeè ér đay

What's that?
  Cái đó là cái gì?   ğaí đó laà ğaí zeè

How much is a kilo of (rice)?
  Một cân (gạo) là bao nhiêu?   mạwt ğuhn (gọw) laà bow nyee·oo

I'd like ...	Cho tôi ...	jo doy ...
(200) grams	(hai trăm) gam	(hai chuhm) gaam
(two) kilos	(hai) cân	(hai) ğuhn
(three) pieces	(ba) cái	(baa) ğái
(six) slices	(sáu) miếng	(sóh) mee·úhng

Enough.	Đủ rồi.	đoŏ zòy
A bit more.	Một chút nữa.	mạwt jút nhủr·uh
Less.	Ít hơn.	ít hern

special diets & allergies

Is there a vegetarian restaurant near here?
Có nhà hàng đồ chay	gó nyaà haàng đàw jay
nào gần đây không?	nòw gùhn đay kawm

Do you have vegetarian food?
Bạn có đồ chay không?	bạan gó đàw jay kawm

Could you prepare	Bạn có thể chuẩn	bạan ğó tẻ joỏ·uhn
a meal without ...?	bị những món không	beẹ nyũhrng món kawm
	có ... được không?	ğó ... đuhr·ẹrk kawm
butter	bơ	ber
eggs	trứng	chúhrng
fish sauce	nước mắm	nuhr·èrk múhm
meat	thịt	tịt
meat stock	nước hầm	nuhr·érk hùhm
	xương thịt	suhr·erng tịt

I'm allergic to ...	Ăn ... làm cho tôi	uhn ... laàm jo doy
	bị dị ứng nặng.	beẹ zeẹ úhrng nụhng
chilli	ớt	ért
dairy produce	đồ làm từ sữa	đàw laàm dùhr sũhr·uh
eggs	trứng	chúhrng
gluten	chất glutên	júht gloo·ten
MSG	mì chính	meè jíng
nuts	các loại hạt	ğaák lwại hạat
seafood	đồ biển	đàw beẻ·uhn

For other allergies see **health**, page 244.

menu decoder

bánh cốm	baáng gẵwm	sticky green rice cake
bánh chay	baáng jay	boiled dumplings
bánh chưng	baáng juhrng	boiled dumplings of glutinous rice wrapped in bamboo leaves
bánh cuốn	baáng ğoo·úhn	steamed rolls made of rice flour
bánh Huế	baáng hwé	rice flour pudding stuffed with minced shrimp
bánh khoai	baáng kwai	sweet potato cake or crepe
bánh mì thịt	baáng meè tịt	meat (usually pork) roll with vegetables
bánh phở	baáng fér	flat rice noodles
bánh phồng tôm	baáng fòm dawm	'prawn crackers' – shrimp chips
bánh tro	baáng cho	sweet cake made of Japanese lily fruit, water, lime & rice
bánh xèo	baáng say·oò	a cross between an omelette & a crepe, filled with pork & prawns & eaten wrapped in lettuce
bò lá lốt	bò laá láwt	minced beef wrapped in betel leaves & char-grilled
bún bò	bún bò	rice noodles with braised beef & chilli
bún ốc	bún áwp	rice noodles with cooked snail meat
canh chua cá	ğaang joo·uh ğaá	hot & sour fish soup
cá quả hấp với bia rau gía vị	ğaá ğwaả húhp ver·eé bee·uh zoh zaá veẹ	rock fish steamed in beer & seasoning
cơm hương giang	ğerm huhr·erng zaang	Huế rice with vegetables
củ kiệu chua	ğoỏ ğee·oọ joo·uh	pickled shallots
chá cá lã vọng	jaả ğaá laã vọm	fried fish cooked with noodles & spring onions in a charcoal brazier

chả giò	jaả zò	fried spring rolls wrapped in a lettuce leaf with various herbs & dipped in fish sauce, sugar, lime juice & chilli
chạo tôm	jow dawm	minced shrimp wrapped around sugar cane
chè bánh trôi	jà baáng choy	sweet pudding with round balls, eaten with sweet sauce (the larger balls are stuffed with sweet cooked green beans)
gỏi ngó sen	goí ngo san	lotus stem salad
lạp xưởng	laạp suhr·érng	sweet Chinese pork sausage
lẩu dê	lòh ze	lamb or goat hot pot
lẩu lươn	lòh luhr·ern	eel hot pot
mứt	múhrt	jam • sugared dried fruits & vegetables
mực khô	muhrk kaw	dried squid
nem nướng	nam nuhr·érng	grilled meatballs eaten with rice noodles & fish sauce
nước chấm	nuhr·èrk júhm	dipping sauce made from fish sauce, sugar, lime juice & chilli
ô mai	aw mai	apricots (or other small fruits) preserved in salt, licorice & ginger
ốc hấp bia	áwp húhp bee·uh	snails cooked with beer
ốc xào cả vỏ	áwp sòw ğaả vỏ	stir-fried snails (still in their shells)
phở	fèr	noodle soup usually served with beef or chicken
phở bò	fèr bò	noodles served with beef
phở gà	fèr ğaà	noodles served with chicken
tôm khô	dawm kaw	dried shrimp
tôm xào hành nấm	dawm sòw haàng núhm	shrimp with mushrooms
thịt chó	tịt jó	dog meat
thịt kho nước dừa	tịt ko nuhr·érk	pork braised in coconut milk

emergencies

basics

Help!	*Cứu tôi với!*	ğuhr·oó doy vér·ee
Stop!	*Dừng lại đi!*	zùhrng laị đee
Go away!	*Đi đi!*	đee đee
Thief!	*Cướp!*	ğuhr·érp
Fire!	*Cháy!*	jáy
Call an ambulance.	*Gọi một xe cứu thương.*	goy maụt sa ğuhr·oó tuhr·erng
Call a doctor.	*Gọi bác sĩ.*	goy baák seẽ
Call the police.	*Gọi cảnh sát.*	goy ğaảng saát

It's an emergency!
Đó là một ca cấp cứu.
đó laà maụt ğaa ğúhp ğhuhr·oó

There's been an accident.
Có một tai nạn.
ğó maụt dai naạn

Could you help me, please?
Làm ơn giúp đỡ?
laàm ern zúp đẽr

Can I use your phone?
Tôi có thể dùng điện thoại của bạn được không?
doy ğó tẻ zùm đee·ụhn twaị ğoó·uh baạn đuhr·ẹrk kawm

I'm lost.
Tôi bị lạc.
doy beẹ laạk

Where are the toilets?
Nhà vệ sinh ở đâu?
nyaà vẹ sing ẻr đoh

police

Where's the police station?
Đồn cảnh sát ở đâu?
đàwn ğaảng saát ẻr đoh

I want to report an offence.
Tôi muốn tường trình một hành vi phạm tội.
doy moo·úhn duhr·èrng chìng maụt haàng vee faạm doỵ

English	Vietnamese	Pronunciation
I've been ...	Tôi đã từng bị ...	doy đaã dùhrng bẹe ...
assaulted	hành hung	haàng hum
raped	hiếp dâm	hee·úhp zuhm
robbed	ăn cướp	uhn ğuhr·érp
I've lost my ...	Tôi đã bị mất ...	doy đaã bẹe múht ...
backpack	ba lô	ba law
credit card	thẻ tín dụng	tả dín zụm
jewellery	trang sức	chaang súhrk
passport	hộ chiếu	hạw chee·oó
My ... was/were stolen.	... của tôi đã bị lấy cắp.	... ğoỏ·uh doy đaã bẹe láy ğúhp
bags	Túi sách	doo·eé saák
handbag	Túi sách tay	doo·eé saák day
money	Tiền	dee·ùhn
travellers cheques	Séc du lịch	sák zoo lịk
wallet	Ví	veé
I want to contact my ...	Tôi muốn liên lạc với ...	doy moo·úhn lee·uhn laạk ver·eé ...
consulate	phòng lãnh sự	fòm laãng sụhr
embassy	đại sứ quán	đại súhr gwaán
I have insurance.	Tôi có bảo hiểm.	doy ğó bỏw heẻ·uhm

health

medical needs

English	Vietnamese	Pronunciation
Where's the nearest ...?	... gần nhất ở đâu?	... ğùhn nyút ẻr doh
dentist	Phòng khám nha khoa	fòm kaám nyaa kwaa
doctor	Bác sĩ	baák seẽ
hospital	Bệnh viện	bẹng vee·ụhn
(night) pharmacist	(Đêm) cửa hàng dược phẩm	(đem) ğủhr·uh haàng zuhr·ẹrk fủhm

I need a doctor (who speaks English).
Tôi cần một bác sĩ   doy ğùhn mạwt baák seĕ
(nói tiếng Anh).   (nóy dee·úhng aang)

Could I see a female doctor?
Tôi có thể gặp một bác   doy ğó tẻ gụhp mạwt baák
sĩ nữ được không?   seĕ nũhr đuhr·ẹrk kawm

I've run out of my medication.
Tôi đã hết thuốc điều trị.   doy đaã hét too·úhk đee·oò chẹ

symptoms, conditions & allergies

I'm sick.	*Tôi bị ốm.*	doy bẹẹ áwm
It hurts here.	*Nó đau ở chỗ này.*	nó đoh ẻr jãw này
ankle	*cổ chân*	ğảw juhn
arm	*tay*	day
back	*lưng*	luhrng
chest	*ngực*	nguhrk
ear	*tai*	dai
eye	*mắt*	múht
face	*mặt*	mụht
finger	*ngón tay*	ngón day
foot	*bàn chân*	baàn juhn
hand	*bàn tay*	baàn day
head	*đầu*	đòh
heart	*trái tim*	chái dim
leg	*chân*	juhn
mouth	*miệng*	mee·ụhng
neck	*cổ*	ğảw
nose	*mũi*	moõ·ee
skin	*da*	zaa
stomach	*bụng*	bụm
teeth	*răng*	zuhng
throat	*cuống họng*	ğoo·úhng họm

I have (a) ...	Tôi bị ...	doy beẹ ...
allergy	dị ứng	zeẹ úhrng
asthma	bệnh hen suyễn	bẹng han sweẽ·uhn
bronchitis	bệnh viêm cuống phổi	bẹng vee·uhm ğoo·úhng fỏy
constipation	táo bón	dów bón
cough	ho	ho
diarrhoea	tiêu chảy	dee·oo jảy
fever	sốt	sáwt
headache	đau đầu	đoh đòh
heat stroke	lả đi vì nóng	laả đee veè nóm
nausea	buồn nôn	boo·ùhn nawn
pain	đau	đoh
sore throat	viêm họng	vee·uhm họm
toothache	đau răng	đoh zuhng

I'm allergic to ...	... làm tôi bị dị ứng.	... laàm doy beẹ zeẹ úhrng
antibiotics	Thuốc kháng sinh	too·úhk kaáng sing
anti-inflammatories	Thuốc chống viêm	too·úhk jóm vee·uhm
aspirin	Thuốc giảm đau	too·úhk zaảm đoh
bees	Con ong	ğon om
codeine	Thuốc côđêin	too·úhk ğo·đeen
penicillin	Thuốc pênicilin	pe·nee·see·lin

antifungal cream	thuốc Diệt Nấm	too·úhk zee·ụht núhm
antimalarial medication	thuốc chống sốt rét	too·úhk jáwm sáwt zát
antiseptic	thuốc diệt trùng	too·úhk zee·ụht chùm
bandage	băng	buhng
Band-Aid	băng dán	buhng zaán
contraceptives	thuốc tránh thai	too·úhk chaáng tai
diarrhoea medicine	thuốc chống bệnh ia chảy	too·úhk jáwm bẹng yả jải
insect repellent	thuốc trừ sâu bọ tức	too·úhk chùhr soh bọ dúhrk
laxatives	thuốc nhuận trường	too·úhk nyoo·ụhn chuhr·èrng
painkillers	thuốc giảm đau	too·úhk zaảm đoh
rehydration salts	thuốc muối hyđrat	too·úhk moo·eé hee·đraat
sleeping tablets	thuốc ngủ	too·úhk ngoỏ

See **special diets & allergies**, page 238, for food-related allergies.

The symbols ⓝ, ⓐ and ⓥ (indicating noun, adjective and verb) have been added for clarity where an English term could be either. When we've given both the southern and northern translation of a word, the two options are marked as ⓢ and ⓝ and separated by a slash. For food terms, see the **menu decoder**, page 239.

A

accident *tai nạn* dai naạn
accommodation *chỗ ở* jãw ér
adaptor *ổ cắm điện* áw ğũhm dee·ụhn
address ⓝ *địa chỉ* dee·ụh jẻ
after *sau* soh
air-conditioned *được không điều hòa nhiệt độ* duhr·ẹrk kawm đee·oò hwaà nyee·ụht đạw
airplane *máy bay* máy bay
airport *sân bay* suhn bay
alcohol *rượu* zee·oọ
all *tất cả* dúht ğaả
allergy *dị ứng* zeẹ úhrng
ambulance *xe cấp cứu* sa ğúhp ğuhr·oó
and *và* vaà
ankle *cổ chân* ğăw juhn
arm *tay* day
automated teller machine (ATM) *máy rút tiền tự động* máy zút dee·ùhn dụhr đạwm

B

baby *em bé* am bá
backpack *ba lô* baa law
bad *xấu* sóh
bag *túi sách* doo·eé saák
baggage claim *thu hành lý* too haàng leé
bank *ngân hàng* nguhn haàng
bank account *tài khoản nhà băng* dài kwaản nyaà buhng
bar *quầy rượu* ğwày zee·oọ
bathroom *phòng tắm* fòm dúhm
battery *pin* pin

beach *bãi biển* baĩ bee·ủhn
beautiful *đẹp* đạp
bed *cái giường* ğaí zuhr·èrng
beer *bia* bee·uh
before *trước đây* chuhr·érk day
behind *đằng sau* đùhng soh
bicycle *xe đạp* sa daạp
big *lớn* lérn
bill *hóa đơn* hwaá đern
black *màu đen* mòh đan
blanket *cái mền* ğaí mèn
blood *máu* móh
blood group *nhóm máu* nyóm móh
book (make a reservation) ⓥ *giữ trước* zũhr chuhr·érk
both *cả hai* ğaả hai
bottle *chai* jai
bottle opener *cái mở chai* ğaí mẻr jai
boy *con trai* ğon chai
brakes (car) *cái thắng xe* ğaí túhng sa
breakfast *ăn sáng* uhn saáng
broken (faulty) *bị gẫy* beẹ gãy
bus *xe buýt* sa bwéet
business *buôn bán* boo·uhn baán
bus stop *trạm xe buýt* chụhm sa bwéet
buy *mua* moo·uh

C

café *quán càfê* ğwaán ğaà·fe
camera *máy chụp hình* máy júp hìng
camp site *khu vực dùng để cắm trại* koo vụhrk zùm đẻ ğúhm chaị
cancel *hủy bỏ* hweẻ bỏ

can opener *cái mở đồ hộp* ğaí mér đàw hạwp
car *xe hơi* sa her·ee
cash ⓝ *tiền* dee·ùhn
cash (a cheque) ⓥ *đổi tiền séc* đỏy dee·ùhn sák
cell phone *điện thoại di động*
   dee·ụhn twại zee dạwm
centre ⓝ *trung tâm* chum duhm
change (money) ⓥ *đổi* đỏy
cheap *rẻ* zả
check (bill) *hóa đơn* hwaá đern
check-in ⓝ *quầy ghi danh* ğwày gee zaang
cheque (bank) ⓝ *tiền séc* dee·ùhn sák
chest (body) *ngực* nguhrk
child *đứa trẻ* đuhr·úh chả
cigarette *thuốc lá* too·úhk laá
city *thành phố* tàang fáw
clean ⓐ *sạch sẽ* saạk sã
closed *đóng* đáwm
coffee *càfê* ğaà·fe
coins *tiền cắc* dee·ùhn ğúhk
cold ⓝ *lạnh* laạng
cold (illness) ⓝ *cảm* ğaảm
collect call *cú điện thoại người nhận trả tiền*
   ğoó dee·ụhn twại nguhr·èè nyụhn chaả
   dee·ùhn
come *đến* dén
computer *máy vi tính* máy vee díng
condom *bao cao su* bow ğow soo
contact lenses *kính áp tròng* ğíng aáp chòm
cook ⓥ *nấu ăn* nóh uhn
cost ⓝ *gía* zaá
credit card *thẻ tín dụng* tẻ dín zụm
currency exchange *dịch vụ đổi tiền*
   zịk vọo đỏy dee·ùhn
customs (immigration) *hải quan* haỉ ğwaan

D

dangerous *nguy hiểm* ngwee heẻ·uhm
date (time) *ngày tháng* ngày taáng
day *ngày* ngày
delay ⓝ *sự chậm trễ* sụhr jụhm chẽ
dentist *nha sĩ* nyaa seẽ

departure *sự khởi hành* sụhr kér·ee haàng
diaper *cái tã* ğaí daã
diarrhoea *bệnh tiêu chảy* bẹng deẻ·oo jảy
dictionary *tự điển* dụhr dee·ùhn
dinner *buổi ăn tối* boỏ·ee uhn dóy
direct *trực tiếp* chụrk dee·úhp
dirty *dơ* der
disabled *bất lực* búht lụhrk
discount ⓝ *giảm giá* zaảm zaá
doctor *bác sĩ* baák seẽ
double bed *giường đôi* zuhr·èrng doy
double room *phòng đôi* fòm doy
down *xuống* soo·úhng
drink ⓥ *thức uống* túhrk oo·úhng
drive ⓥ *lái xe* laí sa
drivers licence *bằng lái xe* bùhng laí sa
drug (illicit) *ma túy* maa dweé
dummy (pacifier) *núm vú giả* núm voó zaả

E

early ⓐ *sớm* sérm
ear *tai* dai
east *hướng đông* huhr·érng dawm
eat *ăn* uhn
economy class *cấp thường* ğúhp tuhr·èrng
electricity *điện lực* dee·ụhn lụhrk
elevator *thang máy* taang máy
email *email* ee·mayl
embassy *đại sứ* dại súhr
emergency *cấp cứu* ğúhp ğuhr·oó
empty *trống rỗng* cháwm zãwm
English (language) *tiếng Anh* dee·úhng aang
English (people) *người Anh* nguhr·èè aang
enough *đủ* doỏ
entrance *cửa vào* ğủhr·uh vòw
evening *buổi tối* boỏ·ee dóy
exchange (money) ⓥ *đổi* đỏy
exchange rate *tỷ lệ hối đoái* deẻ lệ hóy dwaí
exit ⓝ *lối ra* lóy zaa
expensive *đắt tiền* đúht dee·ùhn
express mail *thư tốc hành* tuhr dáwp haàng
eye *mắt* múht

F

face *mặt* muht
far *xa* saa
fast *nhanh* nyaang
father *bố* báw
faulty *có thiếu sót* ğó tee·óo sót
fever *cơn sốt* ğern sáwt
film (camera) *cuộn phim* ğoo·uhn feem
finger *ngón tay* ngón day
first *đầu tiên* dòh dee·uhn
first-aid kit *hộp cứu thương*
   hawp ğuhr·óo tuhr·erng
first-class (ticket) ⓐ *hạng nhất* haạng nyúht
fish ⓝ *cá* ğaá
fly (a plane) ⓥ *bay* bay
food *thức ăn* túhrk uhn
foot *bàn chân* baàn juhn
fork *cái nĩa* ğaí neé·uh
free (of charge) *miễn phí* meẽ·uhn feé
friend *bạn* baạn
fruit *trái cây* chaí ğay
full *đầy* dày
funny *buồn cười* boo·ùhn ğuhr·eè

G

gift *quà* ğwaà
girl *con gái* ğon gaí
glass (drinking) *cốc/ly* Ⓝ/Ⓢ ğáwp/lee
glasses *cái kính* ğaí ğíng
go *đi* dee
good *tốt* dáwt
green *màu xanh lá cây* mòh saang laá ğay
guide ⓝ *người hướng dẫn*
   nguhr·eè huhr·érng zũhn

H

half ⓝ *nửa* nủhr·uh
hand ⓝ *bàn tay* baàn day
handbag *túi xách* doo·eé saák
happy *vui vẻ* voo·ee vả

have *có* ğó
head ⓝ *đầu* dòh
headache *nhức đầu* nyúhrk dòh
heart *trái tim* chaí dim
heart condition *bệnh tim* beạng dim
heat ⓝ *hơi nóng* her·ee nóm
heavy *nặng* nụhng
help ⓥ *giúp* zúp
here *đây* day
high *cao* ğow
highway *xa lộ* saa lạw
hike ⓥ *đi bộ đường dài* dee bạw duhr·èrng zaì
homosexual *đồng tình luyến ái*
   dàwm dìng lwee·úhn aí
hospital *bệnh viện* beạng vee·ụhn
hot *nóng* nóm
hotel *khách sạn* kaák saạn
hungry *đói* dóy
husband *chồng* jàwm

I

identification (card) *giấy chứng minh*
   záy chúhrng ming
ill *đau ốm* doh áwm
important *quan trọng* ğwaan chọm
included *bao gồm* bow gàwm
injury *thương tích* tuhr·erng dík
insurance *sự bảo hiểm* suhr bỏw heẻ·uhm
Internet *mạng internet* maạng in·ter·net
interpreter *thông ngon viên*
   tawm ngon vee·uhn

J

jewellery *đồ trang sức* dàw xhaang súhrk
job *việc làm* vee·ụhk laàm

K

key *chìa khóa* jee·ùh kwaá
kilogram *kí lô* ğee law
kitchen *nhà bếp* nyaà bép
knife *con dao* ğon zow

L

late *trễ* chē
laundry (place) *phòng giặt* fòm zụht
lawyer *luật sư* lwụht suhr
left luggage office *phòng giữ đồ* fòm zữhr đàw
leg *chân* juhn
lesbian *phụ nữ đồng tính luyến ái*
   foọ nũhr đàwm díng lwee·úhn aí
less *ít hơn* ít hern
letter *thư* tuhr
lift (elevator) *thang máy* taang máy
light Ⓝ *ánh sáng* aáng saáng
like Ⓥ *thích* tík
lock Ⓝ *ổ khóa* ảw kwaá
long *dài* zaì
lost *bị mất* bẹ múht
lost property office *phòng đồ đạc bị thất lạc*
   fòm đàw đaạk bẹ túht laạk
love Ⓥ *yêu* ee·oo
luggage *hành lý* haàng leé
lunch *bữa ăn trưa* bũhr·uh uhn chuhr·uh

M

mail Ⓝ *thư từ* tuhr dùhr
man *đàn ông* đaàn awm
map *bản đồ* baản đàw
market *chợ* jẹr
matches *diêm quẹt* zee·uhm ğwạt
meat *thịt* tịt
medicine *thuốc* too·úhk
menu *thực đơn* tựhrk đern
message *lời nhắn tin* ler·eè nyúhn din
milk *sữa* sũhr·uh
minute *phút* fút
mobile phone *điện thoại di động*
   dee·ụhn twaị zee đạwm
money *tiền* dee·ùhn
month *tháng* taáng
morning *buổi sáng* boỏ·ee saáng
mother *mẹ* mạ
motorcycle *xe môtô* sa maw·taw

motorway *xa lộ siêu tốc* saa lạw see·oo đáwp
mountain *núi* noo·eé
mouth *miệng* mee·ụhng
music *âm nhạc* uhm nyaạk

N

name *tên* den
nappy *cái tã* ğaí daã
nausea *buồn nôn* boo·ùhn nawn
near *gần* gùhn
new *mới* mer·eé
news *tin tức* din dúhrk
newspaper *tờ báo* dèr bów
night *ban đêm* naan dem
no *không* kawm
noisy *ồn ào* àwn òw
nonsmoking *cấm hút thuốc lá*
   ğúhm hút too·úhk laá
north *hướng bắc* huhr·érng búhk
nose *mũi* moõ·ee
now *bây giờ* bay zèr
number *số* sáw

O

oil (engine) *dầu* zòh
old *già* zaà
on *trên* chen
one-way (ticket) *vé một chiều* vá mạwt jee·oò
open Ⓐ&Ⓥ *mở* mèr
other *khác* kaák
outside *bên ngoài* ben ngwaì

P

package *đóng gói* đóm góy
pain *đau* đoh
painkillers *thuốc giảm đau* too·úhk zaảm đoh
paper *giấy* záy
park (car) Ⓥ *đậu xe* đọh sa
passport *hộ chiếu* hạw jee·oó
pay *trả* chaà
pen *bút bi* bút bee

petrol *xăng dầu* suhng zòh
pharmacy *hiệu thuốc* hee·oọ too·úhk
phonecard *thẻ điện thoại* té dee·ụhn twaị
photo *tấm hình* dúhm hìng
plate *cái đĩa* ğaí đee·ủh
police *cảnh sát* ğaảng saát
postcard *bưu ảnh* buhr·oo aảng
post office *bưu điện* buhr·oo đee·ụhn
pregnant *có thai* ğó tai
price *giá* zaá

Q

quiet *yên lặng* ee·uhn lụhng

R

rain ⓝ *mưa* muhr·uh
razor *dao cạo* zow ğọw
receipt ⓝ *biên nhận* bee·uhn nyụhn
red *màu đỏ* mòh đỏ
refund ⓥ *trả lại tiền* chaả laị dee·ùhn
registered mail *thư báo đảm* tuhr bów đaảm
rent ⓥ *thuê* twe
repair ⓥ *sửa chữa* súhr·uh jũhr·uh
reservation *sự giữ chỗ trước* sụhr zũhr jãw chuhr·érk
restaurant *nhà hàng* nyaà haàng
return ⓥ *trả lại* chaả laị
return (ticket) ⓐ *vé khứ hồi* vá kúhr hòy
right (correct) *đúng* đúm
right (direction) *bên phải* ben faỉ
road *đường* đuhr·èrng
room *phòng* fòm
rope *xâu* soh

S

safe ⓐ *an toàn* aan dwaàn
sanitary napkin *băng vệ sinh* buhng vẹ sing
sea *biển* beẻ·uhn
seat *chỗ ngồi* jãw ngòy
send *gởi* gẻr·ee
service station *trạm xăng* chaạm suhng

sex *giới tính* zer·eé díng
share (a dorm) *chia phòng nội trú* jee·uh fòm noị chóo
shaving cream *kem cạo rau* ğam ğọw zoh
sheet (bed) *tấm ra* dúhm zaa
shirt *áo sơ mi* ów ser mee
shoes *đôi giày* doy zày
shop ⓝ *cửa hàng* ğủhr·uh haàng
short *thấp* túhp
shower ⓝ *tắm vòi sen* dúhm vòy san
single room *phòng đơn* fòm dern
size (general) *kích thước* ğík tuhr·úhk
skin *da* zaa
skirt *cái díp* ğaí zíp
sleep ⓥ *ngủ* ngoỏ
slowly *chậm* jụhm
small *nhỏ* nyỏ
smoke ⓥ *hút thuốc lá* hút too·úhk laá
soap *xà phòng* saà fòm
some *một vài* mạwt vaì
soon *sắp tới* súhp der·eé
south *miền nam* mee·ùhn naam
souvenir shop *cửa hàng bán đồ lưu niệm* ğủhr·uh haàng baán đàw luhr·oo nee·ụhm
speak *nói* nóy
spoon *cái muỗng* ğaí moõ·uhng
stamp *tem* dam
stand-by ticket *vé chờ chỗ trống* va jèr jãw cháwm
station (train) *nhà ga* nyaà gaa
stomach *bụng* bụm
stomachache *bị đau bụng* beẹ doh bụm
stop (bus) ⓝ *trạm xe buýt* chụhm sa bweét
stop ⓥ *dừng lại* zùhng laị
street *phố/đường* ⓃⓈ fáw/duhr·èrng
student *sinh viên* sing vee·uhn
sun *mặt trời* mụht cher·eè
sunblock *kem chống nắng* ğam jáwm núhng
supermarket *siêu thị* see·oo teẹ
surname *tên họ* den họ
sweet ⓐ *ngọt* ngọk
swim ⓥ *bơi* ber·ee

T

taxi *xe taxi* sa dúhk-see
teeth *răng* zuhng
telephone ⓝ *điện thoại* dee-ụhn twại
television *vô tuyến truyền hình*
    vaw dwee-úhn chwee-ùhn hìng
temperature (weather) *nhiệt độ* nyee-ụht dạw
tent *lều* lay-oò
that (one) *cái đó* ğaí đó
thirsty *khát nước* kaát nuhr-érk
this (one) *cái này* ğaí này
ticket *vé* vá
time *thời gian* ter-eè zaan
tired *mệt* mẹt
tissues *giấy mỏng* záy móm
today *hôm nay* hawm nay
toilet *nhà vệ sinh* nyaà vẹ sing
tomorrow *ngày mai* ngày mai
tonight *tối nay* dóy nay
toothache *đau răng* đoh zuhng
toothbrush *bàn chải đánh răng*
    baàn jaỉ đaáng zuhng
toothpaste *kem đánh răng* ğam đaáng zuhng
torch (flashlight) *đèn pin* dàn pin
tour ⓝ *cuộc đi du lịch* ğoo-ụhk dee zoo lịk
tourist *khách du lịch* kaák zoo lịk
tourist office *văn phòng hướng dẫn khách du*
    lịch vuhn fòm huhr-érng zũhn kaák zoo lịk
towel *khăn tắm* kuhn dúhm
train *xe lửa* sa lủhr-uh
translate *phiên dịch* fee-uhn zịk
travel agency *văn phòng đại lý du lịch*
    vuhn fòm đại leé zoo lịk
travellers cheque *séc du lịch* sák zoo lịk
trousers *quần* ğwùhn
twin beds *giường đôi* zuhr-èrng đoy
tyre *lốp xe* láwp sa

U

underwear *quần lót* ğwùhn lót
urgent *khẩn cấp* kủhn ğúhp

V

vacant *trống* cháwm
vacation *kỳ nghỉ* ğeè ngyeé
vegetable ⓝ *rau củ* zoh ğoỏ
vegetarian ⓝ *người ăn chay*
    nguhr-eè uhn jay
vegetarian ⓐ *ăn chay* uhn jay
visa *giấy xuất cảnh* záy swúht ğaảng

W

waiter *người hầu bàn* nguhr-eè hòh baàn
walk ⓥ *đi bộ* dee bạw
wallet *ví* veé
warm ⓐ *ấm áp* úhm aáp
wash *giặt* zụht
watch ⓝ *đồng hồ đeo tay*
    đàwm hàw đay-oo day
watch ⓥ *xem* sam
water *nước* nuhr-érk
weekend *cuối tuần* ğoo-eé dwùhn
west *miền tây* mee-ùhn day
wheelchair *xe lăn* sa luhn
when *khi nào* kee nòw
where *ở đâu* ér đoh
white *màu trắng* mòh chúhng
who *ai* ai
why *tại sao* tại sow
wife *vợ* vẹr
window *cửa sổ* ğủhr-uh sảw
wine *rượu nho* zee-oọ nyo
with *với* ver-eé
without *không có* kawm ğó
woman *phụ nữ* fọo nũhr
write *viết* vee-úht

Y

yellow *màu vàng* mòh vaàng
yes *vâng* vuhng
yesterday *hôm qua* hawm ğwaa

H

I

L

M

N

INDEX